CM007960230

# The Giant on the Skyline

# The Giant on
# the Skyline

## On Home, Belonging
## and Learning to Let Go

CLOVER STROUD

doubleday

TRANSWORLD PUBLISHERS
Penguin Random House, One Embassy Gardens,
8 Viaduct Gardens, London SW11 7BW
www.penguin.co.uk

Transworld is part of the Penguin Random House group of companies
whose addresses can be found at global.penguinrandomhouse.com

First published in Great Britain in 2024 by Doubleday
an imprint of Transworld Publishers

A CIP catalogue record for this book
is available from the British Library.

ISBN 9780857529152

Typeset in 12/14.5pt Bembo Book MT Pro by Jouve (UK), Milton Keynes
Printed and bound in Great Britain by Clays Ltd, Elcograf S.p.A.

The authorized representative in the EEA is Penguin Random House Ireland,
Morrison Chambers, 32 Nassau Street, Dublin D02 YH68.

Penguin Random House is committed to a sustainable future
for our business, our readers and our planet. This book is made
from Forest Stewardship Council® certified paper.

For Bill and Sally Lee.
And to all the ravers and rebels of the Ridgeway.

*Even in Kyoto*
*Hearing the cuckoo's cry*
*I long for Kyoto.*

Haiku by Basho

# Prologue

I slept with all the windows open and was woken by the dart of a bat as it swooped through the eaves of my bedroom. Perhaps it was in pursuit of some of the small white moths which flitted through the garden, where the sad smell of dead rose petals weeping from their withered heads hung in the air. It circled above me twice, as I lay very still without breathing, before swooping back to its home in the darkness outside.

I exhaled, very awake, as a child moved in the bed beside me. Her long hair was damp at her temple but plastered across the pillow around her in a swirl, as if she was underwater. I reached across to her, murmuring, 'It's too early, go back to sleep.' And then in one silent movement I slipped out of bed and pulled on a t-shirt and shorts, closing the door behind me as I moved through the almost-dark house. Downstairs, the dogs skittered across the wooden floors and I whispered to them too, 'No, too early, lie down,' grasping the metallic reassurance of my keys and gently closing the front door so that none of the sleeping children would wake.

I needed to get to the hill, before it was too late, to make sense of what I was feeling. There should have been no real urgency – it was very early morning and anyway the children didn't start back at school until the following week – but when I reached the hill, leaving my car halfway up on a verge, I wanted to run up the steep slope, to take myself closer to the sound of that skylark, enticing and so high, high above me. The heat did not yet have that soupy feeling which makes August seem flat and unending, and I shivered quickly. Below me, amongst the clusters of red houses in the villages, small lights in windows created awakening constellations of life; to the west lay Swindon, the brightest blanket of light of all, and already the glow of dawn was spreading like melting butter through the darkness, flooding the great plain of the landscape below as morning forced night away.

I ran, stumbling sometimes, as the turf rose to meet me, then walking and jogging as I climbed the steepest ascent of the hill, so that my breath was sharp in my chest. Just once, I stopped, to look over my shoulder, like I was being pursued. Rust-coloured spires of dock seeds, growing precariously tall over their flat, veined leaves, trembled in the faintest breeze, creating patches of red shimmer across the hillside. The hill can be eerie because of all the past that exists around it, though I have never really been scared up there. A few years ago, the body of a girl was found on the edge of a band of nearby woodland, and although I do not associate the hill in any way with the terrible thing that happened to the girl, the fact of her death reminded me this is a remote place. You need to keep your mind sharp in a place like this. I also always like to check the horizon, just quickly, for giants, whenever I am there. Stretching across an expanse of southern England, from Salisbury to the Chilterns and across to the edges of Wales, you'd get an amazing view of a real giant within this space, since a giant would be able to step across the whole plain in one leap. This massive thought always excites me, especially as the view can also be extremely parochial, containing things like the church in the village, the houses around it, wind turbines, hedgerows, railway bridges and barns, pylons, electricity cables and so on.

I was making good progress up towards the Iron Age hill fort of Uffington Castle, to meet that skylark, and as I stopped, it struck me that a giant might be so huge I might not see it at all. A true giant could be too mighty to comprehend in an exact way, as God and the Big Bang are. Big enough to hold a giant, the hill contained huge quantities of time and space that could push a distance between me there, on the hill, and the version of my life which had been disturbing me for a while, and which had sent me there.

I ran faster, making my breath catch in my throat, to punish myself for having been so stupid not to listen. I wanted to hold on to the hill too, to heft myself to it, and find the place where the curve of the top flattens, but before it falls away, steeper still, revealing the chalk pattern of the White Horse. Close to the top, I looked down, to the other side. There it was, like a geometry puzzle on a vast green page, graffitied on to the hill by

men and women three millennia ago. I was heading to
the rink of flat grass, where the hill fort floats above
ramparts as high as a house, dug by men and women
who had no tools to work with other than deers' antlers
and the hip bones of cows.

On the steepest edge of the hillside, there was a spot
where the grass rippled away in enormous mounds and
bumps so strange and surprising they seemed to exist
at the limits of comprehension of a human eye. The
unpredictable shapes made me think of an extremely
beautiful piece of vivid green fabric thrown over a
gigantic mound of mismatched furniture pushed into a
pile in the middle of a room, as someone might do when
painting the walls.

The light was thickening, the air warming with the
first yellow August sunshine arriving as a haze, but even
on the bleakest March days, when it can be cold, dark,
confusing and often quite horrible to live anywhere in
the country, the hill still makes me hold my breath a bit
as that voice in my head that's both me and also disconnected from everything I am says: is it really still there?
Will the hill be as rare and unsettling as I picture it when
my face rests on a pillow in bed? Because the hill, and its
rumpled, crumpled ripples, is the place I go in my head
when I cannot sleep, or I am feeling afraid or angry or
small, or when I want to feel expansive or when I want
rest or to remember joy and awe. Often, I think the hill
might be the place I have needed to find all my life.

Light and time and gravity had pulled me upwards to
the peak, where the air feels thinnest, but also brighter
and purer than it does down in the vale. The tiny

skylark ripped the huge sky open, flooding the view
with pale-white light as I walked across the hill, the castle floating behind me and the whiteness of the chalk
horse glowing brighter on the hillside below. I walked
away from the well-worn track, out into the longer
grass, untrodden by humans, where rabbits left small,
dried pellets of droppings close to the safety of their
burrows. I crouched down, skimming my hand across
the faintest sense of dew, and looked out into the
expanse of the vale, beyond the railways, past the villages, along the darker green lines marking the hedgerows, to search for the shape of my home. My breath
grew shallower. In the broad valley below, I could not
see my house. I could not make it out. I searched the
familiar landscape, since I knew it must be there. I'd
stood on this exact part of the hill, with Pete and the
children, many, many, many times before. Usually, we
could just make out the small, white triangular gable of
our squat, odd-looking house that certainly wasn't
pretty, but had a place that felt just right for us, beyond
the village of Uffington, beyond the railway bridge, by
the sharp curve of road at the edge of our village. Like
locking the last pieces of a puzzle together, I could see
the dark, green tree line of the copse outside Uffington,
and place beside that the paler grass square of our field,
where the horses would be grazing, but I could not see
our house. Instead, the outline of a tall, upright, red-
brick house, on a car-lined street in Washington DC
imposed itself on my view. I blinked very hard, rubbing
my eyes, certain I'd be able to place our home, but all I
could visualize was that American house, its big square
windows like wide-open eyes, smiling at me, as if it was

just patiently waiting for me to abandon my home here and give myself up to its embrace. Very high above me, the skylark persisted, tugging my thoughts upwards as I scanned the immensity of the green view, where my home was nowhere to be seen. The skylark stopped. I was holding my breath.

I don't remember how much of what follows really happened. But I know that all of it is true.

# Chapter 1

I rarely knew where my husband Pete was. Once, I calculated we'd spent no more than thirteen consecutive days in the same place for the previous five years. We might spend a weekend together, three nights if we were lucky, before he'd leave, sometimes for Europe or Asia, but mostly to America. And as I stood in the kitchen listening to Pete's voice, I tried to imagine him on the other side of the Atlantic.

'It was beautiful, the house. We could be happy there, although we'd need to put all our stuff in it and make it a proper home. Make it ours. The agent who showed me around, she's called Sylvia, she can do a virtual tour for you. She thinks it's a really good family house. A blank canvas right now, but a home.'

His voice was distant as he clattered around on the other side of the room. On speakerphone, the Atlantic distances between us felt even greater. He must have been in Washington, since that was where the red-brick house was. He had sent me a link to the house a few days before in a WhatsApp message, and I had seen it, lying in bed one morning, after reaching for my phone, looking for him. Pete had been there, where he always was, on WhatsApp. We typed little messages to each other in place of touching or talking. His message said he missed me so much. That he also felt good to be back in Washington. Then he gave me a small, violent shock by attaching the link to a property website. Drawn into the outline of every red brick of the house was a sense of anticipation. Dark-grey shutters at each of the big square windows, laid out symmetrically around a tall, bright, white front door, were latched back, creating an impression of a wide-open face, eager to be admired. Shiny, clipped laurel bushes edged a lawn which ran behind the house, the grass giving way to a grid of paving slabs, swept clear of the leaves that must have fallen from the trees overhanging the yard. A hose pipe, also bright green like the lawn, was twisted into obeyance beside a tap. Inside the hall, the wooden floors shone, basking in the light from outside, so bright against the pale walls, not a single one of which was painted in a colour, or patterned with wallpaper. In some rooms was the familiar reassuring dark brown of a very few pieces of elderly furniture, tucked quietly into corners, but most of the space was bright and light and empty, waiting for a buyer. In every way it was a beautiful house, and it terrified me.

Because behind its deceptively welcoming face was the fact that Pete had been gathering information, and I had not been paying attention. I hadn't wanted to believe him when he told me how our life together must take us to America, so I had not really been listening. I could also feel within me a resistance which felt like anger because of the ease with which he said, 'Come and live in America.' His words tugged me hard and with great force away from the place I wanted to be. *When we live in America*, or words that represented leaving here, were sitting like landmines all over the thousands of WhatsApp messages we shared. And while I'd ignored the words, or put them aside to think of another day, Pete had not. While I'd been standing still, Pete had been actively thinking about houses and imagining our clothes in the cupboards and our pictures on the walls. During all those months and all that time he had been working in America, he had visualized our life there, the city we would settle in, the district we'd live in, the schools the children might go to, and now, too, the home we'd live in.

Now, as we spoke, across all that water, our children in the kitchen around me argued over who should have the last of the Cheerios, knocking the packet over, scattering them everywhere. Milk-drenched pieces of cereal stuck to the floor around the table like confetti on a pavement after it's rained. The three small pairs of shorts and t-shirts I'd left draped over the backs of their chairs remained studiously ignored by my three small children, even as I reminded them they had two days of sports camp before the end of the holidays; without asking, I knew none of them would know where their trainers were. I'd left the kitchen doors open when I'd got back from the hill, and even though it was not yet eight, the air was starting to feel drowsy with heat, the sun creeping up in the sky to whiten the old, ridged farm concrete in our yard so that through the kitchen windows it was all very bright, although it would be dark for Pete. He had cooked a steak, he told me, and although he'd finished his work, he'd stayed up a bit later so that we could talk. I was grateful for this, and the chance to hear his voice. I had put a row of hearts beside his name on my phone as he's the person I love best, so that whenever he called, a row of multi-coloured hearts flashed at me.

Slicing the crusts from small cheese sandwiches for the children's packed lunches, I imagined Pete's kitchen, the plain, heavy white plate he ate from, a sharp, ser-rated steak knife discarded beside a piece of fat sitting in a shallow puddle of oil and blood. I piled the children's sandwiches on to a plastic plate decorated with an out-line of the Eiffel Tower. The plates reminded me of how separate the rooms we called home had become, so when Pete said, 'We're always together, Clover, remem-ber that,' as he left again, heading to Heathrow, I wasn't always sure what he meant. I knew, deep inside, that we had started out as close together as it was possible to be, but that the accidental circumstances of our divided life had necessarily altered the shape of our relationship. Pete's work had taken him away so much over the pre-vious six years that we had had to learn how to live completely independently. You cannot cry with sad-ness and missing, every day, when you live apart from someone you love as much as I love Pete. I never wanted him to leave, but he did it all the time because away was where his work took him. I loved our partnership, but I had been forced to enjoy my independence too. I had had enough practice – years and years of living with the children as he came and went – so I was, for most of the time, good at being on my own. Often I felt like a little capsule, moving around through the day, getting a lot done, with a tougher shell than I wanted that I'd had to grow to survive. When I was with Pete in the same place, I didn't feel like this at all. When I was close to Pete, I could feel like liquid. When he was near by, in the same house, or we had a few days when we were not separated, I could dissolve and become a part of him, sharing absolutely every element of myself. I certainly could not afford to dissolve like that if an ocean separated us. I didn't want the children and me to drown, which is why it was safer to be a capsule when he was gone.

Now he told me it had been a long day.

'Flying from west to east coast is disorientating. You don't expect jet lag, but there it is. And there was a tornado. We had to sit on the tarmac for a while.'

I wrapped sandwiches in foil, then raked through the drawer stuffed with mismatching plastic boxes and lids, trying to imagine sitting on tarmac with a tornado close at hand. One of our bright-ginger cats sat on the side, mewing at me intently as she stared at my hands, moving as I buttered toast. I wasn't sure whether a cat could be transported to America, or whether she might become disturbed if she too was expected to sit on the tarmac. Pete would be in his kitchen, a laptop open while he read the *Washington Post*, his jacket flung over the back of a white plastic chair. His kitchen would be gleaming and metal, with big windows and highly efficient white goods, I thought, as I walked around our kitchen at home, kicking the wooden drawers by the sink shut as I filled the blue enamel kettle, balancing the phone in the crook of my neck as I folded pairs of pants and tea towels teetering in a basket on the end of the kitchen table, then reached across to take plates for toast straight from the dishwasher on to the table for the children. 'Mum, it's a life hack,' they told me.

I loved listening to Pete's voice, I loved the way he talked, and I loved hearing about his days: how vibrant Bryant Park in New York had been when he'd met a friend for breakfast, how much he missed the children when he saw kids pouring out of school near his office in DC, how badly he missed me when he saw a pair of police horses on the National Mall, since he knew how intensely I would love to see a horse, anywhere. I wished he was in the kitchen with me, making toast for the children, but instead he was in a hotel, or rented apartment, identical to the one he'd called from the day before, in a different city.

I wondered if I'd tethered myself so tightly to home so that I could feel strong even when his absence hurt. Now, I wanted to tell him about what it had felt like, up on the hill, to stand beneath the skylark with my thoughts scattering. I wanted him to understand how beautiful and essential the hill had been, and how confused I'd felt when I'd looked back and been unable to see our home, the one we'd built, together, a decade before. I also wanted to tell him how much I wished he was here for these last days of summer before the children went back to school, because without him it was like a valve in my heart was blocked. I wanted to tell him how cold and bright the river water at Lechlade had been, when I'd taken the children there to swim the afternoon before, and how strange the outline of a heron had been, in the half-light of dusk, when it alighted from the reeds, surprising the children as they watched, silently, as it spread its wide wings above them. I wanted him to know how exquisite the thin, fragile seeds of dandelions had looked, floating through the air as we'd walked back to the car, and how odd yet gentle the black cows had been, turning their heads to watch us, chewing myopically, as we walked past laden with blankets, wet swimming pants, a bag stuffed with empty crisp packets and some left-over biscuits, and also how warm the grass had been as we walked barefoot back to the car. I wanted to tell him about all these things so he might experience them too, but they seemed too distant compared to that red-brick house, pushing our own home aside, so instead we talked about when I might do a virtual tour with Sylvia.

I spread raspberry jam on to three slices of toast, passing them to the children while pausing from listening to Pete to quickly tell them to sit up and sit still while they ate. They looked at me, then continued to roam around the room, wiping their hands on the back of the purple sofa, reaching for the ginger cat, emptying an orange tub of Lego, pulling out large bottles of poster paint from the green chest of drawers. One of the children had yogurt, or milk, on his blue sports shirt, and with the phone clamped against my shoulder I grabbed the child and wiped at the mark very hard with a dishcloth, thinking, as I did this, of the photograph Pete carried with him, of the same child alongside his siblings, which he'd told me he propped up wherever he was, so that another apartment, another hotel might feel in some way like home. I'd felt so sad when I'd seen the photograph, looking lonely on a shiny bedside cabinet, on the screen behind him one evening when we'd been talking

on FaceTime. For him it was yet another Saturday to fill
in a foreign city alone.

I gestured to the children, miming a motion of shoes
and socks, then pointed to my watch and the kitchen
clock. They watched me for a moment, then chased the
cat from the kitchen together. The imprint of the long
summer holidays was still on them and the sports camp
had made them very annoyed, since school was another
week away and they'd mewed and complained bitterly
about getting up and having to contemplate socks and
shoes. I could hear them fighting with each other on the
stairs and I knew they'd all still be barefoot, but I wanted
to talk to Pete: about the house, about his work, about
anything, just to hear him close to me a little bit longer.
There was so little opportunity to do this: by the time
I'd dropped the children at their club in Wantage, it
would be too late in America and Pete would be asleep.
I wanted him to tell me about the house, to understand
how it had made him feel before I told him what it
had done to me. I wanted to tell him that of course I
wanted to be together, but that so much separation had
forced me to create my own life here, in England, and
giving that up would feel like a violent ripping. But it
was a long conversation, and the distances between us
were so great.

'Come closer,' I said to him, tucking a carrot optimistically into a packed lunch bag, then quickly zipping
it up before a child returned to the kitchen and rejected
it. 'Come close to my face.' When I said that I remembered that way the skin on my cheek felt, tight and
crisp, when, on a rare afternoon at home alone together,
I had taken my clothes off, and we'd lain down, and he

had done exactly that. I wanted Pete and his voice right beside me. I wanted to be close to him.

'Opportunities. The chances here are great,' he said. 'The opportunities could be incredible. I think Washington is the right place for us. We can make it work here.' He must have picked up the phone, as his voice was suddenly there, right inside my ear, hands-on rather than hands-free, connecting me to him, a relief his clattering of plates and my handing out of toast were over. Occasionally, when the time separating us stretched from days into weeks, then months, I wondered if there might be another woman, leaning against a kitchen counter in the background, understanding she must make no noise because he was talking to me. I imagined her relief when he hung up, when I was gone, and that feeling of sitting on the edge of a table, laughing, in just your pants in the middle of the afternoon. I thought about her, or the idea of her, quite often. Pete and I loved each other but let each other go all the time; watching him vanishing so often, walking far, far away from me, with other people, into unknown hotels, offices, conferences, restaurants, demanded I have a very high degree of trust in him. Of course, he trusted me too, but I was at home, with children in my bed every night, and rarely went anywhere further than the nearest small town where there was nothing anonymous about my life. Pete could do anything, with anyone. I had to trust him, although I also told him that if he betrayed that trust I would stab him, since the thought of him with someone else destroyed me.

She doesn't exist, I told myself, blinking hard to make myself concentrate as I crooked the phone under

my chin and gestured to the children that we had to
leave, making small sounds of interest at what Pete was
saying before quickly telling him that we were late. I
love you. I love you too. The imaginary woman
returned to my brain as I drove back from Wantage in
the delightfully silent car, having left the children, who
had fought all the way there about the rota of whose
turn it was to sit in the front being out of order, then
complained furiously about having to do football in the
heat. And in that moment, thinking of her, and wondering if she *did* indeed exist, I wondered whether she
would want me and all of my children to move to
America, too.

I stopped at the shop in Uffington on my way home. I
had a parcel to collect that had been sitting there for
three weeks and had not been sent back to the sorting
office in Swindon. I'd thought I was in a hurry, but in
the shop time slipped away; I was willingly drawn into
a discussion with Alex, the tall boy working behind the
till, who wore a leather jacket, about a gig he was playing in the village hall, and whether the pub in Kingston
Lisle was going to get converted into flats, a real shame,
and who had actually bought the big house in the next
village, was it indeed the celebrity make-up artist someone had mentioned, and whether a potential planning
application for the permanent static caravan park on
White Horse Hill, which everyone in the shop agreed
would be outrageous, would get approved, and who
had grazing to rent locally as Luke and Kat were looking again, and Bill's new motor, and the bluegrass band
playing at the church next month, already sold out, and

finally whether it would be the TV trick riders or Lamb National racing sheep appearing as the special act at the White Horse Show next weekend. Everyone was worried about the weather for that one: the weeks of unbroken heat were forecast to break on the day it opened. I left with my package, a strip of raffle tickets for the wheelbarrow of booze at the show, and two bags of plump, black, late-summer cherries, slipping two pounds into the charity box by the till for *Exploring the Pagan Path,* from the shelves of donated books outside the shop.

At the car, Sally pulled up in her truck, grinning at me through the glass, and I waved back as she swung out of the cab, a cigarette smouldering between her fingers. She hitched her tight blue jeans up over her long legs, tucking in her t-shirt which glittered with a sequinned rose on the front.

'Hot, isn't it?' she said, wiping her brow dramatically and laughing. I knew she would have been up for hours, driving to the next village to check on the herd of black-and-white ponies she kept on a patch of rough land behind an industrial unit. She and her husband Bill were gypsies and knew more about ponies than most people. We were the same age, by a matter of days, and she had, I often thought, the strongest mentality of anyone I had ever met. In those vertiginous and lonely months after my sister Nell had died, when Pete had had to go away again, Bill and Sally had become close friends, scooping me up when I was on my own, piling the kids into the back of their truck, amongst the puppies and harnesses, and always making time for me, to chat, to smoke and swig energy drinks, to talk about ponies. When I spent time with them, I'd be left with a sense that they had a secret I wanted to understand, but probably never would. We chatted for a bit about some of the foals Sally had had that summer, about her favourite pony, Blondie, with a mane as golden yellow as her own, and when she asked me if Pete would be back for the bank holiday, I shook my head.

'I bet you miss him something criminal, don't you?' she said. 'Me and Bill hardly spend a minute apart but I know I'd miss him terrible, like, if he was away any-thing like half as much as Pete is.' I nodded, then joked that maybe I'd have to move out there to be with him, and we both laughed, Sally blowing the last of her cig-arette smoke, saying she'd better get on, Bill would be waiting and wanting breakfast.

'Bring the kids down to see the foals, any time, you know you're always welcome,' Sally said, and I gave her a thumbs-up as I slammed the car door.

At home I put the cherries in a bowl, then leant against the side in the kitchen for a bit, flicking through the book on druids, but I was drawn back to my phone. I clicked on the pictures of the house Pete had sent. It looked so neat and tidy, in a strict and empty way I didn't understand. Even the street it sat on was ordered, with parking lines painted on to concrete, and another house opposite, also red-brick, also imposing, also with a laurel hedge clipped into order. In my email was another message from Pete, which he must have sent after we'd spoken, and attached to that, images of more homes waiting for me: tiny, beautiful and violent bombs just ready to go off inside me as I clicked on each of them. Each one exploded beneath my feet, blasting holes into the earth, disturbing clods of the ground I had cultivated into home. Rather than another woman, or another person, breaking our relationship, I realized that a third party was more likely to be bricks and earth than living, breathing flesh. Both of us had become passionately attached to where we were, and the locations of those two places were very different.

All the houses that Pete sent me were in Washington. I tried to picture us in one of them: this time, unlike the red-brick house, a tall townhouse in the middle of a terrace. Bicycles were propped up in a porch and the house next door had canary-yellow window frames. There was a bright-blue child's tricycle in the front garden, where tufty, thinning grass ran straight on to the pavement, and although there was less of the space Pete had talked about, the street had an air of something messy and cheerful about it. When I virtually stepped inside, though, the rooms were small, stacked on top of one another like little boxes. Beside this house Pete had written a note into the email:

Loved walking around this neighbourhood. I think you would like it. Messy and creative. But not sure neighbours would be happy with us in this house – think our children might be too noisy to live here?

Threaded together in the email was correspondence between Pete and Sylvia. Tracing the chain of their emails backwards, it was clear that they had been discussing family homes for a while. He had asked to see a third house, with a white veranda wrapped alluringly around two sides of it, although one of the bedrooms was on the ground floor. There were ceiling fans in all the rooms and diaphanous white curtains in the windows. I looked up from the phone, and around at our kitchen, with the big wooden pine table that had once been in a school, and that had always been in the centre of my mum's kitchen; at the pictures hung in a scramble on all the walls, and the bookshelves I'd painted green one afternoon, stuffed with cookbooks, scrapbooks, maps and novels with broken spines. Our two ginger cats were climbing the curtains, one of them wobbling along the dusty curtain rail then skidding down again like it was a ski slope.

I put the phone face down, pushing it away, as I imagined Pete following Sylvia into each room as she sold the idea of this house, this one, and that one too, being a perfect home for him. I picked up the cat, who resisted, mewing when I tried to cuddle her, scratching me, like she sensed the betrayal going on.

Creating a home wasn't simply putting chairs in rooms, I thought, sulkily trying to fix the kitchen curtains which continually detached themselves from the tiny screws, sagging after the children played behind them, or the cats climbed up them. On every blank space in our home were layers of the small history of our marriage: a paper cut-out of my eldest daughter Dolly's silhouette when she'd had very short hair as a little girl; separate photographs of my mother and father when they were babies, brown and white with age. I'd finally got framed a painting of the Great Fire of

London my youngest son Lester had won a competition
for at school; and there was a woodcut painting of the
Ridgeway framed on top of an OS map that Jimmy, the
eldest of my five children, had submitted for his A-level
art. That had made me feel so happy at the time, since I
felt it had shown me that, somehow, the landscape had
worked its way inside his consciousness and become a
part of him, or at least enough a part of him to make
him want to concentrate on it for his exams.

I let the dogs, Pablo and Stow, tufty black-and-white
terriers, and the lurcher, Cracker, elegant and biscuit-
coloured, out into the garden, then walked through the
house gathering up clothes from the children's rooms
into a laundry basket, popping books back on to shelves,
opening the windows a little further, to try to move
some of the late-summer heat out of the house. In the
yard beyond our straggly lawn, the dogs were in the
longer grass near the hedge, digging frantically under
the corner of a blue plastic sheet I used to cover the hay.
They must have been hunting mice in the longer grass
where the yard gave way to nettles and a tangle of brambles near the hedge. I watched them as they pricked
their ears, looking very intently into the grass, ready to
pounce.

I turned back to the kitchen, where several years of
school photographs were pinned beside a chalkboard
with *Remember How Much I Love You All* written on to it
in my messy handwriting. Underneath it was written
**you smell** in Dash's scratchy writing. On one shelf
running over the cooker, a collection of ornaments
gathered greasy dust: a ceramic lion I'd found in a charity shop, a speckled teapot I'd salvaged when a friend

had been throwing it out, a wooden Celtic cross which
seemed to have arrived in the house, a brass horse
Jimmy had given me, and behind them all, more pictures of the children, a lonely Christmas card, a
handwritten note a friend had sent after a party. As I
looked around at the many layers of pictures and photographs, letters, drawings, ornaments, fragments of
fabric, old envelopes, I could see that creation of home
had become for me an almost frantic attempt to hold on
to all the people and things I loved.

Packing this up, dismantling and permanently leaving it to move to an alien city where ceiling fans chopped
through the air, all year long, and fridges were huge and
an ice machine was necessary and buildings glittered,
where consumption was a way of being, where children
were drilled in shooter lockdown and the highways
were vast and the suburbs massive, felt too distant to
bring into focus. It felt surreal, as if our life had turned
into a cartoon. The ginger cat watched me, her paws
pressed neatly together as if apologizing for the scratch
she'd given me, and mewed pitifully. I wanted to speak
to Pete, right then, now that the kitchen was quiet
enough to think, but he was asleep, in a different time
zone, separated from home, and me, by thousands of
miles.

This was the absolute opposite of what I wanted when
I fell in love with him, a decade and a half before. We'd
known each other even further back, as we'd studied at
the same university at the same time, although that was
little more than snatches of conversations in crowded
student kitchens. I think he'd barely noticed me until he

moved back to Oxford in his early thirties, where I was living with my first two children, Jimmy and Dolly. After a tricky marriage in my twenties, I loved the maternal intimacy of single motherhood, even if my life was precarious financially. And I loved the independence and regular thrills of my life as a journalist. When Pete called me up and asked me to go out for a drink, his name seemed like a distant sound from the past, and I walked into that pub to meet him with no sense of how absolutely he would change my life. Because I realized, very quickly – instantly, in fact – that I needed to reach across the space between us and touch his neck and his face, and then stay there, a physical part of him, or at least as close to him as I could be. Even then I knew I wanted to become a part of his body, like a small, quiet animal that keeps very still so that it can remain safe in its habitat. He made me feel secure, but also wild, and also how completely my DNA needed to become part of his. He was the first person to make me feel truly visible, even when I was at my most vulnerable. I wanted to be beside him, all the time.

I lived like that, close to him, for quite a few years, creating a home within the safety of one another, with Jimmy and Dolly, who were nine and seven when we met. The children filled all corners of the space around them, and Pete completely embraced them for that.

We were all happy in Oxford. I enjoyed the internal poetry of the children's urban childhood: the gentle swinging motion of coloured plastic seats in the playground in the park, the walk to the little parade of shops where Jimmy went alone to buy sweets and fizzy drinks, the clack of skateboards on bumpy pavements. Oxford

had never felt like a truly urban space, anyway. It sometimes felt more rural than a provincial town, with its
busy bicycle lanes in place of a metro, and cows grazing
metres from the high street in Christ Church Meadow,
and riverbanks where geese dabbled between piles of
clothes left by swimmers.

We lived in a house with white plastic cladding in the
middle of a pebbledash housing estate. There was a pub
opposite the house called the Jack Russell, with a huge
empty car park and fruit machines that whirred orange
and pink through the windows from late morning
onwards. When I left the house very early, to drive to
the park-and-ride near the ring road and take the bus to
London for work, I would sometimes see the black
shapes of figures inside the pub, standing close to the
bar, still talking, just very, very slowly, having forgotten that morning had arrived. Sometimes, at night, I
would hear the sound of cars racing in the estate.

For a long while I loved that house. Because we were
so close and so happy, we had more children. But after
Evangeline, my third child, was born, a new preoccupation with place gripped me. She and her younger
brother, Dash, had just eighteen months between them,
born just as Jimmy and Dolly were hitting their teens,
so we were continually losing rooms in the house. Car
seats, highchairs and piles and piles and piles of children's clothes filled the space around me faster than I
could empty it. Babies and toddlers brought a relentless
sea of mess with them, like an ocean swilling into every
room, choking it with single- as well as multiple-use
plastic. Being a mother to many children in a house
with no garden made me feel as if I was being violently

shaken, while also being squashed and always stumbling. It was also both exciting and intimate for Pete and me to think about creating our own home, together, but where to do this made my brain throb with anxiety. He'd grown up in Edinburgh, but moving to Scotland was impractical for his work. I didn't want to return to the exact village, the exact area I had grown up in, since there were ghosts there I didn't want to see every day. But I knew I wanted this growing family to be given a powerful sense of place which they could call home, and which would drench into their little souls in the same way that Minety, the village I had grown up in, inhabited me. Place was spiritual and poetic, while space felt practical. We couldn't afford to stay that close to Oxford, so Jimmy and Dolly changed schools, and we moved further out. That was how we chose the house near the hill. We were also drawn to the Ridgeway, that prehistoric track running high over the green chalk downs close to Uffington White Horse. Lester was born a year and a half later. Although Pete missed the idea of the city near by, moving right out into the deeper countryside seemed, at least at that time, to make sense.

After we'd moved out of Oxford, however, I found I really missed the plastic-clad house and the sounds of the cars and the pub opposite. I regretted the inconvenience of rural life, the mud, the isolation, the time I spent in a car. I thought that moving into the countryside would make me feel at home, but what I found, at least at first, was that I really wanted to go back to the city. Life in the house beside the hill was much more complex than I'd been expecting. Jimmy brought a lot

of other teenagers into the house, trooping up and
down the very steep old stairs like inmates at visiting
hours. The babies became toddlers, and created feelings
inside me, brought on by the chaos of domestic life, that
were like being in a ship rolling on an ocean: I was never
sure if life was about to capsize, and the contents of the
kitchen were almost always all over the floor. I had
something like motion sickness a lot at that time.

It was during this time that Pete's work took him back to
Oxford, and then to London or Europe, at first for one
or two nights a week, and then all the time. As our family grew, so did the demands on him. He started spending longer and longer away, renting a room in London
to work all week, and then increasingly it was west, to
America, that he was pulled, again and again, however
much he tried to pull it back to England. Each time he
passed through St Pancras, he sent me a snap of Tracey
Emin's neon sculpture spelling out *I want my time with you*.
He came and went all the time, arriving for a few days,
when I was happiest, then vanishing, leaving unidentifi-
able foreign adapters in the kitchen and a dizzying array
of mismatching razor blades around the sink.

   Standing alone outside playgroup to pick my toddlers up from their morning session, with the yawning
chasm of a week ahead before Pete would return, I felt
we'd made a terrible mistake. I texted him all the time
and we spoke every day, promising one another that
this was just for the next few weeks, maybe six months.
But we were not together. I became accustomed to
going to bed with the children, sharing their food,
keeping their hours.

At night, with the huge pitch darkness around me, Zoopla and RightMove started to fill my head again. I was certain either of these websites could correct the wrong move we'd made. For quite a while I was certain there must be another house, another place, somewhere else where I'd feel settled. Several times over the course of a few years I tried to quietly sell the house and move us all somewhere else, almost without Pete noticing, since he was away so much. This happened most often when an estate agency dropped a leaflet through our door informing me they were looking for houses to buy in our area and that they had many eager and willing buyers lined up. Those leaflets would excite me so much my palms would start prickling with joy that I might be able to leave the lonely space where I was and find a new place where I would really belong and no longer be so alone. Even now, if I go on to Zoopla, I am reminded by the historical listings that I put our house on the market multiple times between 2016 and the start of 2019.

The children filled every square inch of the new, slightly bigger house we'd moved to, and filled all the cells and molecules inside my brain too. When the need for space overwhelmed us, we spent six months living in caravans while we built a bigger kitchen and three more bedrooms. Pete would return at weekends, exhausted from relentless work, to freezing caravans, mud everywhere and toddlers who loved the utter chaos.

Pete moved around so much, but following him wasn't possible; with five children spread over sixteen years, it was completely impractical. To distract myself from the feeling that Pete, the most important part of

my life, was missing, I filled our new expanded house
with colour, painted the walls and much of the furniture, threw rugs I bought on Facebook on the floors,
picked up Welsh blankets in charity shops to fling over
sofas. I felt grey or teal inside with the loneliness of
the new life we'd accidentally created, and thought
that pink, yellow, orange and blue walls would help
me feel cheerful. I couldn't control Pete's absence any
more than I could control the many different directions
the children pulled me in, but I could create a home
where I felt as whole as it was possible for me to be
without him.

We had a new bedroom, much the biggest bedroom I
had ever owned, with a slanting ceiling and windows
looking towards the downs and the fields around the
house. I covered the walls with bright-green wallpaper,
a wildwood of leaves surrounding me while I slept or
just lay in bed trying to find meaning in a day which had
involved hours and hours of boiling water or picking
up plastic. Babies and toddlers shouted in every room;
teenagers continued to troop in and out. I could not
always attach myself to Pete, as he came and went, so I
attached myself to place instead. The attention I might
have given him if he had been there, I gave to the landscape and people around me. I tethered myself to our
home, lying in the green, green room, thinking about
Pete walking across cities in other countries, along grey
pavements, as the toddlers and children screamed
around me.

During this time I often felt red with rage at all this
parenting I did alone. At the fact that Pete never had
small hands pounding on the door as he tried to work,

or someone whining about how unfair it was that all the biscuits had been eaten when he was trying to have an adult thought. I was infuriated that he had long, long days to devote only to his career, never having to cancel his work, or squash it into a space interrupted by driving to ballet, attending assembly, picking up a sick child from school or volunteering on the school trip. I am ashamed when I remember how blind I was to what he was really going through, taking a train to the airport alone again, waking up in another faceless hotel room in a cold, uncaring, unfamiliar city when he craved the comfort of home. I couldn't feel his loneliness, couldn't hear the silence of another Saturday in a foreign city to fill alone, couldn't understand the pressures he was under on every single one of those Zoom calls, couldn't sympathize with the feeling of missing his children's lives. I became enraged by the compromises I was being forced to make and the shape I had to contort my life into so that his career could work. 'Separate, let's separate,' I would hiss into my phone at him, 'since that's how we live anyway.' But then Pete would come home and I'd feel like liquid again, part of him, joined back together.

Within this environment of change and uncertainty, where I was often alone with five children, the green wildwood bedroom was the place I went to breathe. From my house I could see the Ridgeway, the high skyline of track which originally ran from Dorset to Norfolk, and which human feet have tramped along for thousands and thousands of years. I spent a lot of time thinking about the people who had first walked on the Ridgeway, when it was just one small part of the skeleton of tracks which ran up on the high chalk hills, created by men and women who wanted to escape the dense woodland and heavy clay of the vale below. It became a more distinct track after the landscape was enclosed in the middle of the eighteenth century. A lower route called the Icknield Way was used by the Romans as a military route, and also by travellers who needed to be closer to the water sources and springs below, since the Ridgeway is very high and dry. These two routes – the Ridgeway and the Icknield Way – merge together closer to the Chilterns, where the land flattens.

Being close to the Ridgeway was part of the reason we'd both wanted to move here, and now, alone so often in the house, I thought about the hills a lot. About the ancient people who had moved massive sarsen stones around to create monuments like Avebury, digging into the turf to create the deep trenches of the hill forts at Uffington, Barbury and Liddington, and scraping the shape of a white horse into the chalk on the hill beyond my window. Once, I woke suddenly in the night, certain that those old, old people were standing beside my bed, smelling of mud and animal fat and bright, white air, watching me, their huge dark eyes unblinking. They were in my head a lot, making me desperate to get away from our house and on to the hill, to walk that same track they walked, also used by Saxon and Viking armies, to follow the gentler curve of the hill later used by medieval drovers pushing their sheep to markets. Lying there, with the green walls surrounding me, I could feel as if the outside was coming in, and that soothed me a great deal: gradually, I started to actually

feel the hills and the fields we had moved here to be part
of, but which had felt so alien for a time when the babies
had me trapped indoors, entering my body, flooding
into my veins and inhabiting that liquid space inside my
brain. Slowly, as we settled here, the landscape became
a part of me, so that it moved with me wherever I was.
Often, before they all went to school, the children
stopped me getting out to the fields, since when we
tried they would instantly fall over and drench themselves in puddles, or run in opposite directions down
the road. To escape the claustrophobia of motherhood,
I lay in my room and imagined the feeling of the fields
like bright, glossy, green paint being poured all over
me. I imagined myself vanishing into the green paint,
until I didn't simply walk on the landscape but became
drenched with the colour of it. I began to realize there
were giants outside, as tall as the top of the Ridgeway,
which I might see if I really, really attended to them,
although I couldn't find them at first, since the children
would all have a crisis at the same time and need me.
When that happened, I'd open the windows of our bedroom to look for them, leaning out to gulp the air. As
soon as I did that, the giants would vanish, and instead
many, many tiny, sticky, persistent little hands would
pull me back in.

I only ever wanted to be close to Pete. Sometimes, slot-
ted into a bookshelf like lost souls, I find notebooks I
wrote during those those chaotic, soupy years when the
children were all babies and toddlers. Running through
the lines of every book, in between messy scrawlings
about the details of the next baby's vaccinations, or

notes about a work interview I was preparing for, or
many, many notes about how much it mattered to me
that the children felt a secure sense of home, is the
repeated sentiment: I want to be near to Pete. But in
between longing for him, I resented him too. Sometimes
I called him wherever he was working, in London or
somewhere abroad, just so that he could hear the sound
of the baby crying with reflux, or the toddler screaming
that his t-shirt felt too crispy against his skin. I wanted
him to understand how hard it was, without really
thinking how hard it was for him too. He was working
so hard, but I could be such a bitch.

But gradually, over several years, the babies grew
into children and didn't need me to be in the house serv-
ing them so much, and the adolescents became relatively
responsible, and when that happened, I got up and
walked away from the green bedroom more often, outside to the hill and the fields around the house. I didn't
know the names of that many trees apart from oak,
beech, hazel and horse chestnut, or the names of flowers
apart from dandelion, daisy, bluebell, campion and cow
parsley, or the birds and insects either, apart from robin,
blackbird, magpie, sparrow, thrush, wasp, bee, beetle,
earwig and daddy long-legs, but this didn't matter
because I didn't need to know the name of everything
in order to feel it all moving like green fluid through my
cells. I knew no science, but understood that when I
was outside, in the landscape, something inside me,
which had been very noisy and disturbing and upsetting, quietened. I had read about the idea of inscendence,
something Catholic priest and scholar Thomas Berry
described as 'descend[ing] to our instinctive resources

in order to reinvent ourselves'. In order to withstand my separation from Pete, I felt a part of myself inscending, and that strong little capsule forming within which helped me remain solid so that I didn't dissolve without him.

And the thin strands of community grew stronger, creating a mesh to hold me. I began to recognize most of the people driving the cars that passed on the roads around the house and waved back at them. With the children at school, I had more time to stop and chat in the village shop, or at the market. I made friends with other mums at Evangeline's dance school in Wantage and waiting for Lester outside Beavers at the village hall in Uffington.

The house grew around us, until it was worn in perfectly to the shape I created when I was alone there with the children. I eventually bought curtains for the kitchen, painted another bedroom in a colour that pleased me, and hung pictures of ponies and goats and beaches and trains in the children's rooms. I didn't paint the bathroom but instead hung rows of coloured plates on the walls to cover toothpaste smudges, and I bought a big cupboard with French words for grain and flour painted on to it, filled it with cups and jugs bought from charity shops and hung it over the cooker. Slowly the house made me feel welcome and loved, just as the landscape did, every time I turned in to the gate. Late at night, Pete and I would sometimes chat on the phone about how much longer his work would take him away, but we didn't really have a plan. We couldn't afford to, because the demands of Pete's work were intense, and always somewhere else. I stopped looking at Zoopla. I settled and settled and settled. The children got bigger. Pete was away even more.

I thought of this as I sat in the kitchen, spitting cherry stones into my palm, my laptop now open before me, a Word document I should have been working on up on the screen but sulking with neglect. While I'd been creating home near the Ridgeway, Pete had been settling in Washington. He felt at home there, he'd told me many times. In fact, it occurred to me that for about a year or two, Washington as a place we could really call home was something that had started to come up, with increasing urgency, in Pete's conversations. I remembered the ease with which he had moved through the city when I had gone to visit him a year before. He had booked a hotel, I had taken a cab from the airport, and after leaving my bags I'd walked to meet him from his office near Franklin Square. I'd cried tears of relief when I saw him, and hugged him tight, smelling his neck, pulling him closer as red taxis flashed past over his shoulder, the *Washington Post* building behind us.

Walking down those wide pavements, with so much space between the buildings that every inch of the concrete was flooded in light, even when it wasn't sunny, I had felt like a different person. I was alert but also nervous, the subway unfamiliar as I struggled with the urban geography, stumbling when ordering a sandwich from a dizzying board of options in a fast, noisy deli. It was a delight to have this time with Pete, though. In the mornings we'd walk together to his office, and because I would not want him to go we'd sit at a pavement cafe, eating eggs-over-easy out of polystyrene boxes, drinking cups of weak coffee, grasping these fast little moments we had together.

He was constantly in meetings, so I spent two days alone walking through the damp, intense heat of Washington in August, trying to imagine myself into a different version of life in which I was a mother in DC. I joined a protest in opposition to the Sackler family outside the Supreme Court and walked through rooms of giant black-and-blue Rothko paintings which made me cry, but I was relieved as the chill of the air conditioning dried the patches of sweat that made my shirt stick to my back. Stopping in a chemist's at Dupont Circle and walking between the aisles looking for throat sweets, I felt an electric jolt of memory at that familiar smell of cherry ChapStick and popcorn, which I'd once known so well. America wasn't entirely unfamiliar: when I finished university, I took a one-way flight to New York, then crossed the country on a Greyhound bus, looking for a landscape big enough to absorb all the pain I held inside me then. I found that landscape under the massive skies of west Texas, where I worked on a ranch, riding horses and roping cattle to distract from all that pain. That smell in the chemist in DC darted me back there, making me shiver. Back on the pavement, I tried to imagine driving our children through the city in a big family car, but a cartoon quality to my imaginings took over. Our home beside the Ridgeway was so strong and we were so settled. Moving to DC seemed far too remote to truly contemplate.

Waiting for Pete on the second afternoon, I lingered in a second-hand bookshop behind Capitol Hill, leaving

with a T. S. Eliot, then sat in an Italian cafe eating raspberry sorbet and letting the familiar beat of Little
Gidding soothe the sense I had of being out of place.
The air conditioning hummed behind me as I tried to
imagine visiting the same bookshop with the children
and picking out a book of American poetry that meant
something to me. That evening, I went to Pete's office
and we walked together down the wide pavements. We
dipped into a Mexican restaurant for fish tacos, lingering at high stools pulled up to an outdoor bar where I
drank sugary tea in a tall glass which clattered to the
brim with ice. I was completely happy because I was
with Pete, and there was a lightness sliding between us
which came from having no smaller hands to hold, no
little beings to shuffle safely across roads, no tempers to
soothe or scraps to mediate.

'I like being here, I feel completely at home,' Pete
had said, as we headed to the airport five days later. His
flight to San Francisco was an hour earlier than mine,
and to assuage the hurt I felt in my heart as I watched his
form vanishing through a departure gate, I wasted time
buying keyrings with plastic cut-outs of the White
House and pencils with miniature baseballs on the ends
for the children. Boarding my flight, I decided that the
time in Washington had been a holiday – not a version
of real life, but time out from real life. We'd never really
leave England, I told myself, relaxing into a place of
quiet relief as I settled into my seat and flicked through
the in-flight entertainment. There was too much uncertainty in Pete's work to truly contemplate leaving, I
reassured myself as I drove home from Heathrow. There
was a quickening in my heart as I left the M4, the road

narrowing, then narrowing again as it snaked over the hill, across the downs through Lambourn. There, stable lads and lasses, just off the gallops, bobbed out of Ladbrokes and a girl with a buggy trundled into the butcher's, where a board outside had a special offer for *Best BBQ Bangers*.

I felt something grainy within my deepest nervous system smoothing itself as the road swooped through the broad, unbroken outline of the downs, and I chuckled to myself that I'd often told Pete I loved this road because it reminded me of America, but now, returning to it from the grid streets of Washington, I loved it because it was England and home. We had too much bright life invested in this part of England, our ties to this place too strong, to seriously consider leaving, I said to myself as I passed Sally, in her big white truck on her way to feed her horses, and who waved when she recognized my car. Home, I felt, as I walked into the kitchen, the dogs bounding up to greet me, then I sank into the creases of our pink sofa, brushing off biscuit crumbs the children must have left that morning. Later, back from school, the children and I walked out to the field together, disturbing the tender outline of a muntjac deer, the colour of toffee, which scuttled sorrowfully into the hedgerow. And as my big dun mare walked through the long summer grass towards me, the distinct crooked outline of the hill behind her, the wide streets of Washington shimmered far, far away, back into a distant grid of their own unreality.

I pushed the cherries away, smoothing the wrinkled knot between my eyes with my knuckle, as I remembered that time, and Pete's absolute urban ease as he showed me, the slightly awkward visitor, around. Propped over the cooker in the kitchen was a photograph taken on our wedding day in Oxford, slightly out of focus in a haze of confetti, both equally entranced by the prize in our arms. I reached for it, wiping away the greasy dust which covered the glass with the edge of my sleeve. Standing alone in the kitchen, with Pete in Washington, I felt unnerved by a sense of something precarious unbalancing us. A small, remote but unpleasant thought settled inside my head: maybe leaving the safety and security of my home wasn't, in fact, worth it. Maybe the thing Pete and I had – our marriage, our shared life, our connection – had been altered too much by the long periods of time we'd spent apart. Maybe we were no longer the same people in that photograph.

I was so deep in thought that I hadn't noticed the sound of the postman's van in the yard, but I caught sight of his retreating back as he greeted Pablo. Tiny dots of fruit flies had started to swarm over the bowl of cherries. I swatted them away, dismissing, too, that cold, unpleasant thought about our marriage. In our many conversations about where we might live, we had discussed just ploughing on as we were, with Pete returning home every few weeks. That didn't work either. We needed each other, and the children needed him desperately too. They were no longer little, but Dash and Evangeline were approaching the last years at their village state school, and Lester wasn't far behind. We needed a new plan. I had always known the fields and wide-open hills of the Ridgeway were not somewhere he felt truly comfortable, I just hadn't realized this difference would separate us so absolutely. Our childhoods had been very different, his made up of streets, of cityscapes, of a completely urban environment of theatres and good cafes. Wet fields edged by blackthorn hedges, bramble bushes deep in nettles, tractors splashing down narrow lanes and village-shop chat had played no part in that childhood. I loved it when he knew the waiters at the late-night Lebanese bars we went to a lot on the Edgware Road when we were first together, and he liked it that I could always light a fire in a field, however damp the wood was. Our differences had once pulled us together.

I stared into our wedding photograph, trying to remember the expectation of being that younger couple. Then, as I reached up to replace it, one of the cats jumped from the table on to the side, knocking a small painted jug, sending it crashing on to the floor. The white shadow of milk flooded across the floor as I grabbed a cloth, sopping it up, picking pieces of broken china from the liquid. A tiny, spiked end of a shard pierced the skin on my thumb so that a drop of red mixed with the white. I picked the cat up and put her outside, annoyed, although it had been an accident.

Rinsing milk from the cloth in the sink, I tried to understand how Pete and I had got to this place of absolute separation, since that, too, was an accident. The tangle of family life, which can feel like a knotted web to get through every day, meant that when the children were very small we were just muddling through. We didn't have anything like a five-year plan. We didn't have a one-year plan, or a three-month plan. We were making it all up as we went along. And for several years, we'd been pretending that living apart wasn't so bad, pretending that six or eight hours' time difference wasn't so much, pretending that another three weeks before we saw each other wasn't so long, that Whats-Apping at night as I lay in bed was almost like chatting, that FaceTime was a really pleasing way to be together on a Saturday evening. We pretended this was all OK and told each other it was only for a few more weeks, that this was just a phase. And then six years had passed.

*Six years!*

Resentment began to boil up inside me. It made me want to see his screen shatter when I thought of him quietly logging on to a Zoom meeting from a tidy hotel room, coordinating his team on long phone calls where his background was always silent.

He'd said so often that things would change, soon, and he needed to come home.

From Chicago he'd voice-message, 'I love you, Clover, we'll get through this, and it will change, soon.' From San Francisco he'd call and say, 'Your resentment is killing me, Clover, you're right, I can't do this any more.'

I glanced back at the photograph, then turned it around on the shelf. I didn't want to look at it, didn't want to be reminded of how much simpler it had seemed then. And I didn't want to see any more pictures of houses. I didn't want to think of Sylvia handing particulars to Pete, of her walking him through an interior, showing him the size of the fridge or convenience of a walk-in closet or the space, just here, perfect for a king-size bed. I didn't want to think of him nodding and agreeing with her, or the relief he must have felt at the easy life she was displaying for him.

'This is where my working life is, you must move here, we must sell the house, bring the children and come with me to live close to my work. You must come here, to America, Clover. My work is here. I must be here. This is the only way our life together is going to work. I cannot make the living we need for our big family unless I am in America. I have tried, and there is no alternative. You have to come here.'

We want different things, I thought, as I threw the dustpan and brush under the sink and angrily pushed my hair, frizzing in the heat, back from my face. I was already too hot, and it wasn't yet midday. Out in the yard, a white flat-bed van on the corner by the house slowed down, hooting in recognition. I turned and caught a glimpse of Luke and Kat passing on the road to Uffington, Kat waving as Luke shouted, with an upwards inflection, 'All right, Clover?' I wasn't sure anyone outside a house as neat as the red-brick one would ever hoot or wave, or even if people who lived in houses on suburban streets did that anyway. Sometimes, driving home from school, or to the village shop, or to Wantage to take one of the children to ballet or karate, I'd pass half a dozen cars where I'd see a cheerful grin, a thumbs-up, and it would lift me from the sometimes gloomy concussion the noise the children were making in the back, or the miles I'd driven with them that day, had given me. When Pete talked about America, I had seen something important creating a shape on his face. Washington represented true possibility and a new, comfortable way of belonging for him. It spoke of relief. But I didn't feel anything like that.

I don't see wide, inviting horizons opening before

me, I thought, as I walked over to the hedge beside the field. Overhead, swifts swooped elegantly around the house, creating pencil strokes of movement in the sky which vanished with them. They didn't find it so hard to come and go. I brushed my hand against the hedge we'd planted a few years before, to create shelter from the winds that blew across the flat plain separating us from Swindon a dozen miles away. Once whip-thin sticks, it was thick now, hornbeam leaves unfurled, with the pale-pink paper petals of dog rose scrambling over into the longer grass. Daddy long-legs blundered cheerily through the thick patch we'd neglected, so that it grew waist-high all across the lawn. It had been so sat- isfying to watch the hedge growing, and now, when I was forced to think of leaving, I had a painfully clear sense of my chest being opened with a scalpel and my heart being taken away from the home we had created. And when I looked inside, I could see my heart as many different vibrant colours of green, which were all very beautiful, and reassuring too, since I knew them well. But when I saw my heart being removed from inside me, I could also see Washington from the corner of my eye, and it was unfamiliar and dull like concrete, yet also coloured in patches an intensely shiny, patent grey.

'America? What do you want to go leaving here for, then? If I was you, Clover, I'd never want to let go of this place. Mind you, in this heat, long as you've got a full fridge and a proper fan, you can call anywhere home.' The farrier Aaron's t-shirt was stuck to his back in darker patches, his arms slick with sweat. Sunlight kicked off the concrete in the yard where the dun mare

Mavis was tied in a slice of shade, as Aaron bent forward again to lift her big hoof up. When I'd shown him a picture of one of the houses Pete had sent and asked him if he could imagine me and all the noisy kids living there, he'd made a face, like the children did when they took a swig from the milk bottle left too long outside the fridge.

'No chance,' he'd said, shaking his head as he scrolled through the pictures on my phone. 'I mean, I know you, Clover. But that? House in the city? That is not you. And I don't blame you either. I wouldn't leave my home, not for anyone else. I mean, I almost moved to Wrexham once, when I was applying for my apprenticeship and that, then I realized how far it was from Swindon and I couldn't do it.'

I leant back on the stone trough beside the barn. Some lavender plants I'd dug in there a few months ago had withered in the heat, the soil around them dried to dust. Aaron plunged a glowing red-hot horseshoe into a metal bucket, making the water bubble. 'And rightly or wrongly, Swindon is my home,' he explained, lifting the horseshoe out again and leaning into the anvil as he threw the edge of his hammer around its edges.

The dun mare stretched her neck out, her long, dark mane hanging tangled down her sides, burrs stuck in her hair where she'd been too long out in the field. Still sleek in her summer coat, the outlines of her dapples circled across her back, yellow as butterscotch. In winter, she would become hairy, like a big teddy bear, but at this point in the summer she was magnificent. When I first saw her, on a housing estate near Cardiff, I thought she was the most beautiful horse I'd ever seen. Now, she

lolled her head in Aaron's arms, resting her mouth on
his back each time he leant forward to pick up her hoof
and use huge metal grippers to clip a line through it, to
neaten it, like cutting fingernails.

  He was talking about how he was hoping to buy a
second house in Swindon, with his boyfriend. 'As an
investment because, let's face it, I'm not going to be
doing this when I'm sixty. My arm's fucked already –
tennis elbow from all the hammering.' Aaron stopped,
leaning up against his van, wiping sweat from his forehead with his forearm. 'Don't get me wrong, I make a
good living from this, especially as I was crap at school,
no hope, couldn't pass any exams. I had to do four years
of apprenticeship to get to college, but I knew this was
a good job for me. Especially for someone like me. We
didn't have a lot growing up – my mum was a carer,
Dad was a bin man, but I haven't seen him in years.'

  I asked him why not, and he looked down, kicking
the end of his dusty boot, shrugging.

  'Chalk and cheese. He's a self-taught vegan, never
understood me. But Mum, she gave me and my sister
the best childhood ever, growing up in Swindon. She
worked flat out, too, just like me. And now I'm doing
all right.'

  He pushed himself off the van, picked up a horseshoe
and rubbed it on the edge of the soft, shiny leather of
his chaps, then went back to the mare, making her lift
her leg again. He said he could shoe eleven horses a day
when he was going for it, and I whistled. It costs eighty-
five pounds to shoe a horse. 'But if I can keep on like
this, I'll own my house in Swindon outright in seven
years. I mean, yeah, it's Swindon, but home, innit?'

His short, dark hair was wet with a slick of sweat, his arms tense as he leaned forward with the mare's hoof between his knees. Aaron had an outstandingly strong and capable-looking body, and whenever I posted a snap of him like that on my Instagram the responses always contained lots of hearts. But now, watching him work with the metal shoe, more than hearts Aaron made me think of Wayland. Up on the hill, a couple of miles from the house, is an early Neolithic site called Wayland's Smithy. As Aaron's hammer smashed against the edge of the dun mare's shoe, I thought of Wayland, or Wolund, the Germanic smith god associated with the stones around the long barrow there. The bang of metal against metal rang across the concrete in the yard as Aaron moved between the shoes, stopping sometimes to run his hands down the mare's leg so that she antici-pated his movements, lifting her hoof for him before he pressed the black metal into her. He reached for a small, bright, silver nail with a very pointed tip in a little card-board box and started hammering again. When the shoe was in place, he twisted the end of his hammer, snap-ping the base of the nail off so that the end of it sat neatly against the mare's hoof. I shivered again and imagined Wayland hammering away at a shoe in the same way, unchanged, in most respects, across thou-sands of years.

'Here, open the gate for me on the way out, will you, darling,' he said when he'd finished, packing his tools into a wooden box. He handed me back his empty coffee mug, stepped into his van and slammed the door, his terrier on the seat beside him. 'Does he know, Clover? Your husband, I mean. Does he really know

what you think about leaving all this, leaving the place
that's your home, for good? Because if he doesn't really
know what it means to you, you're wasting your time.
You need to tell him. Show him why you want to stay.
It's fair enough. It's your feelings. Legitimate feelings.'
He smiled at me, then fired up the ignition. 'Never
know, darling. There might be another way.'

Aaron's words were in my head when I went out early
the next morning, while the children were sleeping, to
fill the horses' water buckets and check the fencing in
the field. In an hour, I'd be scooping them from their
beds, stuffing them reluctantly back into sports kit, trying to instil even the slightest sense of urgency about
finishing their cereal. But until then, the early-morning
stillness of the field soothed my agitation as I fiddled
with an electrical unit. Silver-white threads left by cat-
erpillars shimmered in the tall nettles under the hedge,
some stems heavy with fragile strings of seeds like tiny
green beads. Kneeling beside the solar panels clipped to
the electric fence, I felt the dry grass scratching the
inside of my thighs as I strained to hear the deep throb
of current that should have been there if power was
running through the plastic tape. None of the green
buttons on the panels was flashing. All I could hear was
the horses grazing on the other side of the fence, stamping their feet from the flies, and the dogs panting as they
watched me.

   Although the sound revolted me, I needed to hear that
throb of electricity, to reassure me the horses wouldn't
break through into the longer grass growing in the paddock beside theirs. That big artificial click of the electric

current, when it was working, always made me think of electric chairs, and the times I'd been electrocuted on white plastic tape as a child. My sister Nell and I would lay vulnerable, thin green strands of grass on the tape in the field beside our house, daring each other to experience the special sort of pain of an invited shock from an electric fence. The feeling terrified us but we couldn't stop it, and sometimes we'd spend whole afternoons, beyond the reach of adults, shocking ourselves on a fence. It made us dizzy, so that afterwards we'd stretch out in the field, stunned, under the big blue sky with tufty yellow dandelions dotted like litter around us. Nell had an idea we could make ourselves better by wiping the spunky white fluid from inside the dandelion stems on our wrists. For a long time afterwards, I thought the dandelions must be the source of that terrible, electric weightlessness which came from having shocked our small child wrists in the heat of summer on white plastic tape. Even now, I am suspicious of dandelions when I see them on the green near our house. I'm not sure I want my children to touch them, or that sticky, bitter fluid in their stems, even though I know the weightless feeling of nausea we felt came from the shocks.

Frustrated by the fence, I sat back on my heels, pulling my phone from my shorts to re-read the message Pete had sent me when I was asleep.

I'm going to see that house again. I got a good feeling from it.

The message scared me so much, I wanted to throw my phone into the grass as if it was a dandelion or had given me an electric shock. I stood up quickly, brushing dried grass seeds from my legs and flicking a strand of goosegrass which clung to my shirt. I needed to work faster, to do as Aaron had said, to gather the bright, green pieces of my life with Pete and create a picture of them for him, so he could see, beyond doubt, what our home represented. I swore loudly at the fencing unit, so that my dog Pablo looked at me in that guilty way he did when I caught him rolling in a dead badger or eating out of the kitchen bin. If I'd been a more practical woman, I'd have fixed the fence. But I wasn't that woman. I couldn't fix electric fences and I didn't know the names of any of the grasses in the field. I knew nothing about botany, could only name half a dozen wildflowers and was vague, at best, about the types of trees growing in the distant hedge line. I wasn't even that good at the country life I didn't want to give up.

But as I sat quietly, the hedgerow beside me dotted with the pale-pink insides of bramble flowers, a minute black insect magnified as it crawled through the grass knotted beneath my knees, the morning sunlight a milky haze across the field, I realized that knowing these things didn't really matter. They didn't matter beside simply witnessing the gossamer spiders' webs which spun early morning light through the grass where I sat, or spotting the first spatter of orange rose-hips dotting the hedge, or being awake to the plod of the dappled grey mare Sexy Legs as she walked across to greet me, hoping I might have half an apple or the end of a carrot in my pocket, stretching out her thick black lips and sunburned nose to nudge my shoulder. Her black-and-white outline was like a drawing against the cut-out spiked grass of the field, mottled splashes of grey and black hair tracing up her legs as if whoever had created her had been careless while painting, splashing Blagdon spots up her leg. Her foal from the previous spring, Solstice, watched us from further away; she was toffee-coloured, sharing with her mother her Blagdon markings. Sexy Legs nudged me again as I stood up, ran my hand across her belly, trying to sense whether there would be a swelling emerging there, as she'd been out with a stallion earlier in the year. She bobbed her head as I rubbed between her ears, talking to her, but then she stopped to look up, across the railway line towards our house, and the sound of a child. It was Dash, yelling from an upstairs window, his plump, buttery body naked. I shouted back, my hands cupped around my mouth like a cartoon character. 'Get back in the room. Put your feet flat on the floor.'

The grey mare lifted her head, turning away, ears slightly back as if my shouting had disturbed her too, so I ran my hand gently down her side.

'You're all right,' I whispered. 'Good girl.' If I closed my eyes slightly, the roundness of her belly where she might be holding a foal could be wings, folded neatly into her sides. I often thought about her at night, when I looked at the stars, wondering if I might see her in the sky, wings outstretched, proving important things I knew to be true. I remembered the morning when Solstice was born, walking at dawn through the long, damp grass with Dash and finding Sexy Legs shielding her newborn foal. I'd known she was due, of course, but the foal was like a miracle, creating a feeling of awe inside me, of where did you come from, where did you come from? I patted her again, pulling burrs from her mane, feeling her heartbeat in her deep, dappled-grey chest, then turned back to the house.

On the railway bridge separating our house from the field, beside the verge where thistles were sprouting small purple crowns, a man was standing. He wore a black overgarment like a shirt hanging halfway down over his black trousers. In fact, he was dressed all in black, although none of his clothes were ink-black, like midnight, but lighter, as if time had seeped into them and made them paler. His clothes were the colour of dusk. I rarely saw anyone on the bridge that early, the silent moment of the day when I was aware of both the world existing with a tremendous vigour, just before it wakes up, but also not existing at all, like I was the only person inhabiting it. Sometimes, in the very early morning, if I was alone in the house before the children woke, I'd feel there had been an apocalypse and I was the only person alive. That was wonderful. To find myself alone, with no one else there, was a massive relief. In the quiet kitchen, it was disappointing when Dash came in naked but for blue pants worn inside out and one sock, asking for my phone to play *Roblox*. He was never supposed to have survived the apocalypse that happens in my head every morning, only me.

But the man in pale-black clothes had survived the apocalypse too. I watched him carefully as I approached the bridge, where he was peering on to the tracks, as if he was either looking for something or had dropped something like a football down there. The metal barrier against the red-brick edges of the bridge, to stop people jumping, was much taller than the top of my head, but he could look right over it without lifting his feet off the ground at all. Pablo ran over the road – I didn't worry about this as there was no traffic – and twisted his body in a kind of dog greeting, like he knew the man well. I thought of Dash calling me from that upstairs window with his feet not on the floor, but I had time, and I wanted to stay and look over the bridge too, for whatever the man was searching for. He turned to me quickly, then looked back down at the tracks, motioning with his head, smiling in his dusk-coloured clothes.

'Good morning for it,' he said, nodding down to the tracks, and I said, yes, isn't it, but I didn't know what it was he meant. A good morning for what? 'Among the stones. Look among the stones,' he said quickly and quietly. Perhaps he had lost more than a football, a watch or a phone, something that mattered, and it had fallen amongst the stones he gestured to, lying like shingle all alongside the railway track. I paused to look over the bridge too, hoping to communicate a sense of friendliness, without saying much. This wasn't unusual. Often, when I pass a stranger walking on the track through the woods by the house, or up on the Ridgeway, or in a field, I don't always understand exactly what they are saying, but I know it is important to communicate connection. The words exchanged matter less than the fact of being two human beings walking across a shared landscape. When you discuss the weather, you're not really talking about rain or sunlight, but fostering a sense of friendliness or familiarity.

'It's a good time to be out here, in this morning air.

It's important,' he said, and I realized I was holding my breath, waiting for him to complete his sentence, which felt unfinished. 'Good morning to be out there, good to be out there, near the hill, near all this, the hill, the railway, the chalk horse, in this place, isn't it, Pablo?' he said, glancing down at my dog before gesturing towards the hill, the hedges, the field, then back towards the railway line. The way he spoke was inconclusive and reminded me of the way my children had spoken to one another one afternoon when they had been learning about riddles in school.

He turned away from the railway bridge, looking instead across the road, in the direction of the field of horses where I'd come from. 'Look among the fields and the stones and the horses,' he muttered, as if he didn't want to admit to wanting me to hear what he said, and yet also wanted me to know what it was. I looked up at him again, at his big features and faded dark hair. 'Castles, too. Go up to the castles, the ridge. It's all there, you'll find it all there,' he said, words falling almost reluctantly, as if he didn't speak often. In other circumstances, talking to an extremely tall man in a remote place might have been scary, but there was a simplicity to his big features, and the longer I stood in front of him, the taller he seemed. The fabric of his clothes was flimsy, and he didn't wear boots but flat, black shoes made of something like canvas, with the laces undone on one side. He did not look as if he was dressed for the landscape in which we stood but instead had been cut out from a different background altogether.

There was a silence around us, in the heat of the end of summer, and I could hear his breathing until suddenly the first white tradesman's van swung around the corner, whooshing past us, windows open releasing a rush of Radio 1. I was going to ask the man what he meant, but the van reminded me of the minutes I was losing before the children needed to be downstairs eating breakfast, and so I started moving on, towards my house. And when I turned to look back at him, just before I got to the door, he was no longer there.

Later, when I was making peanut butter on toast for the children, all their feet flat on the ground, I thought about the man I had seen on the bridge, and I realized he was too tall to be real. Too giant to be just tall. He had also known that my dog was called Pablo. The giant who had horses and stones and castles in his head and was looking for a lost life, but who didn't look like he belonged here, already knew the name of my dog.

# Chapter 2

The fears of a complete washout for the White Horse Show were unfounded, although the weather did break. Driving the children home from sports camp that evening, unwrapped chips on their laps creating a fug of vinegar and grease inside the windscreen, the warm, mellow light of the sun suddenly sharpened. The colours of the sky darkened to the shade of wet slate, magnifying the yellow of the late-summer stubble fields, polishing them to bright gold. Wind moved the poplar trees on the lane before the house, and some rubbish, blown from a nearby dustbin, skittered across the road in front of us. Spots of unfamiliar rain spat from the rounded clouds on to the windscreen, lubricating the dead insects stuck there, as the children made excited noises at something so novel as rain. It started pattering on the top of the car, and at home the dogs wrapped themselves around my legs, relieved we were home but disturbed by the change in the weather. I moved through the house, shutting those windows that had been left flung open since the start of the summer, pulling a leopard-print fleece blanket from a cupboard to throw over the children's bare legs as they sat on the sofa in the kitchen. They finished their chips, ignoring the dogs staring longingly at them, and while they bickered over a single can of Coke, I pulled out my laptop to answer emails neglected by the drive to Wantage.

Pete and I had not resumed the conversation about the house. Instead, I'd deleted his email with the houses attached to it, imagining I had deleted Sylvia at the same time. If her name didn't appear in my inbox, I could make her tiny figure, walking around in my mind, leave my head and return to her own life in Washington. It was easy to put off any conversation about it, and anyway, since we last spoke, Pete had flown to a conference in Arizona.

It's 108 degrees here. I need some t-shirts. I left my charger in DC.

I worried what he might be wearing, but without him to talk to, instead I tried to remember some of the conversations we'd had about moving to America. Although Pete's voice hadn't sounded amused when we discussed it, looking at houses had ramped up the conversation so that now it felt like an unsettling joke.

We could move to America!

That made it sound so simple, to just sell up, hug our friends goodbye and walk away. OK, let's go now, get your bags, where's your coat, come on, hurry up, kids, we must leave now, we're going! Sometimes the audacity of it made me take a short intake of breath; I regretted the fact I'd only half concentrated when Pete talked about it, as I did when discussing the plot of a Marvel film with Dash, only focusing on what he said with about an eighth of my brain. And since so much of our communication was on the phone, I knew I would have been doing something quite different at the same time that we talked, like lying flat on the floor to reach under the sofa for a dead rabbit the cat had brought in, or running beside a trotting pony which seemed to be lame, or carrying two over-filled buckets of water across the field or fishing matted hair from the shower plug, despite discussing quite complex things relating to cities, time zones, schools, universities, the kind of car we might drive, work, book-shops, what we would eat, who our friends might be, what we would do at weekends, and who I would talk to when Pete was working in a much closer office and his working days were still fourteen hours long.

I felt mean when I thought of Sylvia, walking into my head carrying all her houses with their neat, beige interiors. But I distrusted her because, until she had entered my brain, America had seemed like a dream sequence, and the mighty United States of America actually looked like a great big platter, the biggest platter my mind could ever imagine. In my head, it was all laden with treats and different-coloured sweets, piled into different-sized mounds which we could drive between in a little red car, like a toy small enough to fit into one of my children's hands. The platter glimmered and gleamed and was lit by little coloured lights, bright-pink and green and orange or blue, those strings of coloured lights, like illuminated sweets, that you wrap around a Christmas tree. It was sort of cute and appeal-ing, for sure, I thought, peeling the paper from choc ices for the children for their pudding, but also sickly, plastic and precarious. Like a toy, not real.

Sylvia had brought it into real focus, and much, much more real again was the large brown envelope which had arrived that morning, addressed to Pete but post-marked Washington. I had opened it, dropping the envelope on the floor among three trainers and a flip-flop scattered by the front door. Inside were seven neat, printed pages illustrated with coloured pictures of a school and its pupils. It was a prospectus: an elementary state school with nine hundred pupils, ten times the size of the register at the children's village school. There were pictures of some of the children debating UN climate-change policy, and a headmistress watching from behind a wooden podium. There were images of the canteen, hundreds of small smiling faces, little hands holding sandwiches or apples as they grinned at the camera, just like any of Evangeline or Dash's friends. There was a softball team, a school choir, images of the school litter-pick, and details of a community hub, a call to action for parents to *GET INVOLVED!*

The prospectus made school life in Washington unfold in my hands, as if the platter wasn't just a toy but a pop-up book. I'd looked up the school on my laptop, typing the address into Google Maps, zooming in to a slab of playground, a park, the outline of play equipment like coloured pipe cleaners twisted together. I'd clicked in closer, until the pixels melted, then pulled back, finding focus, stepping from my kitchen into the swampy, hot streets of Washington, holding firm on to Dash and Lester's wrists to stop them running across roads. In our home in the country they were always vanishing ahead of me, down the wide-open, unfenced green running through the village, or under the mosaic

of light and leaves beneath the trees in the wood before
Uffington, or far, far away as they tore along the strip of
chalk path that made the Ridgeway, or dodging between
standing stones in the ritual landscape of Avebury stone
circle or up at Wayland's Smithy, but on pavements,
with cars on either side, they would have to learn to be
different children. I walked through Rock Creek Park,
then zoomed in to the Friendship Hospital for Animals.
I imagined ordering a chicken steak at the Steak 'n Egg
diner and a vegetable-loaded pizza at the New Haven
pizza bar, stopped for a margarita and cheese nachos at
Chipotle Mexican Grill, then walked back to the red-
brick house on Garrison Street through Fort Reno
Park.

I'd zoomed around, leaving northwest DC, moving
east to Takoma Park, scooting back to the National
Cathedral, then on to Capitol Hill, moving through
Georgetown, crossing the Potomac River on to Arling-
ton, and Alexandria, saying the names out loud to see
how they felt on my tongue. But they seemed tower-
ingly urban when placed beside words that made up the
edges of my daily life: Shellingford, Stanford in the
Vale, Uffington, Kingston Lisle, Childrey.

Perhaps we would become a better-organized, urban
family, who took up less space and made less noise. The
children's clothes would be cleaner and never ripped.
The boys would go to barbers, not get their hair cut by
me using the kitchen scissors. The children would be
able to walk to elementary school, but since they'd soon
start walking alone, we'd probably have to get them
mobile phones. On Saturdays, in search of nature, we
would go hiking in state parks. We would have bikes

with ever-ready pumped-up tyres, and chains that weren't rusty. Our car would not be muddy, since we'd never have to drive single-track roads marked with pot-holes that caused punctures, and we'd never get stuck behind tractors scattering clumps of straw on the wind-screen, or splash through deep puddles edging muddy verges, but instead would purr around, probably in an electric car, through the clean, spacious streets. There would be ample parking everywhere. The roads wouldn't twist and snake, as they did here at home, around the hills whose shape had been created by glaciers, but instead we'd know the grid, grow familiar with walk-ing along Gramercy, Garrison, Reno, Connecticut, back to the red-brick house, with its big windows like gentle eyes watching us, and its pale painted walls, just waiting for Dash to plant his hands against them. But I also felt a sense of curiosity, and relief too, imagining how the children might grow as their small world would expand and diversify. They'd make friends from further corners of the globe and become international citizens of the world, although they wouldn't be locals any more.

In many ways, the house and prospectus showed me that the life Pete was creating in America was a good one, but still, I didn't know how to contemplate dis-mantling the life we'd created here. So I stuffed the document into the back of a drawer in the kitchen, hoping it would quietly vanish.

It was hot again that night, the spots of rain all dried up, a sense of late-summer pressure rising. I was still awake at midnight, thinking of what the heat might feel like in that red-brick house. A sweltering, swampy, funky heat which lingered from April to October, was how my friend Patrick, an actor, had described it when I'd asked him. He'd lived in Washington for a few months one summer, performing in two Pinter plays to slightly bemused audiences. 'It's a different kind of scene to the one you are used to. You'll have to get into wearing cocktail dresses and making devilled eggs. Cooking brisket for the school potluck. Just your kind of scene,' he'd laughed and then added, 'Stop being so fucking provincial, Clover, it'll be great.'

I lay in bed, fretting about this now, trying to convince myself I was asleep, then giving up eventually to get up to make breakfast for the children. They cheered when I told them it was Saturday, and that sports camp was over. By mid-morning, I could make out the crackle of a Tannoy in the field beside the football pitch in Uffington. The children pleaded to go to the show, not for the shire horses or vintage steam engines or the poultry tent, but for candy floss, and to go back to Lenny's Lizards, the reptile rescue organization from Wantage, and the rare-breeds trailer, where they had not forgotten the enticing, extraordinary horror of holding the cool, firm skin of real snakes which curled around their wrists.

We parked amongst lines of cars glinting in the sunlight on the stubble field, which was still as hard as concrete despite the previous evening's spattering of rain. The show sat in two large flat fields, framed by the line of the hill and the Ridgeway. Beneath it, a line of canvas tents housed a craft section with people selling honey, hand-whittled walking sticks, home-made felt bags and knitted blankets. The children ignored all this and ran instead towards the main ring, an arena fenced off with ropes where a man with a whistle and a red face was running a dog agility display. A collie with a fervent expression dipped in and out of orange cones, and afterwards the crackly male voice on the Tannoy requested a special round of applause for this the excellent dog and his trainer, all the way from Somerset.

The field moved with people. A child high on his father's shoulders, dripping ice cream on to the man's shiny head; a woman in shorts with a long plait right down her back, carrying a new felt hat and a bag of bric-a-brac from the junk stall in the far corner of the field; a young couple wearing matching purple tracksuits scowling slightly as they queued for chips; a tractor driver from a neighbouring farm sweating in his boiler suit but heading determinedly for the beer tent; families spread out under the oak tree, parents passing foil packages of sandwiches and bottles of squash between them, intently watching the falconry display just getting under way in the main ring. Children, sucking on boxes of orange juice, ragging between their parents, ignoring the falconer's long explanation of the role of the birds' hoods, his voice all but lost in the pop and hiss of the loudspeaker system. The salty-sweet smell of hotdog onions drifted across the field, and further ahead, above the curve of White Horse Hill, half a dozen parachutes, appearing as if from nowhere, floated gracefully down to land, a ribbon of smoke, trailing from a small aircraft, dissolving into the blue sky around them.

The children spotted Iona across the field, detaching from me for a moment to throw themselves at her. She smiled, hugging them all, kneeling down to their height and listening intently to what they had to say to her. She was Jimmy's age, and I'd met her a year before, when she'd come to the house for a party. She had grown up on the other side of the Ridgeway, closer to Avebury, and had worked for a local show-jumping yard. She knew a lot about the kind of things I liked, such as ancient stones and young horses, and she helped me after school when I was working; the children all thought of her as an older sister.

Across the crowd we now saw Jimmy, his golden-blond ponytail as bright as the stubble in the field as he and a handful of friends loped towards us. They were carrying pints and smiling broadly while calling to Dash and Lester, Jake blowing Iona a kiss and raising a pint to me, 'All right, kids, all right, Clover. Nice day for it?', as Kyle scooped out of his pocket a handful of loose change and gave it to the boys. 'Here, let's go and get you some candy floss while Mum's not looking, eh Dash, eh Lester?' Jimmy's friends, who he'd met at the local state school, had watched my children grow up, just as I'd watched them, once a group of young lads who, together with Jimmy, had given me many wild and sleepless nights of anxiety about where their teenage lives were taking them and the secrets they were all hiding.

Funny, I thought, watching them, that now I trusted all of them enough to often get them to watch the kids if I had to nip out, or to take the boys metal-detecting on a bank holiday or pick Dolly up from a bus in Faringdon. For a while they'd created an indoor skate park from old sheets of plywood they used for graffiti in the barn, then grown out of that, instead running speakers from the house and soundproofing the inside of the barn with mattresses to have impromptu raves whenever they could. The next day, they'd fill the kitchen, and I always liked cooking bacon for them while they told me about new jobs, how their mum was getting on, what their younger siblings were up to.

I sat with them for a while as they stretched their long frames out on the grass, Jake rolling on to his stomach and burying his face in his arms as Jimmy patted him on the back, explaining he'd gone straight from a twelve-hour labouring shift to a blow out at the Swan and hadn't had much sleep. Iona sat with Evangeline on her lap, watching the heavy horses, magnificent like gods, being paraded around the ring: a Suffolk Punch, the size of a small giant, red knots of ribbon plaited through his mane; a dappled grey shire spooking so that his handler, a girl not that much bigger than Evangeline, was pulled from the ground before wrestling him back under control.

Queuing for burgers, while the children sat with Jimmy and his friends, I waved to Jack, who lived in a nearby village. He was carrying his new baby son, whose small face was a paler, brighter imprint of his father's. I said I hadn't seen him around for a bit and he laughed, not sure why that was since his dad had made him buy a bright-yellow van just so he could see him driving through the village. When Dolly had worked in the pub, Jack was usually there on a Friday night and occasionally gave her a lift back from her shift. Like the wild west, was how my friend Danny, who sometimes worked for Jack, fixing fences, had described him.

I smiled at Jack, who raised his half-empty pint in

one hand, his baby under the other arm, as if they were
a seesaw. I asked if he was free anytime soon to fix the
broken gate, held up by brambles, in the corner of our
field and he said, 'Is Danny about?' as a shadow suddenly passed across his face.

'Truth be told, I'd do it for you if I could, but there's
a get together, later, for Tom,' he went on. I must have
looked a bit blank because he added, 'Y'know, the lad
killed in his car on the A420 not so long ago? Only
eighteen, just passed his test, bless him. Terrible to lose
him like that. Still, we're getting together.' He paused,
looking away, up to the White Horse, raising his eyebrows and blinking very hard, his eyes a little glassy.
'Me and a few of the lads, we're getting together to have
a drink for him, bless him,' he said again, looking back
at me and smiling, rubbing his eyes. I was sorry, really
sorry, I said, and Jack smiled sadly again, straining to
plaster a smile across his face. 'Just one of those things,
isn't it, really? We've all just got to bloody get on with
it. Still, not a good way to go. Known him since he was
a lad. Not a good way to go. Much too young,' he
shrugged, tipping the last of his pint down this throat,
then making an exaggerated smile at his baby. 'All about
you now, isn't it? I'll be teaching you to drive a digger
before you know it.' His baby laughed, a wide-open
gummy grin, reaching out and tugging his dad's short
hair.

Once, at a party in London, I had a conversation with
a woman with a complex fringe who said she wanted to
move to the countryside for a quieter life. 'City life is so
frenetic, it's completely different in the countryside. I
swear that just living in east London is what gave me

burnout. It's just so . . .' She paused, groping around for the right word '. . . stimulating. That's it. I feel like I'm firing on all cylinders in the city, twenty-four-seven, but since I hit thirty I'm getting to crave what you have, that sleepy living in the country.' She laughed, raising her eyebrows knowingly, and I could clearly sense her turning over in her mind an image of country life she'd formulated following #cottagecore, then simulated after spending weekends at country clubs in the Cotswolds and Somerset. 'Slow village living. Foraging. Wild swimming. Yeah, that's what I want next.'

I'd nodded but didn't tell her about the rat I'd had to kill, that morning, with a brick, as that was all that was to hand, after I'd found it dragging itself around in the barn, rotting to death with gangrene. Neither did I tell her about the etched look of despair my friend Jan had failed to hide when she'd told me about her son selling drugs in the small town where our children went to school, or how surprised she'd been to become a grand-mother to her teenage daughter's baby. Life in villages is full of just as much human longing and misery as any street in a city, and country life is brutal, ripe with death and blood, discarded feathers and rotting carcasses. Life did not feel slow when the ditches running down the verge outside our house were blocked and water started to seep into the yard, nor did it feel slow when the septic tank started leaking, which meant the lawn had to be dug up in January, when it had also started snowing. It didn't feel sleepy when Jimmy and his friends stacked a wall of speakers up in the barn and made the house reverberate with a bass audible not just in the next vil-lage but in the nearest town too. I didn't tell her that life in the country reminded me of the feeling of looking at the bright-purple insides of a dead animal: more brutal and bloodier, but also strangely much, much more exhilarating, than she might have imagined.

Balancing burgers and chips in my outstretched hands, I made my way back through the crowds to Jimmy and his friends. Kyle and Iona had gone for more pints, and Dash cried when he spilled his cone of chips all over the grass. Jake soothed him by sharing the last gulps of a warm can of Coke and showing him how to scoop the chips back into the paper before dipping them into the ketchup oozing out of the side of his burger. Around the main ring, space was being filled by people settling their camping seats and spreading out blankets to watch the motorbike display, while over the Tannoy a clipped male voice was thanking the organizing committee for the hard work put in throughout the year, with special thanks going to Steven Owen Jones, the chairman, for his tireless work raising valuable funds to install defibrillators in the village, make library improvements for the school and supply a new trailer for the local Scouts.

'It's my lucky day,' said Jake. 'I can just feel that I am going to be the winner of that barrow of booze.' He pulled a couple of strips of pink and yellow tickets from his shirt pocket, checking his numbers and stretching his hands out. 'Just imagine it, Jimmy, an entire wheelbarrow full of booze – that should see us through the rest of the weekend, right?' There was a pause over the Tannoy as around the ring people checked whether their number had come up, a rustling sound in the background, and then a voice explained that the winning ticket had been picked and the winner was . . . Steven Owen Jones!

Jake threw back his head, groaning and scattering the tickets around him like confetti. Lester clambered on to him, jumping up and down on his chest, begging him to take him on some of the nearby fairground rides. Jake just groaned some more as Jimmy, wiping ketchup from his hands, said, 'Yeah, we'll take you, mate', standing slowly, hitching his trousers up, pulling Jake up from the grass, then swinging Lester on to his shoulders as they loped towards the fairground, Dash and Evangeline bouncing along beside them, chattering gratitude.

A boy in a tracksuit was leaning on the edge of a waltzer, trying to force eye contact with a girl pointedly ignoring him and instead studying the ends of her thick, dark plait pulled over one shoulder. Kyle and Iona returned, leaving their pints at my feet. Jake declined the Waltzer as much, much too treacherous in his current state, pointed instead to a ride bigger than a double-decker bus and painted with large red-and-yellow letters announcing *THE MOTION THEATRE: THE ULTIMATE ROLLER COASTER* and *FAST SIMULATOR EXPERIENCE*. Techno thumped from around a mirrored door surrounded by flashing lights.

'That looks jokes, though, let's try that,' said Jake, and they all trooped inside, handing over fistfuls of notes and coins to a lad with tufts of hair on his chin suggesting he was younger than them. He was wearing a leather money pouch, tattoos down both his arms.

I sat on the grass, waiting, as the building started rocking and moving. From inside I could just make out, over the techno, the squealing and laughing of the children. I leant back on my wrists, watching the crowds moving away from the main ring, where the falconry

display was ending. In a week the children would
be back at school, another academic year pushing them
onwards. I remembered previous shows, when the
children were much younger, toddlers who needed
carrying and changing, or grew suddenly fretful, lung-
ing out of my arms if they hadn't slept or eaten. Now
they were almost rational, and the hard physical graft
of parenting, involving so much wiping and lifting and
bathing and soothing, was almost over. Pete was missing out on so much. I sighed, pulling at a tuft of grass,
ripping it into little pieces, then looked back at the fairground. The children's squeals reached a crescendo
before the ride shuddered to a halt, and Jimmy and his
friends emerged, rubbing the backs of their heads,
blinking as they adjusted from the darkness inside, the
children dancing beside them in delight, begging to be
taken back in.

'That was the most amazing thing I've ever done!'
shouted Dash. 'We sat in little cars and a big screen played
a film of whoooosshhhhhiiiing down a roller coaster.'

'Yeah, that was definitely worth four pounds fifty,'
said Jake, laughing and making a face as Dash tugged at
his sleeve. 'Maybe next year, yeah? Jimmy and me,
we've got some plans now . . .' And then he, the other
boys and Iona peeled off across the field, promising to
drop by the house later, maybe.

Bereft, suddenly, of those young giants, I bought the
children ice creams, which they ate quickly, racing the
vanilla cream which dripped on to their wrists. Then
they pulled me over to the swirling, blue-and-white
tower of the helter skelter. As we climbed the steps

together, Evangeline paused, late-afternoon sunlight falling on her, as she turned her face to the Ridgeway.

'Look, Mum,' she said, motioning to the curve of the hill framing the field, and the familiar outline of the White Horse. 'I think it's whiter than ever before, don't you?'

I looked back to where she was pointing. From our home, just over a mile away, I could make out Uffington White Horse as a pale shape of tangled lines scrawled on to the green hillside; but high up in the tower of the helter skelter the horse looked new again, more enigmatic, its strange geometric lines moving and changing as I climbed the stairs, up, up. I skirted around the tower, watching the lines of the horse appear to shift on the hill as my perspective changed and changed again. The white plastic of the tower seemed insubstantial compared to the permanent white lines of the horse carved on to the hillside something like three thousand years ago, although in that time no man or woman has been able to figure out why it was put there or what it symbolizes. Archaeologists and historians have theories about it, but Uffington White Horse is a mystery.

'Near to the town of Abinton there is a mountain with a figure of a stallion upon it, and it is white. Nothing grows upon it,' states the earliest reference to *mons albi equi* or White Horse Hill in the Welsh *Red Book of Hergest* (1375–1425). There's no other chalk horse like Uffington. Other hill horses at Cherhill, Alton Barnes and Westbury are figurative representations a few hundred years old at most. No early visual record of it exists, although small, bright, Celtic gold coins have been found decorated with a horse whose outline is like that of the Uffington horse. The horse, which covers almost an acre, holds its secrets. Aligned to the movement of the sun, it's been described as a solar horse, carrying light across the sky; but because it was created in the late Bronze Age, when horses were changing the way humans lived, and fought, what the horse represents is completely open to speculation: it might stand for a god, but could also represent status, kinship or territory. Archaeologists in the seventies dated it using optically stimulated luminescence on silt deposits, but the findings are relatively fluid. They can tell us it was created by people digging deep trenches in the shape of a horse and then filling them with chalk sometime between 1380 BC and 550 BC. But still, we don't really know if it was created as a horse or a dragon or a mythical being.

Staring across to it from the top of the tower, I realized Evangeline was right: it did look brighter and whiter than ever. The previous summer, Jimmy, Evangeline and I had walked up the hill to help out at the chalking run by the National Trust to keep the horse white. Then, the tack-tack-tack of small hammers hitting the hill filled the air as we sat with a pile of gleaming white chalk between us, pounding the horse into a new brightness. It was a remnant of something other people have done for millennia, since part of the beauty of the horse is not just that it exists at all, but that it's been cared for – scoured – for all that time too. Without that care, the horse would have just sunk back into the hill where it came from.

Scooting down the helter skelter, the horse flashed past; and later, as we walked back to the car, as crowds

across the field thinned out and the noise from the beer
tent rose a little in anticipation of a local rock band
playing that evening, I explained to the children that
the show we were at was also a remnant of the 'scour-
ings' which used to bring tens of thousands of people to
the hill. Between 1755 and 1857, they happened every
seven years, and at the last scouring thirty thousand
people flocked to the hill, when Uffington Castle
became the site of festivities, as recorded by Thomas
Hughes in 1859, in his semi-fictionalized account *The
Scouring of the White Horse*. Then, a silver cup was
awarded to the winner of a three-mile pony race, a side
of bacon was won in an ass race, a female gypsy was
rewarded for smoking the most tobacco and five shil-
lings was awarded for grinning through a horse collar.
Carriages, with ladies in their finest dresses, arrived on
the hill, but carters, shepherds and ploughboys also
wandered through the stalls where gingerbread and
apples were sold alongside coloured ribbons, flagons of
ale and salty pork cooked on crackling wood fires. Bare-
knuckle boxing drew big crowds, and even bigger
numbers arrived to watch the peculiar art of backsword-
ing, a speciality in Uffington in which men hit each
other around the head with a kind of stick, one arm tied
at their side. Sometime in the middle of the eighteenth
century, Tim Gibbons, a blacksmith turned highway-
man from Lambourn, beat the reigning champion, only
to gallop off before he was arrested. The idea of this
really excited the children, but was forgotten, very
quickly, when Evangeline found a five-pound note,
crumpled into the shape of a piece of rubbish, lying in
the stubble just before the car. That, they all agreed as

we drove home, was the most amazing thing that could happen on a Saturday afternoon at the White Horse Show. Later, as I walked through the garden gathering up discarded clothes, the light thinning while the distant, tinny sound of guitars rose slightly as the band started, Danny texted me back about the broken gate. He was going to a free party in Salisbury, so could we meet closer to midday tomorrow, not nine a.m.? I texted him back an alien emoji. Of course.

I went out to the field the next day, leaving the children inside sharing a family packet of salt and vinegar crisps they'd taken from the cupboard, and watching a video about mice. Slamming the wicket gate behind me caused a spattering of crows to rise in a single blanket from where they had been pecking in the grass, insistent upon finding worms. Pablo dipped in and out of the hedge line, ears pricked, making starlings scatter from their perches in the bramble bushes as I walked ahead of him, looking to the outline of the hill and the Ridgeway, infinitely reassuring and absolutely eternal, the grid of Gramercy, Garrison, Reno, Connecticut dissolving in my mind like bars being pulled apart.

When I walked through the field, I could always feel my heart deep inside me, green, pounding in exactly the right place. It had taken me forty-nine seconds to walk there, crossing on to the village road for a few metres before turning through the little gate, sitting so deep in the hedge you wouldn't know it was there unless you were looking, into the field. Often, as I crossed the bridge, trains whooshed between Didcot and Swindon, on through the deep railway cutting separating our home from the field. At night I'd not just hear them but also feel the velocity of that engine moving, making our house shake, as if it was a little shocked. They roared very close but so deep in the cutting that they were totally invisible. I thought of them as dragons, moving near to me but just below the surface, out of reach. Often, I was sure they were real dragons, although a few days after moving to the house I stopped really hearing them unless I actively listened out. I'd see them at night, though, when I was driving towards the house, and the dragon would suddenly roar towards me on that short stretch of road where it emerged from the cutting before it tore off across country. Then I'd be able to look right into a carriage, at the outline of people wearing suits or a good dress, a wine bottle or an open laptop on the table in front of them, or moving their hands as they flashed past, ever so quick. Alone in the countryside, it felt good to hear that dragon roaring past. It reminded me that there were people, contained within those trains, speeding towards other lives, all joined together, in cities.

Pablo panted back towards me, his tongue lolling like a strip of raw bacon, looking pleased with himself, as if being a dog hunting through the thick, dark hedgerows was the best thing in the world. Sometimes, when I walked in the field in the early morning, especially in winter, I thought it might be nice if it was lit by glow worms, like that gentle glow of solar lights people have in their gardens. But even when it was dark, I didn't really need lights. I didn't need to be shown the way. I knew the shape of the field, and if you'd given me a felt tip, I could have drawn the shape that the outline of the hill and the Ridgeway made. It rose in the distance, like the shoulder of someone much, much taller, a couple of miles away. The Ridgeway formed my horizon. It formed my furthest view, the edges of my world, every day. The Ridgeway wasn't just a location to me, either: it was a state of being which no other place made me feel. I'd walked and camped on the Ridgeway as a child, danced at raves on the hill as a teenager, returning there again and again for the most important times of my life, so that over time I felt it had absorbed parts of my psyche, and my psyche had absorbed it in return. I am certain the Ridgeway holds vibrations of my soul that I've not experienced in other places, and so it knows things about me, and is sympathetic even, to who I am, in a way I do not have the capacity to find in other landscapes because I have not had definitive experiences there. The big and dramatic expanses of Dartmoor, or the blue and yellow beaches of Cornwall, or the green and purple fells of Northumberland, or the outstanding mountains of Scotland, have no hold over me. These are rich, beautiful landscapes, places I would love to take my children for a holiday, but they do not contain me, and I do not contain them. They don't reveal an internal truth to me which I sometimes find when I am on the Ridgeway; and this was what I was afraid of letting go of.

Moving around the edges of the field as I waited for Danny, I checked for loose fence posts and branches that had collapsed over the wire. It had rained again, just a bit, enough to lift the grass so that it smelled slightly green. I walked to the far side, into the shade of the oak trees near the hedge, where early acorns dotted the dried ground like lost buttons popped from their branches. Apart from the distant sound of the show, it was cool and quiet there, only the rhythmic cooing of a wood pigeon in the tree overhead. Danny had often said it was the perfect field for a rave, hard techno, he said, with the Ridgeway just above it. I'd once spent an evening with him, waiting in his van in a McDonald's car park outside Swindon, drinking cups of coffee as we waited for the location of a free party on the other side of Marlborough to be texted to his phone. We'd chatted for an hour or so, but when his phone pinged he drove, swigging Red Bull, as, close to midnight, we joined a snaking convoy of vehicles passing through Wiltshire villages, then bumping down a rough track, the blackness of Salisbury plain in the distance, cars congregating in a yard, the rain unceasing. The sound of techno, from a stack of speakers as big as a house piled up in an open-sided barn, destroyed the sound of rain hammering on the corrugated iron of the barn roof, distracting from the mud underfoot. No one cared anyway, not the boys and girls in trainers and puffer jackets who danced and danced and danced.

I hadn't been to a free party like that for a long time, although they had defined many weekends in my twenties, when Nell and I had taken the same route Danny and I took that night. It was reassuringly unchanged, smiling faces, pounding music, and the mighty joy of being outside in the night and the mud as the beat filled every space around, echoing into the thick darkness, the light from car headlights dancing on a clump of beech trees, the moon big and vacant and unjudging above. Driving home, wide-eyed with life but totally sober,

Danny told me about growing up in Uffington, biking on to the Ridgeway as a teenager to put on parties like this long before he and his friends could drive. 'We're all in love with the Ridgeway, all of us who grew up here,' he'd said.

I crossed the field, reminded, as I was every single time I went out there, whether I was held by the still, daytime air or the early-evening night-time sky, of that sense it gave me that the land, the place, the space itself, was breathing with me. It was a space big enough to lose the edges of myself in, or at least those edges within me that held all the puddles of anxiety, because it was the size of several football pitches knitted together, a plain almost. The far corners of the field, where the hedge was thickest, where the dogs hunted for mice, were not visible from where I walked through the middle, checking the horses' water buckets. The edges of the field sloped down, quite sharply, to the two corners furthest from our house and the railway line. A scrappy hedge line of beech leaves, spiked with the occasional sharp thorn of holly, and thicker, blacker patches of blackthorn, hawthorn, sprinkled with the confetti of dog roses, ran down the centre. On the far side, separating our field from the neighbour's, was a thick hedge as tall as a double-decker bus. A line of five oak trees dotted that hedge, although one had naked branches, stripped and stunned-looking, where the lightning that touched it had left a physical shock of presence.

I could hear the odd car passing along the narrow road which ran at a right angle down two sides, but invisible, like the train track, obscured by more thick hedges that turned white in the spring with mayflowers.

There was a small wood, a spinney, over the road, which created another horizon underneath the high shoulder of the Ridgeway. In the days of my life, I moved between the house and the field a lot, since there was work for me to do in both places. In the house, I did things like cut up carrots, found paper and coloured paints, ran baths, fought with the children, carried around piles of laundry and piles of books, toys and pens, boiled pans of water, sighed, got undressed, did some writing, watched Netflix, cleaned sinks.

But when I went out into the field, I unfolded into a different person from the one who sat inside writing, or walked around my own house as a mother, often feeling absent. The duties I had in the field, like filling buckets of water, or checking the fence, or walking quietly amongst the horses, gave me much more joy than scraping freshly washed rice out of the dishwasher and finding a single shoe lost from a PE kit or hunting for a tube of toothpaste the youngest children in my life wouldn't reject as too spicy. Walking through the grass when it was still wet, as a pinky blue cross branded the dawn sky, splitting the clouds open as if the world was starting, or stepping through a curl of mist which pulled me towards the horizon, as if I might be walking straight into not simply a new day, but an entirely new dimension, was much more beautiful and certainly more vital than any domestic duty I had in the house. Watching crows lift from the field in a single mottled blanket against the yellowing night sky after it had been raining and they had been eating worms in the sodden grass was so much more incredible and surprising than making beds or folding sheets or kneeling beneath the kitchen

table to separate tiny pieces of Lego mixed together
with scraps of pasta and old dust. Lying in the long
grass, feeling the shape of the ridge and furrow beneath
my body, was a better way to be than kneeling by the
washing machine, raking damp socks from the drum;
allowing my eyes to track along the horizon of the
Ridgeway was a more purposeful way to start the day
than standing in the kitchen scrolling Instagram and
feeling absent.

In the house I could also feel homesick, even when I
was standing right inside the kitchen, or lying on my
bed, or sitting on the edge of the bath as the taps ran,
but in the field I never felt that way. Out there, I just felt
present. I was never resentful, melancholic or annoyed
in the field. I was rarely bored there. Even when I was
doing something mundane like failing to fix the electric
fence or pulling back brambles which had tumbled too
heavily across the wire fence running along the edge of
the hedgerow, I never felt strangled by the demands it
placed on me, in the same way that my tasks in the
house could choke me: the washing, another supper,
clearing up bits of coloured plastic after the dogs had
destroyed the packet of clothes pegs I'd been so satisfied
to buy a few hours earlier from the village shop. The
field contained so many of my big, good feelings that it
often felt more like home than the walls of our house. I
was myself when I was out in the field or up on the
Ridgeway. Inside, I was watching myself from a distance, squirrelling pointlessly around with all those
piles of crap I carried about. When I was in the house
doing that, I was beside myself. But in the field, I was,
always, inside all the best and most right parts of myself.

I glanced back at the horizon, to the familiar lip of land that fell so sharply it seemed artificial against the smooth, ancient outline of the hill. When we'd been driving home from the free party that night, Danny had talked about the way the Ridgeway had always, always been a place where people had come together to make meaning of their lives, and raves were really no different, even though the police would try their best to stop them. That fall, the lip of land of the vast grass ramparts of Uffington Castle I could see from the field, was created as long ago as perhaps seven thousand years before Jesus was born, in the Neolithic Age, then used throughout the Iron Age. The hill fort, which covers eight acres, is surrounded by deep ditches, and when I'd said, imagine living there, Danny corrected me, telling me that it had probably never been inhabited but might instead have been a place for people to congregate, to trade and breed livestock, to be together.

'Like a massive stadium up on the hill, rather than a living village,' was how he'd described it, although no one really knows. I've found books in charity shops, and sometimes, if I was very lucky, on the charity bookshelves at Didcot station when I took a train to London for work, which told me that when you step far, far back into ancient history, every date you meet there is an approximation. When things are discussed in the very ancient past, the dates are sometimes thirty thousand years ago or possibly four and a half thousand years ago. Reading about Neanderthals, I had to recheck dates or recount the number of zeros on a figure. Neanderthals were using hand tools for cutting meat, cracking open bones and working wood four hundred thousand years ago in parts of Britain, as well as forty thousand years ago.

These huge dates suited me. The mega dates with all their zeros were much more relaxing than the precise dates like 1549 and 1653 and 1939 I'd tried to remember at school. Knowing that every fact about these old, old dates, along with the human lives that lived inside them, were all guesses, gave me a warm and easy feeling to live with, as if my own existence was like liquid. Big, big dates dissolved all the hard certainties of life. When I held a huge old date like 7500 BC in my hands, or considered what people were trying to achieve with their days thirteen and a half thousand years ago, today and this moment now would become all fluid, like a pool gathering around me. I loved reading about the ancient past and then letting my mind spool around to enjoy how fucking, fucking massive time is, and that most of those big old dates are approximations anyway, so none of them are truly right or wrong. And that feeling alone reassures me that my place inside this time cannot be wrong, either. Finding anything like a precise date to calculate the age of Uffington Castle has eluded archaeologists; it might have been created about three thousand years ago, although people could also have been congregating there as far back as nine thousand years ago. Let your mind just go there, because feeling big expanses of time is almost orgasmic, if you want it to be. There, you can escape everything human, and, if you try, you can even make your ego vanish. It's so freeing, so I'm not going to put a fence around that free, free feeling and I am not going to even guess the date of the hill fort.

But even the use of the word 'fort' is confusing, with

its associations with castles and walls. Once, I told one of my sons I was taking him to a castle, when he was about three years old, and walked him up the steep hill to a huge expanse of open grass – no pointed arches or flying buttresses, no moats or baileys, no battlements, arrow loops or arcades, no crenellations or drawbars, no shop to buy a plastic sword. He was very, very angry and kicked me hard in the shins.

There is no castle at Uffington Castle. You must imagine it.

Uffington White Horse doesn't look like a horse either. You must imagine it.

Two miles below, cutting string off the gate, pouring water into empty buckets, moving between the horses to run my hands over their flanks, skirting the edge of the field to look for blackberries, I would glance up at the distant white marks on the hillside, which made the horse, and the lip of the castle. They were faint outlines, but in my head they existed perfectly.

I was about to give up on Danny, maybe go back to the show and drag Jack out of the beer tent to help me fix the gate, when I heard his voice approaching from the far corner of the field. Sometimes that sense of the vanishing horizon, hiding animals or the dogs or other beings in that unseen incline, almost felt like theatre. Things appear, and vanish, by surprise. Once, my dun mare had seemed to disappear before my eyes. I'd walked and then run through the field, shouting her name, so angry I'd trusted the gate with a small padlock, one that could easily be smashed with a single blow of a hammer.

But then, as I was frantically moving across the field, shouting her name, she revealed herself in the hidden dip where the land fell.

Danny had come to fix the gate, and after I heard him I could make him out too, broad-shouldered, very specific in his movements, walking towards me through the long grass, then turning back to face the Ridgeway, since the beautiful, sharp sunlight was impossible to ignore. He moved stealthily, so that two magpies, nodding through the grass beside him, were undisturbed.

'The chalk figure is moving. Look at the hill, Clover, behind you, look at the hill,' he shouted, making the magpies jump and cackle, alighting from the field as Danny turned to gesture at the figure then started walking backwards to get a better view of the way that the brilliant, rain-freshened light was refracting off the hill. The White Horse, which sometimes lies flat and almost hidden, was unusually visible. Unusually horse-like, too. Because quite often the lines cut into the hillside, perhaps three thousand years ago, don't really make sense as a familiar animal. A toddler would not be able to name it as a horse. You have to understand what a horse is, how a horse moves, what a horse feels like, to be able to impose this animal on to the outline in the grass on the hill.

Missing its essential horse-ness, it's not surprising people argue over what shape it really is. I'd once argued with Danny when he'd interrupted me, very sharply, when I referred to it as a horse and he told me it was a dragon. I had had different conversations and arguments with people about what it might be but had come to believe it didn't really matter. What mattered was what each person wanted to see in it. Sometimes I think the horse is like God: if you want to believe in something, you will see it, very clearly. If it matters to you that the shape it makes is divine, that is what it will be. It's also a kind of white landscape alchemy, since it makes people stare at the hill and the Ridgeway and imagine magical shapes. Danny wanted dragons. I wanted horses. We both saw precisely what we wanted to believe in.

There was no argument now, though, because when Danny turned around his face was shining. The light was so clear and bright, even though the sky had darkened to a greyish blue, almost as dense as the colour of dark, wet denim when jeans are hanging outside to dry.

'The light, moving on the hill, it makes the horse look, I dunno, it looks real, divine maybe,' he said.

I put my hand over my brow because the light was almost dazzling, making me squint. 'It's beautiful. The way it never changes,' I murmured beside him. He looked at me quickly.

'Yeah, remember that. Because everything else is changing,' he said, and I thought he meant the landscape before us, because the movement of dark, purple clouds with sunlight cutting beneath them was casting shadows over the hill and changing the colours of the field and the hedgerows that ran down the side of it from bright, daytime green to something more like the colour of very old ivy. 'I mean, we're living through a total change in the way we live. Everything is in freefall – the currency, the laws, government – everything is changing. It's happening now, Clover, the transition we are all in, it's happening right now.'

He turned to me, taking his baseball cap from his
head and wiping his brow with great intent, as if he was
at the end of a very hard day rather than a very long
night. I listened while he told me about the way the world
was resetting itself, that it was a terrifying time, the
darkest time we'd ever been through, but that there was
light too. I stood in front of him, able to glimpse the
white dragon-horse over his shoulder, and nodded, listening closely. Danny talked about this often. This reset
worked its way into every conversation I'd ever had
with him. Even when we started out discussing gate
hinges, or where a water trough should be placed, or
the quickest route to Wantage or the size of the new
sound system his mate James was putting together, we
always went to the reset.

I didn't follow everything he said, but I liked his
voice and the way he put words together. I liked his
obsessions: he had been a Morris dancer when he was
younger, and regularly ran ultra-marathons at the
weekends, like they were a little walk. He told me about
the party he'd just driven back from, pulling his phone
from his pocket and showing me a video of people dancing. He'd felt so good, so free, he said. Connected to
everyone else there. I liked his voice and how much it
reminded me of the hills. I liked the way words fell
together from his mouth, shaped by a slight softening,
and rise and fall of vowels that haven't been lost, yet,
from his ever so gently rounded speech. The fields, the
gateways, the woods, the standing stones and the downs
were there in everything Danny said and as soon as he
spoke it was clear he'd spent his life in the countryside.
He didn't have an accent, but the gentle fall of the

landscape and the wide-open shapes of the Ridgeway were there in his voice, the landscape he'd inhabited and walked through since he was a child, then walked away from to take himself to big cities and around the world as a young man, and then returned to as an adult.

I glanced down into the thick grass, thinking of this as his voice dropped and curled around as he spoke. 'You must be sovereign. Currency means nothing any more. Put what you have in silver. And gold. Think for yourself. Make sure your children are sovereign, Clover. Think for yourself. People used to know how to do this, in the long distant past. The answers are every-where, we just have lost the way with knowing where to look. I mean, look at that, imagine the people who made that,' he said, gesturing to the ancient chalk horse on the hill. 'Think of the change that horse has been through. Think of what the horse has witnessed. King-doms faltering and falling and rising again. By the time Roman soldiers were marching along the Ridgeway, that horse was already something ancient and unknow-able. It was already a symbol of the long-distant past. And there's nothing complicated about how we should live now. It's simple. Speak the truth. Question everything. Learn new skills. Think for yourself. Look after each other. Look after children. And love each other.' He brushed his hands together quickly, then turned to me. 'Keep your vibrations high. Go raving, maybe. Love each other. Not complicated, really, is it? Simple.' He shrugged again. 'Don't worry. It's going to be all right too. Now, you got some pliers, Clover? I can't take the hinges off that gate without pliers. Nor-mally, now, I have my tools in my van, but I came straight from Salisbury, from the free party, and they're back at home.'

I knew I had pliers in a tool kit in a yellow canvas bag my dad had given me, and I asked Danny if he minded walking back to the house. He shrugged. Not at all. 'How could I mind on an afternoon as beautiful as this?' he said, and when we got to the gateway back on to the road, Danny was a step ahead, so I said, 'The code is zero zero zero zero.'

'I know, Clover,' he replied, turning to look at me.

I said, 'No, the combination on the lock. It's the code for the padlock.'

He blinked quite hard at me, then laughed. 'Oh yeah, that too.'

As we left the field, he turned again, glancing quickly up to the hill before it was obscured by the high hedges near the railway bridge.

'Beautiful, isn't it, the hill? Perfect, really. This landscape. Is that why you came to live here, Clover, for the hill? Because you're not a local, are you?'

Danny was right. I am not a local. I wasn't born here, although moving here, when the children were babies, didn't take me that far from where I think of as home either. My home, where I lived through much of my childhood and all through my teenage life, was a village called Minety, about twenty miles from Uffington. I didn't grow up beneath the White Horse, but near by are Highworth, Cricklade, Faringdon, Purton, the small, faded market towns which were part of my childhood. I might have gone right back, to live closer to Minety, but my childhood ended very quickly and very violently there one afternoon, and although I loved

Minety, it was more comfortable for me not to live right there, but to be close enough to it so that I could still brush fingertips with the past.

The landscape of this part of southern England has always been home. I have never lived in a big city. I often went to London for work, but I have never lived in London. I was born in Oxford and lived there until I was six, when we moved to Minety. Apart from that time in Oxford, when Jimmy and Dolly were small, I've lived in the country all my life. The architecture of big-city life, with a well-developed public transport system and shops and cafes, museums, libraries, sports centres, cinemas and shopping centres close by, is not familiar to me. I feel home, and at home, when I am standing in long, wet grass or picking my way through a slick of mud around a gateway in a field, and when I can see thick, black hedges near by or when I am driving behind a tractor which is entirely blocking a narrow lane and I am late. I feel at home in a village shop. As a teenager I knew how to get around in the countryside long before I could drive, just as my elder children have done.

And in the ten years we'd made our home there, beneath the Ridgeway with the White Horse in the distance, I had felt that I really belonged. In ten years, I had started to feel that I was, if not *a* local, then *local*. I knew the sharper curves in all the roads and where the ditches overflowed when it rained too much, the exact spots on the narrow lanes where I had to swerve sharply since the potholes were deep. I knew where the best place to see a murmuration was in spring, and where to find mistletoe in the fields near by at Christmas, and where the thickest hedges were for holly too. I knew which plumber to call at 10.07 p.m. on a Friday night when the hot water wasn't working, and I knew the fencer who would come out to help me, even if it was dark and raining, if my horses had pushed through a fence. I knew the house down the green where my dogs should always be on their leads when we went past so I wouldn't be shouted at, and I knew the shape and colour of every car driven by those who lived in the village, and the exact way to wave to them, or not, when I was late, taking the children to school. I knew which handyman I could ask to keep an eye on the younger children when he was fixing a broken tap and I needed to go out, quickly, to pick up an elder child from the bus. I knew where the nearest long barrows and standing stones were, to go to when I was looking for ancient certainty. I knew which stretch of the Thames was still clean enough for swimming, and the bank where the gravel was shallowest for the children to get in. I knew which of my neighbours to call when I was feeling a quiet, Tuesday-morning despair and just needed to chat. I knew the best time to arrive at the village shop to buy asparagus in the spring and the exact time the school bus stopped on the green. I was familiar with which of the charity shops in Wantage were best for books, games or children's clothes, and which one was good for ornaments, cooking equipment and Christmas decorations. I knew, by sight if not name, the kids who played football on the village playing field, and which mother to give their school bags or lunch boxes to when they left them scattered around in the playground. I knew who to contact to remove an infestation of beetles in the

kitchen or swarm of wasps in the roof. I knew which
person to trust in the local pub to give Dolly a lift home
when she'd finished a late shift washing up in the
kitchen, and I knew who to ask in the village to help me
break into my kitchen window when it was dark and I'd
lost my keys, if, that is, I'd bothered to lock up at all. I
knew what day the best home-made cakes were deliv-
ered to the feed shop on the hill, and the time that the
sausage rolls they cook for lunch would be reduced at
the nearby cafe. I knew who to ask about finding a rave,
in a remote field on the Ridgeway, and I knew who to
get a lift with, too. I knew which teenagers to ask for
babysitting when I was desperate for help, which of the
doctors in the local surgery I really trusted with my
family secrets, and which of the guys in Wantage to call
for Valium or strong sleeping pills when I was feeling
afraid and could not sleep. I knew where the bridle
tracks had gates that had been tied shut with binder
twine so messy I had to take a knife to pass through
them on a horse, and the place at the edge of the
ploughed field before the next village where the road
was always flooded, even after a little rain. I knew the
best place to see dawn from the hill above the village in
early spring. I knew which teachers I could really talk
to about how my children were doing in several local
state schools, and I knew which pub was good for pizza
on a Sunday night. I knew the bloke who always knew
where the best sound systems were, and the woman to
borrow a tea urn and wineglasses from when we had a
party. I knew the shapes of the fields and how they felt
under my horse's hooves, I understood the feeling of
the Ridgeway when I walked there at 3.49 a.m. on the

summer solstice, and the best place to hear skylarks on White Horse Hill. I knew about the fresh local eggs sold behind the till in the village shop and the field on the bend where teenagers went to light fires in summer. I knew the place in the woods on the road to Uffington where an early bed of snowdrops always came up, the tree in the graveyard where the aconites grow thickest, and I knew the short cut to the 3D cinema screen in Swindon. I knew where the giant's stairway was on White Horse Hill, and the giant's grave near the Ridgeway too.

I explained this to Danny in a few words as we walked back to the house. 'It took a while to truly settle, to not just meet people but *know* people. For a long time I felt homesick for some other place I don't know and cannot really explain. And to overcome that, living here, I thought of green a lot, and after a while I knew green was the colour of my home, because it was all over my heart and inside me too.' I knew he'd understand the feeling of what I meant. He would understand this sense of sovereignty, as he said, that the landscape and the Ridgeway gave me. 'It's taken time. Much longer than I expected. Meeting people, knowing a place, becoming part of it. You can't rush that. I think it takes four, five years maybe. But now, this place, the hill, the Ridgeway, everyone here. It's my home. But Pete wants us to leave. I mean, I get it. I get it that Washington is where his work is. It's where his life is now.'

'And you?' asked Danny, who always made me feel comfortable even when I was talking to him about big feelings. I didn't feel he was judging me, or Pete either, for anything. 'Don't you want to go? To be with Pete?'

'No, not really. I mean, yes, of course I do, of course I want to be together, I want to have our marriage together, I want the kids to be with their dad, of course I want that. I love Pete. I want to be with him. I need him. But leave *here*? To leave the hill? No. *I* don't want to do that. I'd like to be together, but together here, not there. And I don't want to give up absolutely everything that matters to *me*. The hill, the horses, the places I love. Memories. The walls of this house. The field. The people here who have become my friends. The people, more than anything. You. Everyone. Everything. I don't want to leave any of it.'

Danny glanced at me sometimes as I spoke, looking up from the tool bag he was going through, searching for pliers. I made some tea, and while we talked I laid salted Ritz crackers on a plate beside some pieces of chocolate, then carrots, making a plate of food for the children in place of cooking supper. 'Selling the house would be sad, it would really hurt, but I'd get over that. But to leave *here*? This area I have come to know . . . Well, that's a different feeling. This isn't just a place where I live. It's become the place where I am, where I belong. Where it makes sense being me. And where it makes sense to be a mother to my children. I want them to have continuity and a connection to a place. Leaving this place which is our home feels like a strange kind of destruction to me. It feels like a waste, to leave here, when we have created such a strong sense of belonging.'

'It's a big thing to do, to uproot your family and start all over again. It's not an easy decision. It's easy to think that going away is something exciting, big adventures and all that. But I'm not always so sure. I've travelled all over the world, lived in Manchester for years, moved to New Zealand, Australia for a bit, and, yeah, it was a laugh. But sometimes I look at my friends from Wantage, who've never left, and I just don't know who got it right. I sometimes think I missed out, compared to my friends who are married, couple of kids, settled in Uffington. Still, it could be great. Exciting. An adventure that will change you.' Danny glanced up at me to nod, then took the pliers, moving them in a pincer movement in his strong hand. 'You'll be changed by the experience, all of you. If you ever come back, that is. You'll come back a completely different person.'

I looked across at him quickly, too quickly, so that the knife I was holding slipped and sliced into the very end of my thumb, leaving a bit of loose skin, a flap, although it didn't bleed. I was shocked at what Danny said. I thought of something the children had told me, a few days before, about the fact that all the cells in your body change completely every seven years. In seven years, all the cells in my body would be different from the cells making up my body today. If I went to America, in seven years, the cells that walk through the fields and know the hedgerows and can sense the horses moving in the dark, even when I cannot see them, will no longer be local to the hill and the Ridgeway, since they will all have changed. The idea of that made me feel sick with worry, and I ripped the flap of skin back, to make it bleed. Danny's voice surrounded me in the kitchen, telling me about how he felt when he came back from New Zealand after going there in his twenties, but I didn't really hear what he said. I was thinking about where I would belong if all my cells changed in America. If that happened, I might start to belong to America, as my new cells would be local to Washington. But if my cells did then belong in Washington, or felt most at home in Virginia, or loved being in Maryland, I might not be able to leave there either. If we sold the house, and lived abroad for more than seven years, my cells would all be new. I would become changed on a cellular level by America.

Danny was right. I would become a completely different person. I bit into the carrot, which helped, because beside the red metal taste of blood in my mouth where I'd cut the end of my thumb, it tasted crisp and clean, bright orange. He zipped the tool bag shut and looked back to me.

'You just need to keep talking about it, don't you? Talk with Pete about it. Don't worry so much, Clover. Maybe it won't be as bad as you think. Maybe you'd like it, find a few free parties to go to out in DC,' he said, winking at me, rinsing his cup in the sink. 'Still, it would be sad for us all if you go. You and the kids, bless them. Break my heart, really.' He looked at me quickly and laughed. 'Anyway, I better get back out, get that gate fixed before those horses get out again, eh?'

Across the field from Uffington the second day of the show would be ending; the hard scratch of the Tannoy crackled again, followed by a distant sound of clapping, a whistle, before the applause fell then rose again into a cheer. Earlier, a line of classic cars, as shiny as beetles, had purred towards the showground. More than anything I wanted to call to Danny, to ask him to come back. I wanted him to stay with me in the kitchen, to listen to the rise and fall of his voice, as rounded as the hillside, whether he was talking about brambles on a broken fence, the end of the world, or moving house. And I wanted to ask him what he'd meant – *Break my heart, really* – and to tell him, yes, it breaks my heart too, to think of leaving. But instead I looked up to the horizon, where there was a strange and distant roar as, up above, high in the sky, the sharp, pointed outline of the Red Arrows sped suddenly into view.

I shouted to the kids, 'Come out, kids! Come outside and look at the sky! Look at the sky!'

I heard their feet thundering down the stairs as I flung open the kitchen doors and we spilled out of the house, on to the lawn, the children with their heads thrown right back, pointing high above and into the distance.

Overhead, with the hill below, the aircraft dipped and plunged, leaving plumes of artificially coloured smoke behind them. A vivid, wide stripe of red, white and blue splitting the sky wide open.

# Chapter 3

Pete must have found a charger in Arizona, because two days later, while I was sorting through a pile of school uniform I'd dumped on the bed to organize for the autumn term, he rang from Phoenix. He had left the conference for an hour or two the night before, 'To breathe,' he said, and met some art students running a hairdresser's.

'They were graffitiing the outside of their building. I think Jimmy would like it here,' I heard him say as I folded blue-and-white checked dresses into a separate pile beside stiff, grey nylon skirts and trousers.

'I got the gate fixed, near the far corner. Danny fixed it, where the brambles had broken the hinges,' I said, untangling school shorts from the boys' tracksuit bottoms.

'I go to Santa Barbara tomorrow, for a meeting. I still don't have a hotel there,' replied Pete.

'The children have been doing a sports camp all week. They don't start school until next week.'

'I met someone who worked at the White House today who might be interested in working together.'

'Evangeline has another new teacher this term. Mr Drew has left. She's very upset about it.'

'I might have to go to Chicago at the weekend. I don't have the right clothes.'

'We've almost run out of oil. I need to get the tank refilled.'

We were both silent for a bit as I continued folding clothes, and in the background I heard the distant flutter of Pete typing. Then he asked me what I had thought of the houses. I paused, putting the little pair of shorts aside and sitting down suddenly on the end of the bed.

'The house looks great. It's a great house. In a great area. But so is this one, and this one is our home. So selling here and just throwing everything up to start again in a completely alien place where nothing is significant or means anything feels like, I don't know, an abandonment.'

'It's not abandoning. It's just changing,' Pete replied. 'Not abandoning. Moving. People do it all the time.'

'I know people do it all the time, I just don't want to do it now,' I snapped, as the sound of Lester and Dash's voices arguing over a laptop in a far bedroom spiked. 'Putting down roots and truly knowing a place takes ages. Much longer than I imagined. And now that we've done that, you want us to start again in a place that means nothing to us. I mean, it means something to you, but not me. Everything that I know about how to be a mother and how to exist is bound up with here, with England, with the landscape and the countryside here. I don't even know how to be a mother in a city, in a new country . . .'

'You're a brilliant mother. You're creative and

imaginative. You'd be a brilliant mother wherever you are,' said Pete.

'I'm not sure I would, Pete,' I said quickly. 'I don't even know how I'd be a mother in London. I don't know the things that are significant, the places to go to find meaning. I don't know how to create a relationship between family life and place in a city. I don't have any of the reference points. And Washington? I am not even sure I know who I would be there, let alone who we would be as a family.'

'Can't you just see it as exciting? An exciting new start?'

'Yes, I can see that. I can see the idea of America is exciting. But right now, I don't want a new life. I love the life we have here. I love my friends. I absolutely love the field. I love our house, the way it's so much our home. It's taken so long to feel like we belong here, but now I really do. And so when you say let's change absolutely everything and leave, let's rip up the roots we've planted and start again, I don't see a great value in that. Because I don't want a new life. I want this life, here.'

'But I can't be there, because of my work. We've been through it a million times. This is where I have to be. I want you to be here. I want to see my children. I didn't set out for this, but it's where we are. It's where our life has taken us. These things happen. Life changes . . .'

The spiral of conversation was familiar, although it was no longer circular but moving in a clear direction, forward. Pete was pushing me through doors I wanted to avoid, making the forward momentum of change – the house, the school – impossible to resist.

'Look, I'm seeing a lawyer next week. She's positive about my chances of getting this work visa which will enable us to move here long term, and I need to know you are fully on board,' said Pete, a note of steel running through his voice as another door slammed behind me. Down the corridor, the sound of Lester and Dash shouting about Lego disturbed me.

'I have to go, Pete, the kids, I haven't made supper or anything yet, I have to go . . .'

After the children were in bed, I went back to the kitchen, searching in the bookshelves along one wall for three or four books I'd bought in the second-hand shop in Wantage, about the Ridgeway and some of the giants and dragons that had existed there. I thought they might help me, as the conversation with Pete had made me feel confused and defensive, like I needed troops. I saw the new people Pete was amassing, like Sylvia or the headmistress of the school who stood behind the podium in the prospectus, and the lawyer now too, as a chorus, pulling Pete away from me. I needed to understand, as clear as sharp sunlight through wet, spring-green grass, what it was I was so afraid of leaving. I wanted to understand if it was the chalk track I minded leaving, or the people. I realized that I might be mistaking one feeling for another. Perhaps it was the past that I was afraid of leaving. Because it's impossible not to be aware of the past on the Ridgeway, which hums with humans who have connected themselves to it, in the past as well as the present. And if I, as one lone, individual woman, could have an osmotic relationship with the front doors I have walked through, the sitting rooms I have sat in, the kitchens I have cooked in, the bathrooms I have splashed my face in, the bedrooms I have slept in, the corridors I have lingered in, then there was no reason why the legions, millions and millions, or even billions, of people who had walked on the Ridgeway might not also have had an osmotic relationship with it, and left some of the spaces within themselves up there too.

Lester had grown out of his tricycle, but wanted to follow Dash and Evangeline as they whirred on their bikes down the thread of narrow concrete footpath that ran just outside our gate from one end of the village green to another, crossing through the churchyard then widening out into a huge field, past a pond thick with bulrushes, to the disused water pump at the far end. Earlier in the year, in springtime, the children biked under the spreading arms of horse chestnut trees in the graveyard, their pink-and-white flowers the colours of strawberry Cornettos, but where now conkers, as brown as the buttons on a long tweed coat my mum wore all the time when I was a child, studded the ground. The children liked to stop there, pouncing on the green spikes of unsplit shells, pulling the conkers out from their safe places nestled so cosily within the soft white flesh inside, to pile them into their bike baskets or stuff into pockets.

Dash and Evangeline had learned to bicycle up the green, wobbling along at first as I pushed Lester in a buggy behind them, grateful for the concrete that made crossing the long grass, sodden with water in the winter, possible. A couple of times a year, the local farmer put his cows out to graze, penned by a cattle grid separating the green from the road beyond, which led to Uffington. Sometimes, when I was pushing Lester and shouting words of encouragement to Dash and Evangeline to press on, the children had found themselves surrounded by the snotty, strangely vulnerable noses of a herd of black bull-ocks gazing at them with massively lashed eyes.

'Flap your arms and they'll be scared of you,' I'd shout to the children, suddenly tiny and quiet surrounded by the cattle. Afterwards they'd grumble that they didn't want to walk down the green with the cows there, but I liked the living, breathing mess the cows left and the lack of tidying away. Once, they broke through a wicket gate on the footpath into the churchyard, churning up the grass around the graves, but I was relieved that for once it wasn't my ponies that might have broken a fence, or my dog that had been reprimanded on the village WhatsApp group for chasing a distant neighbour's guinea fowls when they were on the green.

The road on to the green, across the rumble of the cattle grid, is a no through road; a year or two after moving to the village, I knew enough people to wave to every vehicle that passed down there, and crossing the green would often involve a chat with half a dozen neighbours as the children ran or biked ahead of me, and I could relax, since there were no cars speeding past and no strangers to worry about, as their little outlines van-ished into the distance. The green covers eighteen acres, but I once found a map in an old book of local history that suggested it had been bigger as common land, cov-ering the expanse of our field beyond the railway where I walked every day. There are a few houses around the green – a line of three attached cottages, a red-brick converted barn, three bigger farmhouses, dotted distant cottages, a bungalow built twenty or thirty years ago – but the village was probably busier when it was first recorded, in the Saxon charters of 948. St Nicholas Church, where my children biked through the grave-yard, was built around the mid-thirteenth century, and in 1219 the village green, now so empty, was the site of a market held every Thursday all the way through until 1792, just after the common land was enclosed in 1776. The village was still busy, with a schoolhouse opening in 1877, although by 1933 there weren't enough children to support it and instead children went to the village school in Uffington or, as mine now did, to the village of Shell-ingford just further across the field.

Walking down the green, almost every day, I thought of the field bustling with people arriving to sell eggs and vegetables, honey or meat. I might stop to chat to a neigh-bour walking a dog, but the green was only ever that busy once a year, on Guy Fawkes Night, with handfuls of fami-lies from the village congregated at the far end sharing plates of sausages and chocolate brownies around a huge bonfire, sparks sputtering into the darkness, blue smoke swirling. It was my children's favourite night of the year, one that they counted down the days to in anticipation, genuinely thrilled by the chance to meet their friends at the unfenced bonfire, where they would throw their toffee-apple sticks into the flames before daring each other to venture into the further pockets of dark on the green. It was an exciting night for them, especially compared to most of the ticketed, tightly organized firework evenings in neighbouring villages, where children were kept well away from the fire and fireworks would always be set off behind a distant, roped-off area.

Sometimes, walking after school, we'd leave the green and cross a footbridge over a ditch into the field running parallel, behind a hawthorn hedge dotted with weeping willows, into the long, sandy-yellow limbs of miscanthus grass, which the children preferred to call elephant grass. They liked hiding amongst this, which grew so fast and thick before it was cut down, several times a year, to be used as animal bedding or biofuel.

Further across the reed field was the glassy expanse of the lake. When the children were very small, I'd take them to walk all the way around the edge, which glowed orange-pink on warm evenings at dusk, when the flock of Canada geese skidded down on to the top of the water, reflecting the sunset. I could see the Ridgeway from there too, and I liked walking around the lake, to look at that familiar horizon, but from a slightly different angle than at home. It was one of our best walks, through the sweet-smelling poplar trees and the narrow gate where blackberries grew like gemstones, but a few years after we arrived the lake was bought by a fishery who put up high wire-mesh fencing to keep out mink. Jimmy had seen it first and came home looking despondent.

'You shouldn't go and look at it now, with the fencing. It's all fenced off and organized with locks and signs, it's the kind of thing you absolutely hate,' he'd said to me. He was right. I stopped walking to the lake after that. But the green always pleased me, even in winter, when the little pond in the middle of it sometimes froze, and the ground was black and hard.

Biking down the green gave the children a freedom to move outside the orbit of my control, and it was important Lester joined Dash and Evangeline, so a few days after they returned to school I searched Facebook Marketplace and found a shiny, black bike with stickers shaped like bright-yellow dinosaurs on it being sold in a village near Swindon. After I'd picked it up, and with an hour to waste before the children needed picking up, I drove up to Barbury Castle, another Iron Age hill fort, along the Ridgeway towards Avebury.

The road to the fort was narrow, a dark, straight line running away from Wroughton, which perched on the outer edge of Swindon, then passing some barns and paddocks with broken wooden fencing before rising suddenly on to the escarpment of the Ridgeway. Halfway up the hillside, I pulled into a gateway, leaving my car unlocked, to cross the field to a stone sitting on the hill as a memorial to Richard Jefferies, the mystical nature writer who was born near Swindon and wrote extensively about the landscape and life of the downs, and Alfred Williams, the town's hammerman poet who worked for the railway. When we were teenagers, and home was falling apart, Nell and I would drive here from Minety, to be close to Barbury Castle and to read the words on the stone, which somehow made us both feel that all wasn't lost.

RICHARD JEFFERIES
1848–1887
IT IS ETERNITY NOW.
I AM IN THE MIDST OF IT. IT IS ABOUT
ME IN THE SUNSHINE

ALFRED WILLIAMS
1877–1930
STILL TO FIND AND STILL TO FOLLOW
JOY IN EVERY HILL AND HOLLOW
COMPANY IN SOLITUDE

When I pressed my fingers into the grooves of the
carved letters, I felt like Nell might be there too, in
some way, although I shivered because I also felt very
alone. I walked around the stone, wanting to connect
with it, before patting it, feeling a bit self-conscious.
Then I went back to the car and drove on, parking
before the hill fort and crossing the flat field to greet it.

Barbury Castle is a hill fort, and like Uffington there
are no walls or crenellations there, just an expanse of
green surrounded by a deep double ditch. If possible, it
felt even higher than Uffington Castle. The hills around
the steep ramparts of the fort were naked, their curves
so smooth and almost archaic, uninterrupted by heavy
woodland apart from three clumps of beech trees,
which anyone can see, miles and miles away across the
horizon. When we were children, we could see these
three clumps on the Ridgeway from our home in
Minety. I skirted around the edge of the hill fort, completely alone with the grasslands swirling around me,
almost like a sea, although much, much more restful
than an ocean: these hills which stretched between
Oxfordshire and Wiltshire had never surged, threat-
ened or terrified me, and unlike a mountainous
landscape, or even that of moorland, were never craggy
or violent, but instead felt lyrical and sublime, as soothing as they were powerful, tremendous but not
overwhelming.

Soon the children would be surrounding me, needing me for everything, but at Barbury Castle I sat on the
hill, the air and space holding me high above the sprawl
of Swindon below. The fields beyond the castle looked
ragged and hairy, exhausted by late summer, with

clumps of overgrown stinging nettles and bright splashes of yellow ragwort growing too tall across patches of the land below. But up on the hill fort, with handfuls of sheep grazing intently along the ancient earthworks, the turf was cropped and almost neat. I raked my hands through the grass, brushing aside dried up rabbit droppings to part the stems, like hair, and examined the skull of chalk beneath. That chalk was something I had known I wanted to be close to when we moved from Oxford. Our house, down in the vale, sat on thick clay; midwinter, the gateways into the field would be heavy with the water that the clay clung on to. But chalk was something else. When the landmass of Africa slid into the space taken up by Europe, formless floating masses of rock crashed together. The movement of those tectonic plates pushing the land upwards created the Alps, but the shock waves rippled across the new landmass, and when the peaks of those mountains were formed, the downs were formed too. Sometimes, standing on the top of the hill fort at Barbury, or closer to home, at Uffington Castle, I was made dizzy by the outline of a crow wheeling below; close my eyes and it was almost like balancing on a surface that was unstable; I could sense a movement, a rolling, a spinning. The downs made me think of something kinetic, an ever-changing landscape, and sometimes I was certain I could sense, underfoot, the millions and billions and trillions of once-wriggling sea creatures which formed them, since this green of the hills, that dazzled me so much, was once the thick, black bed of the sea. And when I walked on the downs, I often felt the landscape might move again, as it once had, millions of years before, a liquid landscape becoming solid when the moving waters covering it froze into a solid block of ice, then moved again, just twelve thousand years ago when the thaw started. Ice-cold water ran off the chalk as the world got hotter, and the land started moving, like molten plastic, mud sliding so fast it hollowed out the hillside, creating the ripples and dips sometimes called the Giant's Staircase which converged on the pancake-flat land at the base of the hill, called the Manger, where sheep often grazed. When I stood on the hill, these massive waves of green turf made me think of a pot of paint huge enough to fit into a giant's hands. The giant picked up her pot the size of a house and poured the bright, gleaming green paint out so that it fell from the pot in molten waves, which created the hill.

The view from Barbury had changed since I'd first been here as a child. Black sheets of glittering solar farms and huge building blocks of Amazon warehouses were now stamped on to the once all-green landscape. This change was inevitable, but sitting up on the hill I felt a certain fear for other, bigger, more impossible changes that could happen at some point. Embodied deep within the once-living chalk is the distant possibility that the land will change again. Chalk is not solid like rock. If you took a giant sledgehammer to it and smashed it, it could crack open again to reveal the billion-year-old secret life that made it move and buckle, that once flowed inside it.

I stood up, dusting the grass from my hands, then started back across the fort towards the hill. For just a moment, I imagined what it might be like to feel tectonic plates crashing together; to feel them as real, living things, rather than as dimensions of my internal life crashing and smashing against one another each time I thought of Washington. I'd like to see the green earth turning to liquid, like those videos of molten lava we watched during geography lessons at school. I would like to feel the green hill gushing and rushing as live and energetic as a sea beneath me, because in that moment I'd know I had been right all along. If I could see the land buckle and melt then I'd know, for sure, that nothing remains the same, and no feeling is without end. Chalk is a living reminder of this. Flint and granite might shatter but chalk is embodied by living creatures, those tiny beings whose particles could join back together in movement once again, to make the land melt.

As I slammed the door of my car, Lester's little bike jammed in on the back seat, I thought about the way we all walk around as if the pavements we tread on are solid, forgetting that at some time, one day, we will return to a previous shape. Nothing remains as it was. The downs remind me of this thing about human life, which is absolute and clear and obvious, and yet so hard to understand, all the time.

'But, Mum, tell me exactly how White Horse Hill was made,' Evangeline said, later that evening as we followed Lester, very slowly, on his new bike, down the concrete track running across the green. The purple flush of teasel heads coloured the longer grass at the edge of the green, which was itself dotted with scraps

of yellow ragwort. Lester couldn't yet ride alone but
was supported by stabilizers. We'd been talking about
the White Horse as we drove home from school, and as
I stumbled over the correct geological terms to describe
the way chalk downland was created, I remembered
how much my mind liked to seek out the human in the
landscape.

When I was at school, I enjoyed watching the way
the geography teacher created elaborate and colourful
drawings on the board showing a three-dimensional
illustration of Atlantic drift. She wore her hair in a black
velvet hair band, and I was stunned at how neat her
writing was, even as she wrote across the green plains of
a blackboard, watched by a room full of angry, bored
teenagers hunting new ways to humiliate her. Dust fell
gently like dandruff, even when she was colouring in
with blue, yellow and putty-coloured chalk. I didn't
like being told off at school, and had very few friends,
so paying attention to her drawings was easier than pretending I knew what the joke going around the class
was about. And although the science she explained
sucked the feelings from my brain, sometimes I found
images in her words which helped me make sense of
myself and my world. When she talked about ox-bow
lakes, it helped me understand that arching feeling of
relief when the school day was over and I could go
home; when I sat at the back of geography class, with
no friends, missing my mum even during the few hours
of a short school day, I knew exactly how a flood plain
felt too.

My failure to understand the language of ice-cold
facts has not changed. When Dash and Evangeline were

small, I'd bought books on wildflowers or British herbs or plants of the fields and hedgerows, certain I would become a different, more engaged parent than I had been so far. I was certain the books would help me identify things, pulling out the correct names, perhaps even in Latin, that I'd feed to my young children like coloured sweets. Many of the books were small, and I made a mental note I would fit them into a handbag, forgetting, for a bit, I've never owned a handbag. And each time I picked up one of the books, something distracted me, like the dogs barking in the yard, which might mean some more books had arrived from an online bookseller, or that an adult I could talk to had arrived at the house, or I was overcome with a compelling need to look at my Instagram.

As Lester surged forward on his bike, I thought of Evangeline's question, but realized that on the downs at Uffington Castle, or at Avebury or at Barbury Castle, the facts about how this landscape was created ceased to matter. To me, what mattered was an overpoweringly strong sense of the human, all around. It was everywhere, humming in the air, in the ancient remnants of the blackthorn hedges, in the foot-shaped culverts of the old chalk track, in the deeply pleasing human spacing of the beech trees planted in a strip beside Wayland's Smithy. It was this sense of the hundreds and hundreds and hundreds of years of human life and human experiences which had passed there that made the Ridgeway so powerful.

So I told Evangeline what I knew, talking vaguely about the movement of the glacier, of how the rolling downs were formed at the same time as the peaks of the

Alps, of the millions of sea creatures locked in the chalk; but I also said that sometimes, rather than science, I found it easier to think of giants instead. And perhaps, I suggested, there was another world in which that same landscape might have emerged from a time when a giant hammered the mighty bowl of a crucible to create the curves of the hills. Perhaps that intense escarpment of Uffington Castle could have been formed by a giant's furnace heated very hot to melt copper and tin, or the shuddering hammer-marks a giant's anvil made in the earth. But Evangeline was biking ahead of me, catching up with Lester as they crossed the green, Dash tearing ahead of them, all racing together, and I didn't really mind that she hadn't heard me.

When I tried to call Pete later, he WhatsApped me straight back. He was in a meeting, could we talk later. I threw my phone down, frustrated, missing him and annoyed by the absence. I wanted to talk to him and taste him, but I also needed to tell him what it felt like to live with giants in my head. When I tried to write about the way giants walked in and out of my brain, and dragons were there sometimes too, and how worried I felt that they'd leave me if we moved to Washington, it came out all wrong. And yet when I tried again, attempting to weave some sense of history into my email instead, I sounded unintentionally passive aggressive. I had started to think that what home represented was very different for Pete and me. Pete moved much more deftly through the world than I did. He was at home arriving in Ohio or San Diego or Chicago and pulling people together to work, creating a team. He felt at ease in a new city, and although he didn't enjoy staying in four different hotels in six days, he knew how to do it. He knew how to pack light.

'Aren't you homesick?' I'd ask, and he'd say yes, yes, of course, he desperately missed the children and me and wanted us to join him. We both wanted to be together, but he did not feel bound to place, as I did.

I envied the ease with which he left, then returned and left again. I wondered if the extraordinarily strong attachment to place my childhood had given me might not, in fact, be a burden. It might be nice to feel untethered, disconnected from any one place. I felt annoyed with the way the red blood cells in my veins held the shape of the homes I had loved, and I felt a heaviness in the sense that my body was like a vessel for the feelings of the rooms of my life. If I closed my eyes quickly, just like that, blink, I could taste and smell the past and the sensations of home there. But however heavy, or binding, these feelings were, I also was hungry to devour them. Memory itself might be something I could snap my teeth around and take a rich, red bite of, or lick from my lips like sugar left there after a doughnut, or swallow in a gulp like the last cold bubbles in that can of Coke I drank so quickly when it was hot outside and I was so thirsty.

When it was clear to me that the email to Pete about giants was impossible to write, but domesticity felt too clawing, I went out to the barn. Being amongst the hay bales and harnesses was reassuring, and for a while I swept up the straw, rubbed soap on to a bridle, cleared

up the head collars. Before I went back inside, to wash
the children and persuade them to stay in their beds, I
lifted the green petrol canister, kept there for all kinds of
emergencies, to my face, inhaling the fumes inside, since
that was a good way of taking myself away from the
place I was in right then. The petrol smell was fierce and
exciting, transporting me. It reminded me of smelling
the petrol tank of an old motorbike left in the barn at
Minety. The deep, brown smell of creosote and the surprising, clean-but-old smell of a hardware shop made
me feel excited like that too. Petrol and creosote smelt of
the past, but there were other smells I longed for: that of
lightly burned toast and a coal fire in a cold room, or the
smell of the dried soil in a red flowerpot holding gerani-
ums by an open bathroom window, or just that smell of
the way Mum would dry my blue, pure new wool jersey,
hanging it over the back of a radiator when it was still
damp, so that the aroma of wet wool joined with that of
the warming white paint where it was peeling from the
radiator in big flakes shaped like continents. Those sensations were sharper and stronger even than the heightened
smell of petrol as it filled my lungs. I inhaled again, then
put the canister down. For a few moments it had assuaged
the longing and human melancholy for something I
cannot really name, but that's always there, tugging at me,
like tough little tangles in my hair. As I walked back to the
house, the children waiting for me, I thought that if I
could just wrap that sensation up in a piece of tissue paper,
then send it to myself, to open up and consume like that
box of brownies I'd once been sent by a friend, I swear I'd
never feel sad or lonely or at a loss ever, ever again.

                              ★

'Why do you like it here? What do you love most about
it that you really don't want to leave?' Leah asked me, a
few days later. The children were at school, and Leah
had driven from London to my house to take a photograph for a newspaper article I had written. She had
long, straight, blonde hair and wore good trainers and a
black bomber jacket with her shirt hanging out over
close-cut jeans. We had worked together many times
before, but it was only recently that when she held the
camera up in front of her face and turned it to me, I
experienced a strong desire to push it away and instead
cup the back of her neck and put my lips against hers or
even just hold my hand against her jaw and maybe her
collarbone too. Only Pete ever made me feel this. When
she looked at me, I experienced the warm feeling of
being inside my childhood home when I inhabited it
most fully as a child and felt completely loved. Being
near Leah made me think homesickness could be
assuaged by a person as much as a place.

This feeling of wanting to touch her, or at least be
very close to her, had arrived inside me only after Pete
had said we must leave our home. I was pretty sure I
wasn't going to touch her. We were working, and I
didn't want to have to deal with the consequences of
what might happen if I did touch her in that way, since
it might involve a very real, permanent loss of Pete,
which would also be like losing a home. Instead, I
thought of her questions and forced myself to overcome this feeling. I told Leah the Ridgeway was
extra-special to me because of the fact that it was not a
distant wilderness.

'It's a human place. It's very present to the moment

right now, but at the same time all the past is there too. You should go up there, on your way home. Even the marks big tractors make there are beautiful, in the late summer when the fields are burned gold and it's harvest time. The plough lines are like massive mathematical symbols scouring the ground in a strange and beautiful way.' I told her it was one of the most solitary but also most human places I'd ever been. 'You feel humans all around you when you are there, in the lives of the many, many people who have walked there across thousands of years, just like we do today, feeling anger or boredom, or their frustration and lust and exhaustion or hunger and comedy. The people who have been there in the long-distant past are always pushing and jostling at me. They want to keep up and be part of what we're all doing now, even though they might have died three thousand years ago.'

Actually, I felt the people who had died there three thousand years ago, or eight or ten thousand years ago, were the ones who did more jostling and agitating to be part of the present than the real, living people I saw walking there. But I didn't say this to Leah, as I wasn't quite sure how to explain it, even though I knew exactly what it felt like in my head. Snap snap snap, went Leah with her camera, moving in front of me, and I pressed my palms on to my legs to keep my hands still and stop them reaching out to touch her.

'You wouldn't lose that feeling if you went away, though, Clover,' she said. 'We carry the places that matter, they don't leave us. You don't have to be afraid of losing anything, just think about the things you would gain. The new experiences. Your life with Pete and the kids together. And you could always come back later. The places here will remain. They're inside you.'

After she left, and because there was enough time before the children came out of school and back into the kitchen, their book bags and uneaten packed lunches landing beside them on the floor, I knew I needed to go to the Ridgeway, quickly to make sense of what had just happened.

I drove past the Blowing Stone pub in Kingston Lisle, and then past the Blowing Stone itself, sitting, with a little lack of dignity, beside some creosoted fencing belonging to two attached cottages that look out on to the hill. I'd passed it many times before and, like the White Horse, it's another mystery of the Ridgeway. King Alfred was born four miles from here, in Wantage. The Blowing Stone was taken from the Ridgeway, where local legend said that Alfred himself had blown into one of the crevasses in the stone to alert his troops, camped a mile west at White Horse Hill, about the arrival of the Danes before the Battle of Ashdown in 871. Thomas Hughes wrote about the stone in his famous book *Tom Brown's School Days*, describing the landlord of the Blowing Stone pub, who blew into the stone to make 'a gruesome sound between a moan and a roar, that spreads itself away over the valley, and up the hillside, and into the woods at the back of the house, a ghost-like, awful voice'.

I barely noticed the stone, since I'd passed it so many times, but each time I was near the cottages I always wished I lived there. They were the houses closest to the Ridgeway for many miles around, separated from the

track by a wall and a strip of beech wood which tumbled into the verge, running beside the road. In the
spring I'd see foxes and badgers in the wood, and one
winter, just four years earlier, Nell and I had ridden our
ponies along the strip of the Ridgeway, parking very
close to the cottages, which now made me think she
must be close when I was there. If I lived there, I told
myself, parking on top of the hill, I'd keep them as two
separate homes I could walk between, depending on my
mood. One would be plain, neat and minimalist, with
wooden benches, linen curtains, all-natural stripped
woodwork. Rows of plain bookshelves would cover
some of the walls, but I'd avoid books with spines that
were too bright or patterned. Next door, I'd paper every
single inch of the walls, skirting boards, cupboards and
banisters with floral wallpaper, so that walking through
the front door would be like the sensation of stepping
inside pass-the-parcel. The window frames would be
the green of spring grass on the downs, so that there
would be no real division between the room inside and
the hill so close, which would seem to pour through the
windows. In that garden I would keep a pony and I
would at least try to grow some vegetables there, and
herbs, and perhaps even roses, though I have no love for
gardening. The minimalist house would have nothing
in the garden, not even a rosemary bush, so it would be
very easy to care for. I realized, walking away from my
car, that I was associating the cool, minimalist house
with Leah, and the house full of flowers and the pony
with my children. Pete would return from America and
be at home in either house. I was sure I could live like
this. I imagined this would be the place where I would

feel completely satisfied, and America would never have come into the picture.

I thought of Pete and the different ways I missed him, even when we were arguing or were at odds with each other, as I walked west, with Blowing Stone Hill behind me and White Horse Hill before me. The Ridgeway was almost the first place I took Pete, when we were falling in love with each other, and I wanted to show him the curves of countryside which mattered as much to me as the way he touched the shape of my body. This was the stretch of this old, old track I knew best, which led to Wayland's Smithy, and on from there to Liddington Castle, another hill fort which inspired much of Richard Jefferies' writing, and then Barbury, and on, further from there, to West Kennet long barrow and the standing stones at Avebury.

A woman with two dogs passed, pointedly keeping her eyes on the track, and then a cyclist, in yellow Lycra, who smiled and nodded but didn't say anything when I said, 'Hiya', just cycled silently on. Apart from them there was no one else there, and no one on the horizon either. I walked, feeling confused. The air felt static, no birds or insects around, and I couldn't feel those old, old people I was looking for. The Ridgeway is like this. It is like creativity. Sometimes it just doesn't appear. Sometimes it's just a distant chalk track with the shoots of fresh green wheat growing near by or heavy, brown ploughed fields on either side, just as sometimes – often – writing is just a computer screen with a lost cursor and black letters that will not move where I want them to go.

I walked on, feeling a bit embarrassed about what I was asking the Ridgeway for. Did I expect the green hill to crack open, revealing all the secrets of life? What a stupid idea, I told myself. 'It's just chalk, leaves, mud, flint,' I said aloud, while also silently admitting that, yes, I did want the hillside to split open. Of course, I did. I want the giants to be there. I want a goblin to appear and talk openly to me.

Instead, the path ahead looked pinky grey, the lightest rainfall of night having made the chalk greasy, stretching ahead, reminding me of the way my cat had brought a half-eaten baby rabbit through my bedroom window, leaving its guts stretched across the carpet, glistening in the dark when I felt them under my bare feet, shockingly cold and slimy, like standing on a dead alien.

I stopped by the strip of beech trees that ran alongside one edge of the Ridgeway, then slithered in my trainers down the deep chalk ditch separating the strip of trees from the track. That ditch was so deep, it could be mistaken for ancient earthworks, but I knew it wasn't that. This deep ditch, like the displaced sarsen stones the size of bedside tables moved into gateways, had been put there with tractors, by landowners, to stop people about the age of Jimmy taking speakers to this place and creating music here, to dance in the darkness and then in the light too. Walk here, but do not dance. Do not seek, let alone find, that peculiar and precious place of freedom you will only touch hovering above a field, between the place where the bassline and a repetitive beat meet. Don't camp either, or at least not outside designated sites. Do not attempt to sleep with a smoky crackle of sticks in a fire beside you or experience the glimmering cobweb of dew settling around you in the earliest morning. Do not try to take one step outside the footpath allocated for you. Jimmy had tried to pitch a tent here once, with one friend. They didn't make a fire, had a bivouac they planned to sleep under, just a single sheet, but still they were kicked off at midnight. No camping here, in this ancient place, where people have lain down and slept for thousands of years.

I grumbled about this to myself beneath the orange copper beech leaves, their long, strong trunks stretching like single, straight bones to a sky where the clouds were skittering away and blue was breaking through grey. I would have gone on feeling angry about the effort put into digging those deep ditches and heaving those huge stones about to stop the raving and the dancing, if I had not seen, ahead of me on the path, a tree, braced against the wind that whipped up the edge of the downs, covered in small yellow apples. They clustered along spindly, leaf-stripped branches, each fruit no bigger than a large marble. In the grass around the trunk more had fallen. I crouched down to turn a few over in the grass, looking for one unbruised I could eat straight away, since I could hear Mum, in the garden at Minety, telling me and Nell, 'Don't pick the apples from the branches, girls, save them until later in the autumn, eat the windfalls first.'

I paused. There, on the Ridgeway, where there was only me, who, exactly, was I saving the apples for? Giants and goblins and thousand-year-old women walked this space, but, however much I wanted to bring them to a place in my life, even I didn't think they would eat the apples.

I defied my Mum's voice and picked handfuls of the small, sweet apples, taking one or two bites from the plumpest flesh then flinging them into the grass to eat more, stuffing into my pockets the choicest apples I could reach from the highest branches. The apples pressed inside my coat pockets as I walked onwards, towards the ridge of the hill. I fished one out, rolling it in my palm as I walked, and, in a moment, I was in the kitchen of my house when Nell visited and the apple tree through the window above the sink was fully ripe. She said she'd like to paint the tree, motioning her hand across the pane as if she was reaching out to touch the fruit. Those apples were also small, yellow, ripe in late autumn, and two months later Nell died.

Standing on the Ridgway, I knew this was what I must communicate to Pete: that this landscape wasn't just hills and grass and trees but a physical act of memory. This place which he wanted to take me away from was where I found the women I loved so much, who are all gone and dead. I was concerned about how I would keep my relationship with the dead strong if my home was Maryland or Virginia. This landscape, which Mum brought us to and which had formed Nell and me, would be so far away that it would be like losing a final but strong connection to my dead sister and my dead mother. The Ridgeway was exquisitely precious to me because, when I was there, for a few moments I could be with the people I loved most; this landscape itself was them, in some form, not only their dead bodies, buried deep beneath the soil, but the living memory of their lives.

I turned away from the apple tree, back along the Ridgeway, back towards home. As I walked, I felt satisfied, and excited. I had found something clear to communicate to Pete. I could explain to him that I'd walked down Connecticut, Gramercy and Garrison both on my computer and in my mind, and that I had seen and understood a life we might have there in the red-brick house, that I'd seen how appealing the school prospectus had looked, I could see a good life in America, but that I couldn't understand how it could ever, permanently, be home.

# Chapter 4

I was so sad when Pete had to stay in America, missing the last weekend of the holidays and then the children's return to school too. He had tried so hard, but it hadn't been possible. Dash burst into tears when I told them all that Dad had really tried to get back, but he wouldn't be home. I swallowed the ache of melancholy that rose inside, concentrating instead on making plans with the children – swimming in the river at Lechlade after school, a picnic in the beech trees beside Wayland's Smithy where we'd cook sausages, milkshakes at the new cafe opening in Faringdon – which we could use to leapfrog from one weekend to another, to get through the weeks until he came home. He'd wanted to come back to England for the last days of late summer, which stretched beyond the start of the new term, lingering in late September with the temperature sitting high and hot and still. The light spattering of rain a couple of weeks before had been a brief mirage, and the ground in the field was still cracked, the dried-out clay like a crazy-paving jigsaw which persisted into early autumn. A letter from school informed parents all children were expected to take a hat and filled water bottle in every day, and that sun cream should be applied every morning. Enforcement of a winter uniform for autumn term was quietly dropped and Evangeline returned to wearing her summer dress.

Jimmy had been a vague presence in the house over the summer. He worked for a gardener in Oxford, but as autumn approached, and university started, his place in the small solar system of our family would change again. I saw him more after the White Horse Show, as he started spending less time out and away with his friends, and longer at the house. Sometimes we chatted about the vague possibility of America, which made him laugh like he, too, thought it too distant an idea to really contemplate. I was relieved, in some ways, that Jimmy still saw home as a place that didn't change. He hadn't yet fully experienced the feeling of the tectonic plates of life, which felt so stable, moving precariously underfoot. Change would always happen, nothing would ever remain static, but I felt Pete and I had achieved something by giving him a sense of security. Selling our house and moving to Washington would take that away. Home would no longer be a place he could return to. That would happen sometime, of course, but remembering how that had felt to me, when I was an adolescent, younger than Jimmy was now, I felt I'd do anything to protect him – and all his siblings – from it.

Much more pressing to Jimmy was looking for the spare can opener, a sharp knife, a few plates, a saucepan and the spare frying pan with the bent handle, which he had started packing into boxes, to head for Manchester and his new life at university. Things that belonged to him, but which were part of the daily fabric of our house, started vanishing. There were gaps, like missing teeth, in some of the bookshelves in the sitting room where he plucked copies out, and odd, lighter spaces started appearing on the walls, staring blankly at the room, marking those places where he'd taken down pictures that were his. A blue-and-red oil painting of a gas station against an American landscape, which Pete and I had given him for his eighteenth birthday, and a framed photograph of Nell holding him when he was two or three years old, standing on a riverbank, were both packed away in the cardboard boxes that sat on the landing outside his room. I preferred not to look at the boxes, his offerings to a new life. Autumn rolled on, the date for his departure stepping closer every day, until suddenly I could see, all too vividly, the way that this part of motherhood, with a grown child living under the same roof, ended. It would happen very quickly, overnight, and those endless, endless days that had come before would suddenly, abruptly, be over.

Sometimes I tried to imagine what Jimmy's ongoing absence would really feel like, but when I tried the thought of that overlapped with my own confusion about leaving for America. Putting the Atlantic between myself and two of my children would once have been unthinkable, but if we did move, it was unlikely Jimmy and Dolly would want to come with us. They were both on the cusp of adult life, pulling forward, moving on. The speed of the movement of time confused me, especially in relation to motherhood. Sometimes it was dizzying, racing away from me so fast it left me feeling winded, and struggling to keep up; yet often, when I sat in my car, waiting for the school day to finish, I imagined I would be right there, waiting in the car, for ever, waiting for the rest of my life.

When time became something scary like this, I soothed myself by walking out to the field, even though the crunch of dry grass at this point, in early autumn when the land should be wet and wintering, upset me too. Mole hills had appeared as small, brown bumps in patches of the field, but fewer than usual, since the ground was so hard. I edged around the field, searching the hedgerow pointlessly for blackberries. They'd arrived six weeks too early, purple glistening jewels beguiling everything around them, growing heavy on the bushes around the gate as early as July. By mid-September, when they would normally be plump and shiny, they'd grown wizened, hairy and red. Sour, as if the Devil had thrown his cloak over them. Blackberries, which used to arrive in September with the first crunch of frost to pierce the white mist of a chilly autumn morning, representing all the optimism and sweetness of a new academic year, pencil cases and a good crumble just needing custard, were long gone by the return of school. Instead, dark-blue sloes hid themselves behind their soft, silver dust in the hedgerow, as clumps of starlings whistled and chattered on the highest branches.

It was cooler in the evenings, but during the middle of the day the horses sweated through their hair, even in the shade, as I walked between them, running my hand over their flanks. I felt strong and certain of my place inside the day when I was needed by the animals, and I had no idea how to arrange my brain when I thought

about leaving them for America. If we sold the house, if
we left England, we'd have to sell the horses too. Crossing the field, I sought out the big dun mare, who was
standing in the shade of the weeping willow. I lifted her
mane away from her neck, twisting the coarse, dark
locks together as she blinked at me slowly, nestling her
soft, butterscotch-coloured nose into my short pockets,
looking for something. I leant my face against her side,
trying to imagine a life without her, without the field
to walk through, without the landscape to find and lose
myself in.

'People leave the places they know, people move all
the time,' Pete had said to me in exasperation the night
before, after I'd snapped at him that I'd deleted the email
full of houses he'd sent for me to look at. People move
all the time, I thought, pressing my face closer to the
mare's flanks, listening for her heart beating. People sell
up and leave that which is familiar every day. The usually muddy and stagnant pond near the hedge line,
where the willow emerged from the water for most of
the year, had drunk itself months before, cracking and
drying so that absolutely nothing of the water there
was left. Sometimes Canada geese honked and waddled
across the field, but I'd not seen them since the pond had
emptied. The horses stamped on the cracks, nodding
constantly as currants of flies clustered around their
eyes. They watched me as I walked amongst them, running my hands across their bellies, raking tangles from
their manes. Against the dried and exhausted grass of
the field, they looked like animals displaced, as odd and
off as a giraffe would look, picking its way amongst the
daisies on springy, cropped, downland turf. All the

dampness of the land had seeped away, as if it had been liquid itself and the plug had been pulled, cracking the dried mud where there should be water.

I left the horses snoozing in the shade and went to the water butt in the middle of the field, holding my wrists under the iron-grey water pouring from the blue piping as I filled water buckets for them. To avoid thoughts of selling them, I thought instead of a conversation Jimmy and I had had, days before, about lost villages. He had been reading about hunger stones, hydrological landmarks buried in riverbeds by people hundreds of years ago as a warning of what droughts and long periods of dry weather could do to humans and their communities. *If you see me, then weep* are words carved into a rock buried in the bed of the Elbe River in the Czech Republic, sometime close to 1616. Jimmy told me that during the hottest part of August, just a month before, the droughts across Europe had been so intense that parts of lost landscapes were revealed. In Lake Como, the 100,000-year-old remains of deer, hyena, lions and rhinos returned, like long-lost ghosts of the past, and in Lombardy, the foundations of a Bronze Age building rose up through a dried riverbed. In Rome, the ruins of a bridge originally built for Nero reappeared as the Tiber fell. Jimmy had spent weeks of that summer driving through Wales and up the west coast. He told me about the lost village of Capel Celyn in the Tryweryn valley, near Bala, which had emerged again, a terrible apparition from the past, after it was completely submerged in water in 1965 to create Llyn Celyn, a reservoir supplying water to Liverpool and the Wirral.

Perhaps nothing really changes, I thought. Perhaps

the imprint of character on a place is always there, however much the cosmetics and outline of a landscape seem to change. Dragging buckets of water to the horses, I thought of a young girl who might have grown up in Capel Celyn, someone who had never known English and had only Welsh words flowing from her mouth. Now I imagined her standing waist-deep in water, as it gushed in around her, where once her home had been, although in reality they would all have been forced to leave their homes long before the water consumed them. She and forty-seven of her neighbours lost their homes that day the village was flooded. I tried to imagine what she might have felt as the water of the new reservoir rushed across the place where the horse-hair bristles of her mattress had been, sloshing into the wooden bucket where her mother had crouched, morning after morning, to milk their goats, and cascading over the school desk where she had had her palm caned. I tried to feel her dismay as oozing, slippery mud submerged her home in the torrent of water that poured through it, and her horror as she realized that the water levels would rise until fish, blubbery and mindless, swam in and out of the now-underwater church and through the village post office. Water overtook the place where her home and her village had been.

If I closed my eyes, I could see the water submerging the village, like one of those fast-forward and slow-motion videos simulating the effects of climate change which the children watched on YouTube. The water robbed Capel Celyn of its definition as a village that day in the sixties, but, decades gone, deep underwater, perhaps the village itself was never really lost, simply waiting. I wondered how much of the spirit of the village, and the girl's home, and her friend's and neighbours' homes, was still there, in the foundations and stones emerging from the dried-up lake. Perhaps the water had washed everything away. Perhaps the mud had congealed and destroyed every sense of place that the school, the church, the girl's home, the post office had contained when the village was a living community. Perhaps the sense of home of that place was congealed then destroyed when the water and mud rushed in. Perhaps the village had been dissolved for ever in the years that the houses and the buildings sat silently under water. Or perhaps they were still there, in some way. Perhaps the life that had been lived in the village had once been so strong that the sense of place had remained, despite the flooding.

To postpone the inevitability of the moment Jimmy really left home, I tried to stall the end of his childhood by engineering picnics with pizzas on the riverbank, or visits into Oxford, promising noodles and a trip to an art shop, as if I was setting up playdates to engage my near-adult son. I was also looking for ways to imprint home into him, one last time, so that it would be inside him, when he left, for the rest of his life.

Late one night, reading in bed, a photo of a friend fell from the pages of my book. It was of Davina, black curly hair and a very direct smile, looking straight into the camera. The last time I'd seen her she'd told me about a lost village near the Ridgeway called Snap. She'd been sitting at a wooden table, folding a piece of card she had cut out in three swift cuts using a very sharp Opinel knife, from the edge of a box on that table holding jars of honey.

'Stick that under that leg, would you,' she'd said, motioning to the corner where the table leg did not sit flat on the uneven floor and pushing a book across the table with her elbow at the same time. 'Make it balance. Look, Snap.' There may have been a slight stain on her forefinger as she pointed to the book again, either from tobacco or more likely from gardening, and I picked the book up and flicked it open. 'A lost village, close to Bishopstone, close to you, near Liddington, near Barbury Castle. Deserted, not lost, not that long ago either. Full of homes until very recently. Relatively, I mean. A hundred years ago, perhaps. Time is relative.'

I had flicked through the book she handed me, trying to decipher a badly printed OS map with text in a wonky line across the pages. Davina said I could borrow her book, after she had read it, and we'd decided we would go and find the lost village together. But she died, suddenly, two weeks later. I didn't know what happened to the book, but looking at the image of Davina, I remembered the name: Snap, the lost village.

Jimmy was in the kitchen, cooking fried eggs, and he looked massive.

'Lost village? That sounds cool. Near here?' he said, flipping two eggs over, sliding them on to thick slices of toast dripping with golden butter.

I knew a lost village would appeal to Jimmy; it was almost as enticing as a crop circle. Since he'd passed his driving test, he and his friends often set out to explore parts of the landscape, as if by reaching backwards, to the deserted factories, old airfields, abandoned houses, they could make sense of the fractured, changing shape of home and understand their place in it. Jimmy had shared photos with me of some of these trips, precarious images I found unsettling to look at, of a half-ruined underground corridor they'd scrambled down in an old munitions factory, of the outline of his silhouette inside a Second World War pill box standing over a high drop, of three of them walking across a high beam in a derelict building covered in graffiti, of Jimmy laughing, much too close to a cliff edge.

Now he threw his frying pan into the sink as I spread an OS map on to the table, tracing my thumb along the bone of track of the Ridgeway, looking for new places hidden in the ripples and lines of the paper. 'A lost village,' he repeated, squeezing bright tomato ketchup on the yellow yolks of the fried eggs. 'That would be great. We could go and look for it before I go.'

The OS map still confused me as we drove in the direction of the hill forts of Liddington and Barbury, those names Davina had talked about. I gripped the steering wheel as the road swooped down to the village of Aldbourne, crossing the blue pulsing vein of the M4, the swell of the downs all around. Orange and yellow beech trees fluttered beside the road like flags in the outstanding autumn sunshine against a cobalt-blue sky. It was a rare and precious thing to be with Jimmy on my own for a whole day. I wanted to be proficient, to have worked out a circular route we could cover in five hours or so, not to get lost, to have funny and interesting things to say, to make him laugh, not to squander the

beauty of the time we had by frowning over a map or
searching for a phone signal in a field, or behaving like a
cliché of a middle-aged woman, flustered, out of place,
irritable, lost. I wanted him to remember the day we had,
but a very small part of me thought he might only be
coming for a walk because he felt sorry for me, because
my preoccupation with a lost village made me sound
vague, like it was me who was lost too.

   This feeling wasn't helped by the realization, as I pulled
the car over in a lay-by near the Ridgeway, that I'd left the
correct OS map on my desk in my bedroom. The map we
had with us sliced off Aldbourne, close to where we might
start our walk. I hoped this might not matter and the
route would simply reveal itself, since the Ridgeway is
straight. You just walk and it's all there. But when I looked
at an older map, with *Medieval village of Snap* faintly printed
on it in Gothic letters, I could also see that we weren't
looking for the Ridgeway anyway. It didn't run through
Snap but lay some way apart from the old track.

   'What are we looking for?' Jimmy asked as I squinted
over the wrong map, trying to match the corner of
what we had with the curve of the hills before us. I
didn't want to tell him that I didn't know. Or that what
I was looking for was a feeling as much as a place, that
of home after it had vanished. I wasn't sure if I should
confess that, while there might be nothing left of Snap,
I wanted to see what the place of it felt like. I wasn't
sure which idea made me seem madder – looking for a
village that wasn't there or trying to sense a feeling of a
place long gone. Because when I'd looked up Snap
online, there wasn't much to go on. There were, of
course, lots of villages that had been deserted, all over

the country, but Snap was unusual because it was still, just, a working village at the start of the twentieth century, having evolved as a small settlement of agricultural workers on the arable farm around it since the fourteenth century. Children born there went to school up the hill, in the slightly larger village of Woodsend. The census of 1861 recorded a population of fifty-three in Snap, which dropped to thirty-four by 1881, when there were just six families, their names recorded in the last census as John Jerram, George Fisher, John Plumber, John Bates, George Ebsworth, Robert Fox and James Fisher. By the end of the nineteenth century, Snap was vanishing, families leaving for Swindon, to work with the heavy chains of the new locomotives heaving on to the horizon. In 1905 the village was effectively killed by Henry Wilson, a butcher and sheep dealer from Ramsbury, a village near Aldbourne. He needed fewer workers to care for his sheep than had worked there when it was arable land. The last person to live in Snap, I read, was a woman called Rachel Fisher, who stayed, living alone, even after her husband James died. Apart from being used for military training in the First World War, the village was lost.

Looking for Snap, we stopped in Aldbourne. In the village shop, beside jars of Oxfordshire and Wiltshire honey, I queued at the food counter. A man in orange overalls was buying three sausage rolls and ham-and-cheese sandwiches, 'for the lads on site', he explained cheerfully. I paid for a pamphlet on circular walks from the village and bought Jimmy, waiting in the car, a brownie.

'Oh, yes, there are plenty of lovely walks around,' said a woman with her hair piled into a messy bun, smiling and nodding. 'But Emma, she's who you want to talk to. I'm not from here. Hold on. Let me see if Emma's free . . . Emma? Emma, there's a lady for you here, about walks, Ridgeway walks,' she said, calling into the back of the shop. Emma emerged, and I told her I was looking for the lost village at Snap, as I was going for a walk with my son.

'Yes, Snap's wonderful, just as the Ridgeway is. I walk there with my children quite often, although it's a fair way from the road, a mile or more along a track. You might have to carry your son for a bit of it,' she said, motioning in a direction along the road, then putting her hand over her mouth to giggle, very hard, when I pointed out my son in the car outside. 'You can walk and walk on this stretch of the Ridgeway and never know it all. I've walked it all with my little son and run it on my own too. Just follow this road, up out of the village. There's a gateway you can park in, where the verge narrows, beside a big black barn, then walk up the track towards the Ridgeway and you'll see a fork, take that left, you can't miss it.'

I thanked her, quickly, as there was a small queue forming, but wished there had been more time, since I wanted to ask her what the Ridgeway made her feel like and why, precisely, she lived here, and who else she walked with, and whether she was married and if she still loved her husband, and how big the Ridgeway felt on the horizons inside her. But Jimmy was waiting, and someone behind me had started to shuffle their feet, and a voice in the back of the shop was shouting, 'Emma,

Emma, order for two bacon rolls and a white Americano with one sugar.'

Emma was right. The gateway near the narrow verge was easy to find, and beside that the black corrugated barn, packed full of fat straw bales curled together like a pile of cinnamon buns on the counter of a coffee shop. Outside the car, steadied by my feet on the track, the fears I'd had about what we were looking for vanished. Warm heat fell on to the stubble, bright yellow in the mid-morning light of late September. The little walking guide I'd bought had a photocopied map taking in the hill beyond the village, with the word *Snap* clearly marked, although there were no buildings, tracks, or any signs of a village ever having existed. There might be absolutely nothing left of Snap, I thought, as I grabbed a plastic Minecraft-branded backpack taken in a rush from Lester's bedroom and stuffed with a flask of tea, a package of sandwiches wrapped in foil and two apples. Whatever we found, it didn't really matter anyway, since the sun was so bright and nothing seemed to matter, apart from that delightful feeling of it being a Thursday morning, not even the weekend, and there being a track ahead of us. This carelessness felt as luxurious inside me as the curve of the hill before me, where a metal sign, edged with red rust, optimistically pointed in the direction of 'By-way to Snap & Ridgeway' at a point where the dusty chalk track, so very dry, forked in two directions.

We walked, chatting then silenced by the sight of a crumbling barn locked in behind big metal crash barriers, as if a rave had been anticipated and prevented before it was even a distant beat. Sparrows darted in and

out of the building. Brambles scrambled over the corrugated iron roof. And although I could see nothing there,
Jimmy nodded, motioning with his chin to graffiti on
the back wall.

'Imagine this as a place for a party.'

His voice rose, and in it was all that yearning of being
young and wanting a place to be separate from the
world while you are also part of it, to escape the reality
which holds us all so tight. It was so silent there, standing by the barn, no sound at all but a cow in a field far
away bawling distractedly to another; but I could
remember the feeling of beats filling every pocket of
space around me as I danced in a place like this on
another stretch of the Ridgeway when I was Jimmy's
age. I wished he could experience that again, just
quickly, before he left for Manchester. But I also
thought of 'Emma, Emma' and the rolls she had to
make, the early mornings she didn't want disturbed.

'Imagine, a long time ago, the sound of a cart, or
horses and wagon wheels rumbling along here,' I said to
Jimmy. He reached down, saying, 'Look,' and picked
up a metal band a few inches long and an inch thick,
rusted and battered flat and smooth, as if it had come
straight from a cartwheel. Beside it was another stone,
the size of a pat of butter, but with curved edges and a
smooth shallow dent in the middle.

'It looks, don't you think, like the hole was made by
something? Made by someone, even?' Jimmy asked.
Maybe a man had taken a stick and rubbed it between
his hands on top of the stone to create fire. Or maybe it
was just an unusually smooth stone with a strange dip in
the top of it. Because I wanted something to hold on to,

to remind me of the day, beyond the pictures I took on my phone, we put it in my backpack, so much heavier now as we tramped onwards. We talked about whether the stone might be a talisman, and if it was possible to pick something up from the world and take it home, and if it could retain its power, or if, in doing that, removing a stone, a flower, a leaf, and taking it into a kitchen, it took all the beauty from it anyway.

'The stone is beautiful and kind of majestic here, on the track, but it could also just turn into another stone on my window ledge, with me not remembering where it came from or why it was special,' Jimmy said, as the track changed again, the open fields closing around us, the long horizons vanishing as the fields squeezed in. Hazel and alder trees wove together into a single tunnel as we walked on, talking about stones and repetitive beats. There was no evidence of Snap anywhere, though, so we paused again, to pore over the map in the village pamphlet, then stopped for longer, hunting for a signal of Snap on our phones and finding nothing.

'Maybe we missed Snap. Maybe so much of what it had been was lost, we didn't even notice it,' I said, turning back to retrace our route a little, pulling away from the track, clambering over a baggy barbed-wire fence. I walked among the hazel trees, staring hopelessly into bushes thick with brambles and leaning down to peer into the dense, green overgrowth, like I was looking for an elf crouching there, not an entire lost village. When I'd looked online, I'd found optimistic descriptions of a long-abandoned windmill, and even the foundations of houses rewarding those who looked hard enough.

In that moment I felt so disappointed. I had wasted

this morning with Jimmy. I could have taken him to
Avebury, or even Stonehenge. Instead, I was hunting
around under the bright-green light of hazel trees for
something I didn't really understand. I shrugged.

'Still, it's been nice to get out, hasn't it?' I said as we
pressed on, and Jimmy nodded. Around us, the tunnel
of trees had spread out. We walked back into the wide-
open countryside, where golden-stubble fields, dotted
with specks of crows pecking for seeds, bristled alongside the chalk tracks, and we kicked the black insides of
flints as we walked. Smaller tracks appeared, labelled as
by-ways on the dark wooden posts which marked them.
These tracks crossed the valley, their routes less well
walked, overgrown with the brittle stalks of hemlock
and thistles with ferociously huge leaves. Hedgerows
grew tufty and thick across some of the tracks, mottled
with splashes of scarlet berries, and the yellow flash of
a goldfinch alighted on a hedge then was tantalizingly
gone.

I had wanted to take Jimmy somewhere surprising,
to show him that, away from the younger children, I
was still capable of adventure and suddenness, but it
hadn't worked. We wandered on, talking less about
Snap and instead about what lay ahead for Jimmy, his
move from home to a new part of England. We both
had our eyes to the ground as we walked, and I was
thinking that soon, maybe, we could sit in a field, eat
the sandwiches Jimmy had made, then find a short cut
back to the car and forget the village, that this would be
the best thing to do, to go back to reality. As we walked
under the dappled light of an oak tree shading the track,
the mottled green froth of a strip of woodland appeared

before us as the way curved sharply to the left. There was a rusty five-bar gate in front of us and I stopped.

'Look, Jimmy, look, look, look! Jimmy, look! Jimmy, look, this must be it. This must be it. This must be Snap.'

How could some bent and misshapen metalwork, twisted into the shape of a windmill, rising from the green below it, like the outline of a small giant, once used to pump water for the village of Snap but now unused, forgotten, abandoned, make my heart pound like that? What is the source of the power that things, spaces, places, objects hold in them? Because as I stood gazing at the broken outline of the windmill, I sensed emanating from it a phenomenal energy of place that made me feel something approaching awe, as tears slid silently down my face.

The pointed triangle of the windmill, which touched the cloudy blue sky at a point no higher than one of the oak trees in the wood beyond it, rose, almost like a very old spaceship, from a mess of elder bushes clinging around its legs. It was just a tower, teetering on those thin, rusty limbs, yet somehow still standing, the smashed pieces of its wheel a metal mangle in the brambles at its base. Jimmy dropped his bag, swinging over the five-bar gate into the field, approaching the windmill slowly, as if quietening himself so as not to startle it, the actual alien from the past that we had been searching for. The dried ground around its four metal legs was pitted and potted with the cloven-hoof prints of the cows, who scattered further out, on the far side of the field, some turning to stare at us from their distance.

Jimmy began to climb it, reminding me of how he'd

always climbed as a boy, scaling the metal chain-link fencing beside the ground where he'd played football on the ring road outside Oxford, or scrambling up trees, up buildings, on to roofs, scaring me but never himself. 'There's a good view from the top!' he shouted down to me, and when he returned to earth we ventured into the trees beside the windmill, and the lost village emerged. Hidden under a tangle of nettles was a well, with blocks of stone piled up in a round, but throttled by brightest-green ivy. '*Snaep*' was the Anglo-Saxon word that lent its name to the village. It means 'boggy land', but high in that chalky valley, with the water table several hundred feet below, Snap would have dried up to nothing without the wells. As the silence in the clearing was broken by the sudden crack of a stick, the rustle of our feet through the fallen leaves, I tried to listen for the past, to hear the clamour around the well, children bumping their wooden pails against one another, women with metal buckets fetching water, the source of their daily survival, all silenced now.

Picking our way between bumps and mounds of collapsing earthworks, we found the startlingly straight lines of red bricks, some broken but still a memory of the foundations of houses now stripped back to nothing but ruined old bones. Moss and ivy carpeted the ground, springing and snaking over lichen-covered tree trunks, and we stepped over the remains of a rusted barbed-wire fence, silently straining for the sound of the past, shocked suddenly by a bright flash of blue-and-white fragments of broken china lying deep in the ivy: a tea set, a dinner plate, a jug, the shattered pieces of homes.

Afterwards, we sat for a long time on a log in the

clearing, neither of us wanting to leave Snap. While Jimmy unwrapped cheese sandwiches, we talked about the little I knew of Snap, and about Rachel Fisher, the last person to have lived there. She and her husband James had first appeared in the census of Snap in 1871, when they were in their mid-forties. I had seen a photograph of her, her face sharp, standing beside James, his face round and white as a floury bread bun under his wide-brimmed black hat. He seemed cheerful, oblivious to the forces of fate and corn prices and the whims of Henry Wilson, the butcher, that would make his village, and his home, vanish. Unlike Rachel, James looked like he would welcome life right in, while barely noticing what it was doing to him.

I imagined them in Snap, before Henry Wilson bought the land, the rise and fall of their lives defined by the fields which flowed seamlessly into their village, into their house. Finishing my sandwich, pouring tea from a flask, I thought it must have been a heavenly place to live in summer, surrounded by a rippling sea of wheat which would change to the rich, brown clot of plough after the harvest. Tougher, no doubt, in the cold, hard, dark desolation of late January, when there were still weeks and months to endure before the bright-green optimism of early spring heralded the rhythm of change which would bring summer. Then, the children who ran sticks along the fence behind her cottage would have been the children of the ploughman and the shepherd. Those children would have known every rise and sighing fall of the track Jimmy and I had wandered along. As we sat quietly in the clearing, I thought of them walking across spring turf to the schoolhouse at Woodsend, humming to themselves, then suddenly out of breath as they ran, grabbing each other's hat or bag, following little paths made by other children growing up in Snap before them. I tried to imagine how Rachel might have felt when the schoolhouse at Woodsend closed, and the voices of the children grew quiet, since there was no work for the ploughmen after Henry Wilson bought the farm, turning the arable fields over to sheep.

Across the clearing a blackbird chattered suddenly, perhaps aware of our presence. Each sound – the birds moving with intent, the faint breeze moving the canopy of leaves above us, the crunch of dried leaves as I stretched my feet again – was amplified by the silence. I imagined Rachel watching the last deserting figures vanishing down the track, one lifting a hand in farewell without turning around, as she went back to her cottage where James was breaking up sticks for the fire, the two of them the last inhabitants of Snap.

I stretched my legs out, the luminous orange Adidas stripes of my trainers so bright against the earthy, soft browns of the oak, beech and hazel leaves making a carpet around where we sat. Rachel remained in Snap long after her neighbours, and their children, had left, staying on there, alone, even after James had died. I tried to imagine myself into her space, sitting by her fire, the thin curtains of the cottage windows left open because the pitch darkness of Snap was where she felt safe. Snap was her home, and as the final inhabitant of this lost village she, too, was Snap. Perhaps, walking amongst the walnut trees near her cottage, remembering the sound of children humming as they waited at the well, and the patter-patter of sheep feet across the field, she did feel sad, although never so sad she wanted to leave. For some time after James's death, Rachel stayed alone in the clearing where Jimmy and I sat, passing a metal cup of tea between us. She pulled water from the well, and must have lived on very little, perhaps gathering berries and hazelnuts, and sometimes taking a visit from a villager who walked up the track from Aldbourne, bringing her some bread, cheese, a bit of bacon. Tending the fire in the grate in her cottage, searching for kindling in all the familiar places, picking her way along the path into the field, once muddy from the marks the children made but now smooth with disuse, which must have marked the edges of her world. She was an old woman by then, who had seen saplings grow into thick trees and knew that same valley, and the intimacy of its relationship with the old village, as well as she knew the inside of her heart.

Sitting there in the silence, I understood why Rachel Fisher had gone on living there alone until her nephew persuaded her to move to Cooks Yard, in Aldbourne, in 1909. She hadn't wanted to leave her home amongst the trees, the smell of leaf mould just outside her cottage, where she always slept with her window open, even on the coldest night, better to hear that strange and beautiful sound of foxes barking. She wanted to wake to the sound of a dawn chorus that was only hers, and walk out, alone, after it had been raining, to sense the watery green smell of the hazel leaves, still dripping, just a bit, as the first light of dawn broke through them. Of course she missed the children, her neighbours, the rumble of cartwheels on the flint track, the clash of buckets beside the well, the cheer and crackle of a village bonfire, but missing them was not as bad and as sharp as the feeling of leaving her home.

It started to rain as Jimmy and I packed our lunch up, leaving Snap behind, walking slightly north as the track closed behind us. Flints and chalk underfoot gave way, a little later, to a concrete track which skirted a yard with a large blue tractor reversing in and out of a barn, carrying huge, round bales on prongs as carefully as if they were live beings. It started to rain harder, fat drops settling on furry hazel leaves, darkening the blue of my pale sweatshirt, and we laughed, huddling into a thicker hedge of blackthorn as the rain hammered on to the chalk track, puddles suddenly forming, reflecting the glassy light above. In the distance we could make out Aldbourne, our car close to the black barn, but at that moment I'd have done anything to continue walking. I'd like to have continued through the curve of the chalk valley, to walk to the Giant's Grave, the Bronze Age long barrow overgrown with ivy and nettles near the hill fort at Liddington Castle I'd found once with Pete, a long time before, and to hold on to that moment I had with Jimmy for longer.

What I found when we returned home, though, was that while we left Snap – Jimmy peeling off to meet friends, the children and Iona, who had picked them up from school, a clamour in the kitchen, Dolly returning from college – Snap did not leave me. The outline of the lost village moved inside me like a shadow.

Sometimes, in the early mornings, in the days after our walk to Snap, I found myself lingering a little longer on the bridge before the house, hoping I might see the tall man dressed in the colours of night. That tall man had told me to look on the ridge and the hills for something that was lost, and I wanted to ask him about what he had meant. But more than him, I kept thinking of Rachel Fisher, in the last weeks of her life, walking the back paths which run from Aldbourne towards the Ridgeway, and always wanting to be in Snap. After she died her nephew was quoted in a local paper saying that once she'd moved to Cooks Yard, she missed the sound of birds singing, and the bark of foxes in the dark. Maybe her mind, so used to the quiet spaces of the downland landscape which had enclosed her so tightly, started to let go of the feeling of her home. Maybe the fluster of village life in Aldbourne, where children chased the fat white ducks that waddled and gussied in the mud around the pond, and the sound of the neighbour's baby crying rose over the noise of village boys fighting over a ball in the yard, distracted her. Perhaps the sound of a pedlar calling out as he walked through the village, and the noise of the rag-and-bone man arriving to carry away metal, or the rumble of the milk cart in the early morning and the shouting of the butcher boy at lunchtime, muddled her. Perhaps the pattern of the blue-and-white china she and James had used in their cottage cracked and dissolved from her mind, and finally the memory of walking across the downs with James on a sunny day drifted away from her too, formless and forgotten.

Or maybe, I found myself thinking as I waited at the bridge, she made herself forget as she moved closer to the end of her life. Perhaps remembering it represented a dangerous pull towards the past she could never return to now that Snap was gone. I thought about this as I stood on the bridge, feeling the exhilarating whoosh of an early-morning train zooming to a city while I waited for the man in black, since I wanted to tell him what it felt like to forget about home.

Because I, too, have sometimes chosen to forget. I don't remember the feeling of walking down hot tarmac roads as a teenager, on nights so white with moonlight it never truly got dark. It was the middle of the night, and my sister Nell and I walked along the roads barefoot, the tarmac warm against our soles, a sweetness of poplar leaves heavy around us in the dark, but I don't remember it. I don't remember the way buttercups grew so thick and tall that they stained our hands dusty yellow when we walked through the paddock together behind the house, and neither do I remember the broken pattern of mottled light falling beneath the apple trees as we stepped barefoot through apples hidden in the longer grass, daring each other to move faster, avoiding the wasps in the rotting apples like hopscotch. I don't remember the true sound of the screaming of swifts in the summer sky when we lay on the lawn at dusk, and I don't remember that precise feeling of the way the heat suddenly left the air, turning the evening too cold, making us quickly stand up, brushing grass from one another's backs as we walked inside. I don't remember the green smell of parsley where Mum would tell us to go and pick some before supper, or the oily smell of harnesses in the stables in front of the wooden box where we hid sweets taken from the kitchen. I remember none of these things. I don't remember the sound of my mother's voice calling something to me from a far corner of the garden, beyond my vision, to 'Come, quickly' and look at the bright crimson of the poppies that were growing everywhere – '*Everywhere!*' – and I have forgotten the sound of Nell laughing, in an upstairs attic room. I don't remember the very narrow slit of a window, on the curve at the bottom of the stairs by the kitchen door, wide enough only for a small child to hide in, and neither do I remember the cold white tiles in the kitchen where we'd press our faces to cool them on the hottest days, or that patch at the top of the stairs, where the carpet was threadbare, under the criss-cross lead in the landing windows where we played with plastic toy ponies. I don't remember these things because I've found it can be safer to forget.

Now the memory of the lost village I carry inside me hurts my mind, and not remembering enables me to rest it, to stop it straining for the past, to guide it into the present, to force it into now. These places, these rooms, these spaces of home are imprinted inside me, a haunting that feels like an internal language I can only read when I touch the past, like a memory of braille. My childhood home vanished when I was sixteen, when my mother had a terrible riding accident. She lived for twenty-two years after it but she no longer looked like herself, behaved like herself or was able to be Mum. She was alive all the time in which I took A levels, went to university, ran away, got married – twice – and became

a mother, but she was not present for any of it. Before
then, love defined the way she mothered us. Once,
when I was about fourteen, I cried about going to
school. Mum was so upset to see me sad to leave her,
even for a day, that she went out and bought me some
potted primrose plants with bright red and yellow
petals. She arranged them in a bowl, like a little garden,
and left them in my bedroom, to come home to. I think
of that quite often as a small but extraordinarily beautiful thing to do for a child.

Losing my home also made me do things I hope my
children won't do: it made me hurt myself in unneces-
sary ways for a long time. But I have found a way of
calming this desire to hurt myself when I write. When
I write a true and beautiful sentence about what loss
feels like, I exist in a state of pure happiness and my life
feels like it has total meaning.

In my twenties and thirties, I dreamed all the time
of the home I had lost. Sometimes, at first, it would
seem familiar, sweet and friendly, but then something
would be wrong. Doors and windows might be missing, a room in the wrong place. Or I might find new,
unfamiliar rooms I'd never been into as a child and
what had felt delightful was replaced by the implicit
sense that the rooms would reveal something I really
shouldn't, mustn't, see; the beautiful and familiar
mutated into uncomfortable and threatening, a once-
reassuring place made grotesquely scary or just wrong.
Sometimes the house I dreamed of appeared to me,
but far beyond in a distant valley, out of reach. Home
never appeared to me as a place of warm, nostalgic
peace or ease; home, in my dream state, was always

disturbing. And the essence of home was always lost in some way.

'Even if I could go back to Minety, I wouldn't find the people there that I'm looking for,' I said to Pete, that evening when we were lying in bed, staring at one another. We had been discussing our days. I wanted to reach into the phone and touch him. Outside, one of the dogs was barking repeatedly, so I stood up and shut the window, the square figure of Pete on FaceTime following me. Dash and Evangeline were biking in circles after one another around the yard, Lester following them in a smaller circle. Occasionally one of them stopped to point out something about the other's bike or kick the other's tyre. I leant against the green window frame, picking at an area of peeling paint, watching the children. They had spent much of the day plugged in to separate computers, jagged and furious when I whipped through the house that afternoon, grabbing the screens from them, kicking them out into the yard where they cycled, livid with one another.

I'd been explaining the powerful feeling of Snap to Pete, and how a sense of home remained there even though the houses, and Rachel, were long gone. It was like the imprint Minety had left inside me. 'The past is so hypnotic,' I said to him, 'it's as if we don't know how to resist it, let alone have the strength to leave it, even if we did know how. Even when we are looking away, looking at the future, doing our own thing, we recreate it, by accident.

'And what I'm really scared of is that if we move, I will be recreating the loss of the past,' I told him.

My mum was in her early fifties when she had her accident, and it was just that – an accident. She didn't mean to vanish. She didn't wilfully bring a state of violent trauma into our lives, but ever since I've had children I've been afraid that something beyond my control will make me vanish from their lives and destroy their home at the same time. I fear reaching my early fifties in case the urge to recreate the same circumstances of the past simply overwhelms me.

I never felt this as a younger woman. Then, I was certain I was creating a life all of my own. I felt bold and original. But as I reached my mid-forties, I could see that I'd created a life very similar to my mother's: she'd had a big family, five children from two marriages, and my dad, like Pete, worked away for much of our childhood. I had recreated all the good stuff of the past, no doubt. It was not just by chance I had a messy, mismatching kitchen surrounded by muddy fields and thick black hedges, dogs on every sofa, a bond to the village shop, ponies moving in the garden outside. These were the things I grew up with that I wanted, whether I knew it or not. And perhaps vanishing, or violently dismantling home so that it left a permanent imprint of loss on my children, was also something I'd reach for without even realizing it. I told Pete I was scared that by moving to America, we would be wilfully making home vanish, just as home had vanished for me. I said that selling the house and dismantling the children's home might mean that it would become a place they would be looking for for ever, just as I was.

Then I told Pete about a poem I had been reading, 'The Ruin', describing a once-magnificent but now-

destroyed city, and the lines I loved that spoke so loudly
of the loss I was afraid of:

*Wondrous is this foundation – the fates have broken*
*and shattered this city; the work of giants crumbles.*
*The roofs are ruined, the towers toppled,*
*frost in the mortar has broken the gate,*
*torn and worn and shorn by the storm,*
*eaten through with age.*

'I'm afraid we are willingly weaving loss into the
children's lives, especially Jimmy and Dolly's, since they
are the ones we are leaving, and that's the thing that
scares me most of all.'

Outside, the forked, dark tawny outline of a red kite
wheeled in the sky, and at that moment the children
stopped as one, turning their small, pale faces to the outline of the bird. The light fractured, the pressure of
moisture rising in it as wind lifted off the wide, flat field
beside the house, making the tendrils of weeping willow
hanging over the yard move suddenly. The window rat-
tled and the children, sensing I was watching them,
turned their faces from looking at the bird to me. Then
they threw their bikes on to the yard as the first spots of
rain burst through the flat clouds which had scooped
overhead. Quite suddenly, it felt like the very end of
summer. I looked at Pete, inside that brightly lit little glass
and plastic square. I wanted to reach inside and touch
him. I didn't want to be apart, living through one another's screens, our skin separated by thousands of miles.

'Go to Minety,' Pete said, his voice reaching me
through his screen. 'Take yourself back to Minety, go

there. It's still there, Clover. You can go back, and it won't be the same, but it won't be gone either,' he said, and I could hear an echo behind him and see the vast space of a big meeting place or conference behind him. 'You know it always makes you feel better to go back there. Go to that wood where you take the children when the bluebells come out. Or just go and drive through the village. It will reassure you, maybe. It usually does.'

The verges were wilder as I drove along the narrow road, the hedgerows moving close enough to touch my car windows, grasses and thistles making a metallic scrape along the door as I pulled closer into the potted edge, sticky with wet clay after the thunderstorms and days of rain. A faded burgundy tractor pulling a flatbed wider than the lane humped towards me as I pulled up, my car tipping into a rut while the tractor slowed right down, clumps of damp straw from a split bale on its bed scattering on the road behind it like sodden ticker-tape confetti. A man – more of a boy, really – with cropped dark-blond hair sat high in the cab, wearing oily, dark-green overalls, and lifted one hand to wave at me without taking his eyes from the narrow road. I knew his face, or at least his imprint; I remembered boys like him, who drove tractors around these roads when I was the same age, a grown-up teenager. He might have been driving the same tractor, for the same farmer, whose land Nell and I had ridden across as children.

After the tractor passed, I stopped, pulling my car into the edge of the road by a farmhouse we'd passed so often as children. I turned the engine off, stepping out to look at the house, which was the approximation of a child's outline of what a house might look like: five windows around a front door, a pitched roof, chimney pots at either end. Behind the house I could see the striped ridges of a rusting red corrugated-iron Dutch barn. When Nell and I were children, this house and the family who lived here fascinated and repelled us. Then, the window frames were peeling with faded blue paint, the garden below them a mass of dog roses and black-berries in conflict with the thick, dark crosses of a blackthorn hedge. There were quite a few houses like this around Minety, big and often half-empty places with broken panes in upstairs windows that were never replaced, and outdoor loos and gardens overtaken with thick laurel hedges or dense mats of brambles. In some gardens the outline of an overgrown vegetable patch, or the dried-out stalls of empty cow byres, were still visible.

But life has changed. Now, at the farmhouse, there was gravel raked in even stripes across a drive once wobbly with the broken mottles of agricultural con-crete. Peeling paint had been replaced by gleaming white window frames, the blackthorn banished and replaced by clipped box hedges under each window. A wooden-framed car port had been added beside the Dutch barn, no longer red but now painted a glossy black, housing electric-car-charging points. Beside the front door were two child's tricycles lined up beside a custom-made rack for wellington boots.

I shifted slightly, kicking the end of my damp train-ers, remembering the silence that would suddenly overcome Nell and me, snatching away our chat about what last happened on the school bus, when we'd pass

this house, straining, always, to get a glimpse of the
family who lived here. They stayed on the top floor,
we'd heard from one of the boys who drove tractors,
because their pigs and cows stayed in the downstairs sitting room. 'That family, they're perverts,' he told Nell,
after he'd stopped to chat to her as we walked back from
the school bus. 'Three brothers and two sisters live
there. Have sex with each other, they do,' he'd said,
taking a swig from a bottle of very diluted orange
squash. Nell told me he'd said they had sex with the pigs
too, although he'd made her promise not to repeat this.
'No, not true, not true at all,' Mum said, when Nell
told her. Perhaps it was true, she conceded, that their
pigs did occasionally wander into the kitchen, but there
was nothing wrong in that, and it certainly was not a
reason to think they had sex with the animals, or each
other, she told us in a tone that made it clear this was
a fact.

Sometimes we'd see the shadow of a face at a window,
or a vanishing outline of one of them whistling to one
of their dogs in the barn behind the house, as she hung
washing out, in the place that was now the car port. Or
we'd pass one of them walking, with his head down,
moving his shoulders with a sharp, small movement, as
he returned from the village shop, where the family
were known to stop very occasionally for a few weeks'
supplies. All of them, both brothers and sisters, wore
faded rubber boots, wide-legged brown trousers and
tweed jackets too long in the arms, with shiny patches
on the shoulders, elbows. They walked and moved outside the safety of their farmyard as if trying to make
themselves invisible against the landscape, hunched

slightly, braced, if not for attack then for some part of life to impinge on their worlds. It occurred to me that the brothers and sisters were about the same age then as I am now, three decades later. To us they looked like very old people.

Even as a child, before I knew what a lost home felt like or the ferocity of the imprint it leaves inside a person, I understood that this house, and its inhabitants, represented a kind of life that was rare and disturbing but also beautiful. I understood, as Nell and I tried to steal glances into the windows, that what we were witnessing was a kind of vanishing. But despite the irrepressible movement of time, when I stopped my car I somehow expected nothing to be changed. In fact, everything was, of course, completely different.

Overhead, I heard the hard, almost guttural cawing of a crow. Looming close to the house, on the far side of the road, were the outstretched arms of a line of pylons, buzzing with an electric energy I could feel in my nerves. I turned to look for the crow, which was suddenly silent, the pylons towering above me, giants moving forward. I took one last look at the house as a shiny, black Tesla pulled into the drive, pausing for a moment before I raised my hand in a quick greeting, unable to see back inside the dark-tinted windows as the car crunched across the gravel and into the car port.

I abandoned my journey into the village. There was no point in going further, to the house I grew up in. I knew I could look right into the upstairs windows there, if I went into the graveyard, where the house looked over the church walls. I've done it many times before: staring up to the bedroom window that was

mine, knowing the stretch of corridor that led to the
bathroom where once a pigeon had flown straight into
the glass as I sat in tepid water, as a young girl. There's
no point in going back to look for the past there, I
thought, as I reversed my car, turning around in a gateway beneath the pylon. I didn't want to think of what
might have happened to the brothers and sisters in the
farmhouse, and being in Minety wasn't showing me
anything. I realized I had been trying to locate my
mother and my sister, their actual beings, but when the
people who were in a place when it mattered have gone,
then what was substantial and important holding you
close to that place has gone too. Most of home will have
gone from that place when the people leave it.

Going back, trying to re-find a place in time and to
impose the present on it, usually hurts. And as my
childhood home retreated behind me, the scene of the
crime of Mum's accident vanishing, I realized, as I had
realized before but often forgot, that returning to my
childhood home, and to the feelings of being in that
place as a child, would always be like trying to grasp
hold of water. It isn't possible, but instead there is the
consolation of holding a sense of that place within me
for ever, wherever I am. The walls of the house I grew
up in, and the tracks through the fields around it, the
tarmac on the road outside it, the angle of the bend in
the road, the colour of the stone, the clotted, peculiar
quality of the clay in the area around the house, are
inside me, I realized, as Minety retreated.

I wanted to pull over and text Pete that I was feeling
less afraid. In my mind, I can still become seven years
old, the age I was when we moved there, when, if you

walked into the kitchen, you would find me with Mum and Nell. Mum would be cooking something, Nell would be leaning over the kitchen table, her long, unruly hair tangled across her face. We would have just walked back through the village, past the shop, past the pub, from the school bus. In my mind, it is possible for us all to exist at that moment in the past, and for nothing to have changed. I can go to that place at will, if I promise myself not to hang around too long. It's crucial I do not try to test the dimension which I am existing in when I take myself there. If I just step into it, and do not push on the edges, or try to speak to Nell or Mum, all will be well and I can sit in that kitchen with them both, because in that dimension nothing has changed, and all is as it once was, and is very beautiful.

I cried when I spoke to Pete, late that night. We'd been talking about our house, tentatively picking at the scab of what it would take to sell it. It hurt, yes, but not with the violence of a few weeks before. 'I felt separate from the past, like a bank of time was pushing me forward. And I can see it will be different for Jimmy and Dolly if we move. It won't be the same. It's not the same thing. It's not a destruction. I can see that. You were right. It was necessary to go back to the village and think about how separate our life is from the one I had there, in the past. That they're not the same thing. That the past is not the present. That my life is not my mother's. I know this, rationally, I know it, but it's like my brain needs reminding, again and again.'

After we finished talking, I re-read 'The Ruin', lingering over the Old English word *dustsceawung*, to understand what had been lost and the impermanence of things, the contemplation of dust, saying it aloud as I lay alone in the dark. Going back to Minety had made me shake the snow globe, but now the transience of everything lightly settled around me, imperceptibly tiny flakes that would be shaken again, but settle again too.

# Chapter 5

Pausing in front of the estate agent's window in the market square in Wantage, as the statue of King Alfred, stone-still, stared at my back, I watched a woman with blonde hair moving her hands in an animated way to explain something to someone she couldn't see down the telephone line. I registered a little feeling of shock, not at the estate agent, but at the fact that I hadn't seen anyone talking on a landline for several years. All I needed to do was push the door open, sit down in front of her, and start the process of selling the house, as Pete had said. But when I looked at the houses in the agent's window, visualizing ours reduced to a 'characterful home in a sought-after location', I couldn't do it, and ducked away instead to the hairdresser's, where Tina was waiting to colour my hair.

I spend hours and hours in Wantage, every week, stalking around cafes looking for electric sockets and spare tables, so as to sit with my laptop for several hours at a time to work when the claustrophobic domesticity of home is too distracting. When I'm not working, I'm

waiting for one of the children to finish a dance lesson
or a basketball session. I know the women by name at
the best charity shop where I have wasted a lot of time
buying stacks of plates decorated with a certain pattern
of blue roses that pleases me, or cereal bowls just the
right depth to stop the children's cornflakes spilling all
over the table. When a school play or book day
approaches, I go there to look for cat ears, or a shepherd's tunic, or a king costume or a bright-yellow
t-shirt a child could wear to become a duckling. I like
talking to the men and women who drive up from
Guildford to sell vegetables on the weekly market stalls.
I like listening to the patter of their chat and am always
impressed by their neat and speedy mental arithmetic,
and the precise, fast way they move their hands to meas-
ure out brown paper bags with black grapes or new
potatoes or heads of clean, palest-green chicory.
Sometimes I'll stop to chat to a neighbour, or one of the
children's teachers, or the man who cleans our windows, or Danny, who will pull on to a double yellow
line in his van so we can have a proper long chat. These
people matter a lot to me, their friendships have
formed a cocoon around my family, like a bird's nest, in
the years we've lived there. I find it reassuring that, unlike several other small market towns in neighbouring
counties, the high street in Wantage has absolutely no
boutiques selling cashmere jerseys or high-thread-count
Egyptian-cotton duvet covers. Instead, I can watch
teenagers from the secondary school emerging from
Greggs with hot sausage rolls mid-morning, or men in
heavy boots and work jeans, splattered with paint, nip-
ping into the bookie's or out of the Bear at lunchtime. I

like sitting in Costa, the clatter of my fingers overlapping with the squawks of the teenage girls, their hair straight and stiff and shiny like new straw hanging down their backs, as they slurp milkshakes, tapping on their phones, laughing too loudly as they reveal Snapchat secrets.

I know Wantage at night too. Jimmy knows, and his friends know too, that I'll go to any lengths to stop them getting into a car with a driver who has been drinking. There's a taxi rank in Wantage, but if it's late, and there's no floor to crash on in town, Jimmy might call me. It had happened a few nights earlier, when he messaged me, apologetic, late, because there were no taxis and a few of them needed somewhere to stay and Jake's mum had said no.

I hadn't minded getting his call: within a few days he wouldn't be calling me from Wantage at 1.37 a.m. on a Friday night, and probably never would again either. I'd parked in the marketplace, waiting in my car, a black puffer, pulled hastily over my pyjamas, rustling every time I reached for my phone. I'd left the wipers running, clearing away spots of rain as I watched a tabby cat dart across the town square as a couple, leaning into one another as if they were sharing a conspiratorial secret, vanished down the alleyway near the King Alfred pub. Jimmy and a handful of his friends, Jake and Kyle, Benji and JP, hadn't emerged for a bit, but then stumbled out of the narrow doorway of Delaney's, Wantage's one nightclub. They stood under a streetlamp, to huddle together to light cigarettes, smoke drifting around them in the streetlight as someone dropped the lighter and they all laughed loudly in unison. More figures emerged from the room above the pub, like inmates released, blinking and gasping. Everyone who wanted late-night drinking in Wantage went to Delaney's. I'd been once, queuing beside the bar with other school-gate mums, stable lads from Lambourn, bricklayers working on the big new estate outside town, the girls who worked in WHSmith and the MD of a local accountancy firm. I loved the all-embracing nature of local life: everyone together, a big messy jumble so that no one felt left out, no one felt too cool, classes and cultures and lives sliced right across and mixed together. From the car, I watched as someone leant forward suddenly, with his head between his legs, before staggering onwards and arranging himself on the steps beneath the stone statue of King Alfred, who stared across the square, marble-eyed yet also slightly affronted. Two younger figures joined him, one scrambling on to the other's shoulders, to climb the statue. In the early morning, King Alfred would be wearing a baseball cap jammed on top of his stone helmet. I watched for a bit, curious to see how they all moved around one another, until Jimmy suddenly spotted the car, lifting both hands in greeting. I flashed the headlights at them, and they ran towards me, hands clapping over their heads as if a great victory had been achieved. Then they had all fallen into the car, saying I was 'decent, decent', a high smell of beer and tobacco drenched through them, laughing, again and again, as we drove into the darkness of the road twisting between the fields separating Wantage and our home, at the inherently ridiculous fact, at the absolute jokes, of being twenty, and drunk, in Jimmy's mum's car, at near enough two a.m.

★

I have not always liked being in Wantage. When the children were babies and toddlers and moving around required nappies and snacks and changes of clothes I struggled to organize, and browsing anything was out of the question, Wantage was the place I would dash around grabbing wipes, milk, a roasting chicken, some tracing paper, all of which it had been a matter of great urgency to get out for. I did not like Wantage when I was called there, six years ago and 39.5 weeks pregnant with Lester, by Jimmy's headmistress, to be informed he was being expelled. Wantage had seemed alien then, a distant place where I had no reference points, no true, strong memories to call up, no allegiances, no real friends. But, with time, those bonds have grown, and grown strong too. Now, I like popping down a back alley to the junk shop behind the square, stopping for rye bread and really good coffee at the Marcopolo bakery, lingering to chat to the boys in the nail bar who tell me about their family in Vietnam while they turn my nails bright pink, or following the memory of a cobbled street, out to the small arts centre in the car park behind the square, where I have spent huge chunks of time standing in the foyer examining posters advertising a belly dancing club, a film screening, the next Brownies meet-up, a call-out for local carers. I've stood there watching parents carrying kit bags and trailing small children dressed for karate or ballet while I've waited for my own children and seen them grow up.

The layers of years I have spent here have settled over one another like coloured sand, making up the bands of a decade of my life. So many of the days of my life have been spent waiting in Wantage, and it is in those years that I've found the shape of my life too. I thought of those days as I pushed the door open to Tina's salon, anticipating, with relief, two hours in which I could drink milky Nescafé and flick through thumb-softened copies of magazines left piled on every seat while Tina told me about what had been happening in town, because she grew up here and knows everyone.

'I say everyone but I mean I know most people as you do if you live in a place as small as this makes sense not big-city living is it people know each other they make a habit of it make friends with everyone you do when you live in a place like this and that has its advantages although not always there are times I just want to leave just want to put these scissors down and to get out to Didcot or Oxford get a bit of air go to the shops and see life a bit though saying that I love Wantage been here all my life not like you moving here with all those gorgeous children now how is that lovely little Lester bless him and Evangeline is she still dancing she loves her dancing doesn't she and Dash too how is Dash getting on now?'

She paused, running her silver metal comb through my hair, lifting the strands straight upwards, snipping the ends, standing back to check her work, running the comb quickly over it all again. 'All the pubs too. People like being in pubs here, not as much as they used to, but the pubs are still busy, come the weekend they're all busy, people in Wantage like going out, drinking, getting together for a chat, maybe a dance, and all that,' she said, and laughed. And then she added something else, and her words made me look up at her so quickly that the tip of her scissors nicked the edge of my neck. 'Black Wantage,' she said, standing back, then leaning forward to slowly snip some longer lengths she'd missed first time. 'Black Wantage, or so they say.'

Black Wantage. The name hung in the air, a name I'd heard before, written on an information board in the local museum, where I'd spent many wet afternoons at half term with the children. It had emerged more than a century ago because the town had no lamplights, but also because of the sense of lawlessness and wildness that lingered over it, something I had been reminded of when waiting for Jimmy and his friends as the pubs spilled out. The salon filled up; a woman chuckled, lowering her voice quickly because she'd been telling her lady, whose hair she was cutting, about some things she'd seen her neighbour doing only last night, 'You'll never guess what he did next,' although as she launched into the answer the salon fell surprisingly quiet, the gossip oozing with riches too ripe to resist.

Tina, who had heard it all before, stepped backwards, checking her work, reaching for a mirror as she moved around the back of my head, pointing out the honey-coloured stripes of blonde she'd painted on to my hair, then nodding, satisfied, as she reached forward and ripped open the Velcro at the neck of the salon gown. 'No one would call it Black Wantage today, now, although mind you, it can get busy on a Friday night. *Very* busy. The pubs are normally full. And then there's the bar above the Swan, the cocktail bar. And the night-club. Delaney's, it's called now, although before that Hush, and then it used to be the cinema, years ago. Now, I won't lie, I have seen some scenes outside there on a Friday night that would make all our hair stand on end,' she said, then nodded at the girl sitting in the seat

beside me, quietly turning the pages of the magazine in
her lap, whose straight, black hair fell almost to her
waist. 'Even yours.'

Black Wantage, I thought, pulling a scarf over my
hair. The ground had that peculiar, gritty smell of rain
on dry concrete as fat drops fell. I dodged a teenager in a
school blazer biking down the middle of the pavement,
then dipped into Greggs for powder-pink glazed dough-
nuts covered in yellow sugar strands the children loved,
before threading through the covered alleyway from the
square, with its red-and-black checked tiled floor, on to
cobblestones past the Bear, past the Swan, apparently so
small on the corner by the church but heaving like a
Holbein painting come Thursday night.

'Black Wantage,' I said to myself, stopping at the big
charity shop behind the square, where buggies, books,
plastic chairs, cooking pots, toasters and table lamps
divorced from their shades were piled up, three washing
machines deep, against the walls of a huge Dutch barn.
I would have liked to have bought a dark-brown chest
of drawers for eighteen pounds, to replace one propped
up by a pile of books in the children's room, and was
almost persuaded when the man at the till told me he
could deliver for an extra five pounds, as long I lived
within a seven-mile radius. I resisted, remembering the
house in Washington with its careful pieces of brown
furniture already tucked into bedrooms, although this
was a shame, the man said. I could have got myself a
bargain there, adding that the barn had been bought by
a developer and would close soon enough. And Black
Wantage was still echoing in my ears when I drove
home, remembering the figures falling out of the pub,

scrambling up the statue, laughing in the lamplight when I'd picked Jimmy up, and the fact it was always Wantage, not Faringdon, where Jimmy returned for a proper night out. When he was expelled from school, he'd said that smoking weed on the playing field wasn't exceptional. 'Everyone was doing it,' he explained after he moved to another big state school, in Faringdon. 'It's quieter there. People are more likely to be in the school choir.'

'Black Wantage,' a local historian repeated, sometime later, as I squeezed into the back of a room in a community centre, gently shaking rain from my coat. I took a seat behind rows of people, some carefully taking notes with neat handwriting, others simply listening, arms crossed. The lack of lamplights meant the town was lit instead largely by a smutty swirl of bonfires. This darkness was exploited by vagabonds, the man explained, who knew they could quickly vanish in the poorly lit streets, where itinerant canal workers relished fighting with the hungry and increasingly desperate townsfolk as the local industry of the tanneries started crumbling. Children in the workhouse were starving, and gambling, drinking, cockfighting and badger-baiting were rife. The absence of a town police force meant that the Bow Street Runners, London's earliest law enforcement, headed first for Wantage when they were looking for criminal runaways from the capital. It was, the historian suggested, a name which Wantage earned at the start of the nineteenth century.

Wantage wasn't black before this. In fact, for at least two hundred years before then, the historian told us, readjusting his papers behind a lectern, pulling up a slide on an illuminated screen in front of the hall of

people, Wantage was golden. By 1500, it was thriving as
part of the fast-growing leather industry, and for the
next three centuries the town was industrious. Skin and
blood brought wealth to Wantage, where more cows,
pigs and sheep were slaughtered than anywhere in the
south of England. The biggest tannery, Sylvester and
Ansell, employed more than a third of the town's working men. Shoemakers, glove-makers and a thriving
rope-making industry brought prosperity and put meat
and beer in bellies and clothes on backs, for not just
keeping warm, but for looking elegant, fashionable
even. Shoppers jostled through the market square,
heading for watchmakers, cobblers, weavers, tobacco-
nists and apothecaries, which all sprung up as the town
flourished. When Wantage was golden there were banks
and butchers, and better transport links than there are
now, with daily coaches to London, for which passen-
gers waited outside the wine merchant's, where the bell
over the door jangled all day. Wantage was glistening
and glimmering, and everyone knew it because of the
arrival of two separate firms of solicitors, a sure sign
there was gold in the town.

The town was thriving, but boisterous too, thanks to
the cheese and cattle fair in the spring, the cherry fair in
July and the quarterly fairs too. At the hiring fairs in the
autumn, wagoners with whipcord twisted into their
hats, thatchers wearing a wisp of straw woven into their
shirts, shepherds carrying crooks, and maids carrying
mops, all jostled through the square, signalling their
skills. By the end of the eighteenth century, more itinerant workers arrived with the canal, men with a past,
tough enough for work that kept them on the move,

now striding into town, notes in their pockets, looking to feel alive, to drink and gamble and fight and fuck. The fairs brought horse traders too, strong young men leading strings of ponies, who vanished, soon after, taking more than their gold coins with them. Word was you could get away with things in Wantage, since there were no policemen, no local corporation, no squire, no charter, in short none of the local infrastructure found in other towns near by to quieten things down, to keep the peace, to confiscate the cockerel or badger, the booze and the gambling cards, to break up the brawl.

The forty-four pubs across the town heaved with men flinging coins on to the bar, incited by the yeasty smell of beer which mixed with the smoke from bonfires out on the street. There, men with shining red faces, bundled out of the bar for drunkenness, gathered on the unpaved, rutted street, excited by the clatter of coins falling in the marketplace, where money changed hands around wooden cages, and black-and-white-striped badgers with long snouts were goaded into a snarling, furious ball, sharp white teeth snapping until crimson became the colour of the night. Gambling was a way to feel alive, and the Lion or the Brandy Butt were the establishments to visit to really drink, where drunkenness wasn't just abided but encouraged. The Camel and the Jolly Waterman were known to be good for gambling, with dogs, badgers and cockerels fighting to the death for coins and blood running down the pavements. Even by day there was blood in Wantage, since the butcher in the square was paid more for the meat of a bull whose blood was up when it was slaughtered. There was little peaceful death.

The texture of life on the land, that slid seamlessly
from the downs into the town, and in rooms in the cottages dotted across that land, and in the barns and stables
in each of the farmyards which met the alleyways running from the market square, was changing rapidly by
the end of the eighteenth century. Cottage industries
quietened against the rumbling cogs of the approaching
Industrial Revolution. Grain dealers arrived, wearing
conker-coloured shoes, examining their golden pocket
watches, piling plump sacks of yellow corn on to painted
barges, to exploit the rising prices. They discussed news
from France, where word was that neater, faster tanning
methods meant leather from across the Channel was getting much, much cheaper.

The certainty of bustling, confident, golden Wantage faded. Human and animal shit ran through open
culverts in the market square, the air thick with the
malty stew of the breweries mixing with the hot stink
of dog and pigeon excrement used in the tanneries.
Bonfires swirled in the streets, sparks destroying thatch,
and the stocks in the town square were rarely empty,
with crowds congregating near the pond and the pump
there, for it was good sport, to see a neighbour pillo-
ried. The tanneries lumbered on, struggling to compete
with the new steam-driven industry in the north of
England and crumbling altogether by the time new leather traders arrived, not a rumour from the grain
dealers' chat but now actual people walking through
the marketplace selling cheap European leather. In 1811,
the largest tannery in the town – the largest tannery in
the country, in fact – went bust, and more than a third
of families in Wantage were bankrupted overnight. A

year later, when the last shoemaker went out of business, he had six hundred pairs of beautiful, handmade leather shoes, all unsold, sitting in stock.

This, then, was why there were children in the workhouse starving. The lack of law enforcement made them brazen, their fast, grubby little fists snatching watches and penknives from pockets. Those same daring little hands followed women through the marketplace, women too distracted by the open drains and lack of pavements, the cart sploshing through a culvert, to feel those small hands reaching into baskets to swipe bacon, cheese, a loaf of bread. The pubs grew louder, brawling breaking out so that sometimes it seemed the beams were straining, and the walls themselves were being pushed outwards. Wantage got wilder and blacker every day, so much so that the town was forced to impose a curfew from eight p.m. to five a.m. It was isolated, too, when the road to Oxford flooded. No other town had such lax rules; badger-baiting, dogfighting and cockfighting remained legal in Wantage long after they'd been banned from every other town in the county, and across the country too. How quickly a place can change, I thought, listening to the historian who told the hall how the golden time of Wantage, with its apothecaries and watchmakers and tanneries making gloves, had slid into Black Wantage, somewhere a local judge noted there was more crime, drinking at all hours and gambling than any other town in Berkshire.

'No one would call it Black Wantage today,' Tina had said, and I thought of this, a few days later, with time to kill before Dolly's bus from Oxford arrived, as I slipped into the long corridor of the second-hand

bookshop, its floor-to-ceiling shelves stuffed with thousands of books. There are almost no second-hand
bookshops left in Oxford, and when I remarked on this
to the owner, he said the success of the shop had been
down to buying the lease several years ago. 'No way
we'd be able to survive if we were paying rent,' he said,
popping a stack of Russian novels back on to a high
shelf. He'd started looking out for local history books
for me, after I'd spent an afternoon kneeling in front of
a section of faded hardbacks on old Berkshire and
Oxfordshire.

After I'd paid for the books, I watched Wantage from
my car, sitting in the marketplace, waiting for Dolly's
bus. I could hear the voices of the market traders trying
to sell their last punnets of mushrooms and boxes of
bananas for just a pound. A woman was queuing for a
cappuccino at a little horsebox selling organic coffee,
and the man who sold high-vis jackets and fleece blankets decorated with a horse's head or a roaring lion was
packing up. The lady who sold trays of plants and boxes
of eggs had already left.

Opening one of the books, I pored over line drawings
and a few photographs illustrating the development of a
small, thriving market town. I read descriptions of the
hard-working grocers, butchers and teachers who made
their lives in Wantage, weathering the closure of the tanneries. I thumbed through the index, looking for a
reference to Black Wantage, and found nothing. And I
remembered how the historian, at the end of the talk,
had suggested that 'Black' Wantage may well have been
an approximation, rather than fact. It was true that the
town had had a reputation for debauchery, horse dealing,

gambling and drunkenness, but there were also plenty of
local people who sold vegetables or wine or watches;
there was a local solicitor, and the town had its own bank
up until 1817. But between the lines I read of a sense that,
in the nineteenth century, the town needed a hand to
hoist itself upwards. In 1828, Parliament passed the Wantage Improvement Act 'for the better Lighting, Watching,
Cleansing, Paving and otherwise improving the town of
Wantage', led by William Ormond, a solicitor who nailed
his proposals to the church door, removing the fire
engines that were being stored there, and extending and
rededicating the church while he was about it too.

With the help of just a handful of others, Ormond
changed the town: the bonfires were put out, and
lamplights, upright and respectable, erected, although
sometimes they were smashed. The new local constabu-
lary were also sometimes found drunk – remnants of
the old Wantage, Black Wantage, snarling and uselessly
lashing out as the whole town was pulled and pushed
and buckled into obedience. The new vicar, William
John Butler, founded a convent, whipping idlers into
shape and rallying a new congregation. Sharp grey slate
replaced the thatched roofs, and the cards and coins and
dice were banned. Landlords were fined for encourag-
ing excessive drinking, so the pubs calmed down and many
closed; the Camel had its licence revoked after bull-
baiting was recorded, again, there. There were no more
fireworks in the town square, even 'odd-shaped' buildings and jutting-out windows were abolished; anything
that encouraged the slightest sense of civic disrespect
was closed, squashed, quietened. The children running
hoops down the alleyways were told to stop and walk

quietly. When the church was rededicated in 1857, over a thousand people turned out for it. Hairdressers and milliners, lawyers and engineers opened shop in the town, and in 1877 the Prince and Princess of Wales unveiled a new statue of King Alfred, standing fine and proud and a touch defiant, above the town square, something that would have been unthinkable a few decades before.

I closed the book. Dolly's bus was late. On the street a mother hurried past, motioning to the teenage girl behind her to hurry up, both turning suddenly at the metallic crash of a shop front being lowered. Headlights illuminated the square as rain spattered the windscreen. While I knew that teetering on the brink of complete civil disorder and moral debauchery was no way for a small town to exist, I'd always liked imagining Black Wantage, and constantly found myself looking for imprints of the wild place the town had once been. Often, at half term, I took the children to the Vale & Downland Museum near the church, where a display about the town brought it alive, with small wooden boxes attached to the wall with flip-top lids containing little squares of hessian sack you could take out to sniff the past. Lifting the lid, and touching the hessian, the children would gasp at the sudden stench of the tanneries, or urine, and the sweeter, more familiar smell of woodsmoke. And Danny had told me plenty of stories about the wild Wantage of his twenties, a decade before, claiming it was quieter now. 'All the new houses, isn't it? Some of the old local life got lost when all the new houses were built. New people coming in don't like wild old Wantage, I think,' he'd said.

As Dolly's bus shuddered into the town square, and I turned on the car engine as my daughter, bag slung over her shoulder, hands stuffed into her puffer coat, picked her way through the rain towards me, I realized that I saw in Wantage what I wanted to find. In the same way Danny saw a dragon on White Horse Hill, while I saw a horse, I have made Wantage the place I want it to be. In its past I find the colour and energy which bring it alive, transforming it in my imagination from a conventional little market town two hours from London into an alluringly exciting place of bonfires and horses, vagabonds, rebels and wildness. Wantage wasn't my hometown as a child, but I'd made it into a place in my imagination, a place I deeply cared about and felt connected to – and that I loved. If I could do that here, perhaps I could do that in Washington.

I was back, a week later, for a funeral. It was market day, and the town square was criss-crossed with people making their way among metal stalls whose grubby canvas coverings shielded fold-up tables laden with boxes of purple aubergines, shiny green apples, outsized bunches of celery and the ghostly white faces of cauliflower. I picked my way through the stalls, remembering how I'd first met my friend Liz, on another market day, in a queue in the bank on the far side of the square, before it was shut down. Evangeline and Dash were with me, pulling handfuls of leaflets instructing them how to apply for a mortgage from the racks near the cashiers while I jogged Lester on the spot, his arms and legs clawing the air with a pain in his tiny baby belly. Liz had crouched down, distracting Dash and Evangeline by pulling one of the small gold rings from her fingers to let them try on while I comforted Lester. Her dyed red hair was cropped short to her head, her large eyes accentuated by the thick black eyeliner she'd drawn in flicks around the delicate folds of her lids. I was so grateful, and afterwards we walked through the market together, where one of the boys on a stall stopped to chat with her, slipping her a box of strawberries she immediately gave to the children.

I'd bumped into her again and again after that, and we'd always stop to talk; she'd want to hear how the children were getting on, bless them, and tell me about her grandchildren, who were visiting from Australia, where their parents had moved three years earlier. She'd moved to Wantage from Pinner as a much younger woman, in the sixties, she told me, after her father had got work as a train driver in Swindon. Liz never left after that, travelling into Oxford every day to work, first as a cleaner in one of the colleges, and then later helping to run a kitchen for a homelessness charity. She'd brought up her two daughters in a village outside the town, until her husband left her for a woman who worked in Budgens in Faringdon, and she'd returned to Wantage. 'There was everything I needed here when the girls were at home, more or less,' she'd explained. 'And once I'd made my home here, it seemed a shame to start again anywhere else.'

I last saw her in the bargain superstore, buying multi-packs of mini Mars bars and colouring books for her grandchildren, who she was going to visit in Melbourne. She'd been planning the trip for almost a year. 'You never know, I might not come back,' she'd said with a wink, as the last of her items were swiped through the till. She'd just come from the hairdresser, and she made a little gesture, like a film star or fifties glamour model, pushing her hand behind her head, cocking her shoulder, smiling extravagantly.

After the service the upstairs community room, just off the town square, was packed. It was difficult to squeeze across the room to the trestle tables on the far side, covered in white tablecloths, where platters of sausage rolls, egg sandwiches and slices of fruit cake were laid out beside a hissing tea urn and lines of delicate white cups and saucers. Rain had pattered on the church windows during the service, but suddenly the sunlight outside was so bright, making colour pour through. I'd been listening to a man in a faded black canvas jacket and a trilby, with a feather tucked into the band, telling me about how especially good Liz had been to him after they met at the shelter. As the light glistened through the tall windows, he lifted the little glass of red wine he was holding and raised it, smiling, the burgundy liquid suddenly as bright as a ruby. 'To Liz,' he said, as I bit into the sweetness of a glacé cherry in a slice of crumbling fruit cake, trying to distract myself from the prickling sensation around my eyes, brought on by the thought that I'd never bump into Liz or walk through the market with her ever again. Instead, I focused on a woman beside me who was talking about how she'd first met Liz at a disco in the early seventies in Letcombe Regis village hall. 'A beautiful woman, so full of heart. Difficult to believe it, just gone like that, in a flash,' she said, brushing flakes of sausage roll from the sleeve of her jacket.

As I was leaving, pulling my jersey closer around me because, despite the rain-freshened blue sky, it was suddenly cold, I knocked the arm of a woman who was standing smoking on the pavement outside. She looked around quickly, pushing her curly dark hair back from her face, saying, 'No bother, no bother' as I apologized. She had a small, neat face, black eyeliner drawn carefully beneath her eyes then finished with an exclamatory flick. She was wearing high heels and a nipped-in black suit, a smudge of red lipstick resting around the end of her cigarette.

'Someone's in a hurry,' she added, smiling and looking at me more closely as she ground the end of her cigarette under the ball of her black patent-leather shoe, nudging the butt into the gutter. 'Not really supposed to do that any more, am I? I'll have to assume you're not going to tell on me. Want one?' She held a packet of cigarettes towards me, and I did want one, very much. I wanted to pluck one from her packet, snap open a lighter and inhale so that all that smoke filled my lungs and nicotine hit my bloodstream. No one offered me cigarettes now.

I shook my head but lingered for a moment anyway. There was a little time to waste. The children were at an after-school club. I motioned my head, to the upstairs room, and we talked about Liz, and how much duller life would be without her in it.

'Just the way it goes, though, isn't it? We're all heading that way, got to make the most of the days we have, I suppose, although God knows it's not always easy. Go on, have a cigarette,' she said, motioning the packet towards me again with more intent, but I put my hand up.

'Honestly I'd love to, but if I did, I'd be back on twenty a day by the weekend,' I replied, and instead we carried on talking about Liz, about her peculiar ability to recognize everything that was even slightly golden in life. It was a tragedy that she never got to experience Australia.

'Or that Australia never got to experience her,' said the woman, with a shallow laugh. 'She was desperate to see those grandchildren. I'm not sure she'd ever quite made peace with her daughter moving away, but each to their own. Anyway, life is for the living, that's something Liz always said to me, although I think it broke her heart to think of those grandchildren leaving Wantage.' Her words reminded me of what Danny had said, and I looked at her quickly as she tilted her sharp, enquiring face at me, small black studs like onyx in her ears, glinting, as she folded her arms in front of her, shrugging her shoulders up a bit and stamping. 'Touched a nerve, have I?' she added, and so I told her about how much I, too, didn't want to leave, to move to a city where I knew no one like Liz, had no connections, no roots, no wider family or friends. The woman watched me as I spoke, pulling another cigarette out, tapping it on the box before lighting it. When I stopped, she exhaled, blowing smoke between us.

'It's a difficult decision. A very difficult idea. And believe me, I know where your head's at right now. I know what it's like. I was in your position. I didn't have kids, like you — still don't — but I had a fellar, a man I thought I was crazy about. A bit wild. And funny, really funny. Worked in construction, building and that. A tradie, I'm sure you know the type. Sexy, you know? And believe me, I loved that man.' She tipped her head back, swallowing a laugh. 'Mad about him, I was. Then one day he upped and left for the Middle East. Dubai at first, then Saudi Arabia. Because there was work there, a great living, he said. And he promised me a life with him. Made it all sound super-duper; swimming pools, two cars, sunshine. Never-ending sunshine. Not like here.' She snorted, glancing above her as if it might rain again at any moment. 'I wanted to go. I broke my heart over wanting to go, but something stopped me.'

She looked away, staring across the marketplace where the metal stalls were being packed into the back of a lorry, and three teenagers were sitting below King Alfred's statue, all poring over a single screen, laughing.

'This place, Wantage, the downs, the town and the people who belong here, they're my home. This is my home. I loved that man, and I meant to go with him, but I couldn't. I could not make myself leave. I talked about it for months. Bored all my friends to death, I should think. Well over a year I was talking about it. But when it came to it, I couldn't do it. I knew I'd lose part of myself if I did. I'd lose everything, in fact, that really means something to me.' She pulled her jacket close. 'He went on that he was moving for a better life. Quality of living, he always said. Sun, sea and sex, he said. That sounded all right. Mind you, he was working on building sites here at the time, and mid-February, that's hard work. Really hard work, in the cold. But it was weird. The more he talked about swimming pools and shopping or beaches and quality of living, the less sense it made to me. An easy life. That's what he said he wanted, and he was convinced he was going to find it over there, in the sun. That would be enough. I just didn't think it would be enough for me. When you feel part of a place, it's in your soul. It's part of your bones. That's what Wantage makes me feel anyway. Strange old place. You can't really put a price on that, can you? That's a quality of living you can't buy.' She paused, then leaned forward, closer to me, and laughed very quickly. 'But, hey, don't look so glum. I'm not you. And I didn't have kids, we weren't married, and I don't always know I made the right decision. Sometimes I think of the path I could have taken, out there in Dubai or where have you, somewhere hot, and I wonder, honestly, if I did make the right choice . . .'

She brushed her curly hair away from her face, where it had fallen across one eye. 'Here, let me help you. Take this,' she said, fishing in the black leather bag slung over one shoulder, peering deeper then pulling out a small, brown bottle the size of an egg cup. She unscrewed the top and squeezed the dropper cap, nodding at me. 'Go on. Trust me. I promise. I wouldn't do you wrong. Put your hand out.' She put a drop on my palm, watching it intently, as though it was a ladybird crossing a leaf, not making eye contact with me until every bit of the oil, which sat on my palm in a fat, thick bubble, had been squeezed from the dropper. 'Go on. Try it.' I raised the oil to my face, sniffed it, then licked it, flat across the palm and on to the fingertips. It tasted bright green. It tasted the way my breath felt once when I buried my face in the newest bank of grass in the field in early spring and filled my throat with something of the earth. It made me feel pure herbivore, and, despite the taxi rank near by, where drivers in dark glasses passed the time between fares, leaning into one another's cars to chat, I felt suddenly connected to something of a world that was entirely separate from the hard and jagged slabs of concrete we stood on.

'What's in it?' I asked the woman, who had slipped the oil back into her handbag. She laughed.

'Don't worry. I know what I'm doing. Trained as a herbalist. Of sorts. I'm Cathy, by the way. And this oil, it won't hurt you, not at all. It might even help you. Having said that, it could do nothing. Or it might just be like a cigarette. Not addictive, though.' She laughed again, with her mouth open.

'Why does it taste so grassy?' I asked, because the oil was so sharp and leafy it felt like the hillsides around the town had slid right down into the marketplace and then on, down my throat, right into me.

'Because it's made of the deep earth. Go on. Take it,' she said, gesturing to me to take the bottle. 'Think of it as a bit of the land, in a bottle you can carry with you wherever you go.'

A week or so later, on my way back from the dentist in Swindon, I went to see Cathy at home in her ex-council house, 'the one I wouldn't give up for a penthouse in Dubai', she said, her shoulders shaking as she laughed. I wanted to buy another bottle of oil but as much just to be in her presence. We sat outside, behind her house, partly because she liked to smoke, but also because her house sat just below the Ridgeway, almost close enough to touch. The first oil she'd given me was mugwort, connected to the element of water and the moon. 'It's relaxing, rooting, you know? Good for the nervous system. I like it because it grows in abundance here. It's very English.' A child kicked a ball against the back of the house next door, but it was still quiet enough to hear the chattering of sparrows in the hedge at the end of the garden and feel a coolness from the ripples of the Ridgeway. 'I've got a new oil you might like. Nettle. It just popped up to say hello one day, last week after I got your text. A bit of fire and sun in there for you. You can mix them if you like. They're opposites, but both as green as grass.'

My conversations with Cathy made me think more closely about how powerful the connection to place is, and the kind of things we'd give up to keep hold of it. Sometimes, after I'd left her house, if Iona was around to pick up the children, I'd postpone returning indoors and go to the field. The oil Cathy gave me made me want to lie down, so that I could enjoy the squelchy wetness of the landscape as it seeped through my jeans, pressing my cheeks into the grass to inhale its green flavours. At those times, if I could have buried myself in clods of earth, I would have done, because lying there made me feel part of Nell. My sister's body was of the earth now. Not near by – she was buried in a churchyard on a hill near her home in Stroud – but the exact geography mattered less than the fact she was still inside the earth. When I lay face down in the grass, I imagined she might feel my heart beating. I thought my heartbeat might join with hers, which was part of the earth. Sometimes I'd lie on my back, on the far side of the field where oak trees grew in the hedge line, their mottled leaves creating a canopy above me, enjoying the feeling of giddiness as their branches moved above me, my arms and legs outstretched below them so that every limb of mine was connected to the ground, but my face was turned to the light. I liked the feeling of grass growing around me, rising green right above my eyeballs, like

little giants everywhere. And often, in the early evenings, I'd walk out there when I should have been
inside, reading to a child, running a bath, but instead
leaving Dolly or Iona in charge so I could unpack my
brain from where it felt screwed into a corner of my
head. When I lay pressed into the earth, listening for
my sister inside the ground, I was sure I could feel Nell's
heart beating too, and from there, if I looked up to the
patchwork of various greens on the hill, I'd see the pale
scrape of the White Horse. Perhaps it was the oil, or
perhaps it was just Cathy, and the reassurance I'd found
in her words – that it was made of the deep earth and
that I could carry that sense of the earth with me, wherever I was – but I started to feel a more certain and solid
sense that I was connected to the earth and to my sister
wherever I was, not just there in the field but everywhere I walked.

Two days before he left for Manchester, Jimmy had a
party in the field. On the far side, where the land drops
down towards the small woodland close to the road, he
dug a fire pit and stacked old sleepers he and Jake had
pulled from the hedge to create a grid to lift their speakers off the ground.

'Best use I've ever seen for a pile of fucked old gateposts,' Jake said cheerfully as they stood back to admire
their work. The speakers had been left in the field during
the summer. Moving across the field, tracing narrow old
tracks made by muntjac deer which ran parallel to the
hedge line, or walking into the middle of the field, over
the gentle roll of ridge and furrow as my trainers damp-
ened slightly in the longer grass, following new tracks

the dogs made before me, I'd see the speakers as black blocks, alien against the softer green landscape. When it occasionally rained, Jimmy covered them with a big square of shiny blue plastic, which would flap hopelessly like the loose fabric on a sail when the wind gets up. Sometimes, if I found the horses rubbing against one, or threatening to put its hoof into the box, I'd suddenly feel intensely annoyed by the blue flapping plastic and send Jimmy shrill little WhatsApp messages asking him to remove them from the field immediately. He'd agree to do it that night, and they'd still be there weeks later. Mostly, though, I liked seeing them, as they made me think of Jimmy, and I didn't mind at all, either, when he filled the night sky with sound so loud the noise seemed to stand up alone in the dark sky, as if Orion and his belt were suddenly lit up, and he had started moving.

I went out to the party with the younger children, who were excited by the ravers, Dash jumping up and down on the spot for a while, until the music got louder and Dolly took them back to the house, promising popcorn, although Dash screamed. I stayed a bit longer, joking around with Jake and Kyle and Iona as more friends from Uffington arrived. Luke and Kat had driven down with their three young sons, friends of Dash and Lester, in the back. I'd spent a lot of time with them the previous summer, when Luke had helped me bang posts into the ground to strengthen the electric-fenced paddock I'd created. We stood in the darkness, Luke clutching a can of lager, Kat's blonde hair pulled back from her face, as we chatted for half an hour about a pony they'd seen for sale in Cricklade. They'd wanted to buy it for their boys, but they weren't sure,

since it could be so hard to find grazing locally. I talked
for a bit to the son of my good friend Louise, who
worked in the village shop and had helped me out with
babysitting the children when they were younger. Her
son was fourteen, and when I'd been in the shop buying
pasta and stamps earlier that afternoon she'd asked me
to look out for him at the party if I saw him. Jimmy
sometimes skated with him at the park in Uffington. He
was just staying for a couple of drinks, he said, and in
the light Jimmy had rigged up by the speakers I could
see his sandy-coloured hair falling across one eye, a lad
emerging from the little boy he had been. He was still
there when I left, but Jimmy said he'd keep an eye on
him, and having watched that group of boys grow up, I
knew that looking out for one another at parties was
something they were good at. It's their time, I thought,
as I walked through the night, back towards the house,
the moon a distant silver disc of mottled light high in
the sky.

When I got to the bridge, he was there again. The tall
man, standing with the moon's light bathing his clothes,
so that now he was the colour of midnight on a full
moon.

'You know that shape the light makes when it's cast
by moonlight?' he said, without turning to me. 'I've
always felt it was more like the memory of shadow,
rather than the way daytime shadow looks. Shadows
have much sharper outlines that follow you when the
sun's shining. Moonlight shadow is just there, like it's
part of you.' He turned his head towards me, smiling a
little, but I paused, silenced by the much more direct
way he was addressing me than he last had. He swept

one palm, then the next, down his long arms, the gesture someone might make admiring a fine new silk shirt.
'And maybe much more of the true memory of a place
is held in the landscape than we realize. Maybe a landscape holds the shadows of the people who've lived on
it for ever,' he added, as if he was sitting inside my mind
and observing the work going on there. Then he
glanced down, looking around, dismissing what he'd
just said. 'No dog with you this time?' he asked, flicking
his head sideways to smooth his hair from his eyes. 'No,
not this time,' I replied, then laughed, nodding over my
shoulder towards the field, adding, 'Just my son, out
there in the night.' I turned back to where the sound of
a quickening beat was mixed with the spikes of laughing and shouting, good-natured noises of people
celebrating together. 'He likes to play loud music in
the night in the field, just over the hedge. Sometimes
the neighbours complain but people are generous here,
generally. As long as it's not every weekend,' I said. The
man smiled a little, nodding a bit, then turning to look
back over the edge of the railway bridge, as he had when
I'd seen him that morning a few weeks before.

'What are you looking for?' I asked, leaning on the
bridge wall beside him. 'Last time I saw you, you were
looking down there, on the tracks, just as you are now.
What are you searching for?'

Tipping my head right back to see his eyes, my neck
cricked, because he was so tall, but just as before I didn't
feel afraid to be alone in his presence. After I spoke he
looked down at me sharply, as if surprised I'd noticed
his search.

'I lost a few things, down there, over time, so I come

back here as often as I can to look for them. I've lost
stuff. Things that matter. I might find them, maybe not.
Perhaps it doesn't actually matter, since all that we have
is now. Still, better found than lost for eternity, isn't it?'
he replied.

'And what is it that you've lost, down there on the
tracks?'

'Well, it's difficult to say. But time, you might call it.
I have lost a lot of time. Thinking I could change things
beyond my control or exert my will to make matters
different. That's a quick way to lose time. I won't get
that time back. I know that now. Still, I come here to
look because I'm hopeful I can bring a resolution to the
loss.' He raised his eyebrows quickly, smiling down at
me and moving his head again, to flick his hair from his
eyes in that small, swift movement. 'You could lose a lot
of life, worrying about time. You could lose a life itself.
Now, I have lost those too – lives, I mean. And that's
why I come back here, to look for those lives, to carry
on with me, so that I can't lose them again.'

He paused, and sighed, long and low from a place
deep within him, far away from me. There was so much
more I wanted to ask him, but the music was suddenly
rising in the field, reaching a deeper pitch, a louder
thud, too loud, beyond the volume Jimmy had said
they'd stick to so as not to keep the entire neighbourhood awake all night. I turned from the man, mumbling
apologies as I texted Jimmy, then called him, raising my
voice over the sound of music and laughter behind him.
The dirty yellow light of my phone was a hard glare
under the cooler white light of the night, and I regretted the sudden intrusion of technology into the

moment. It had created a distance I didn't want between me and the man. Maybe he minded as much as I did, because when I turned back to him he'd left me, and was walking further down the bridle track that ran parallel to the railway. He must have sensed my dismay, though, because for a moment he paused, turned his big, pale face and called back to me.

'Don't worry. I'll come back. Another time, I'll come back. I won't just vanish.' As he lumbered off, shoelaces undone, I was certain what he said was true.

# Chapter 6

On the last night Jimmy spent at home, I decorated the table with a bunch of sky-blue speedwell I'd found growing in the nettles outside the house and made roast chicken. Even more than cups of tea and digestive biscuits or spaghetti with a rapidly cooked tomato sauce, or faintly burned white toast with globs of melting yellow butter on it, or bacon and eggs, or a brown roll with a sausage sliced longways and ketchup inside it, or half a bar of fruit-and-nut chocolate, roast chicken was what home really tasted like. I'd wanted supper to be celebratory for Jimmy too, lingering longer than normal to tidy away piles of damp laundry sulking in the corner of the kitchen, to unhook the children's coats from the kitchen chairs and actually return them to the front door, to gather the odd assortment of shoes scattered across the floor, to lay the table neatly, with proper places rather than simply dumping a metallic crash of tangled knives and forks in a pile in the middle. I wanted Jimmy to feel how much he was loved before he left home, but creating an orderly space was difficult. A jug of water was spilled by someone reaching for the potatoes, and a chair knocked over with a terrible crash when the water was being mopped up. Lester cried inconsolably about his gravy touching his broccoli and everyone spoke at the same time, or in snatches of nonsense, conversation as broken as a Beckett play. When the children pushed their chairs from the table, I was more than happy to release them. And afterwards, when the younger children vanished, cradling bowls of pale-yellow ice cream, into other rooms, I didn't stop them but stayed for a bit in the kitchen with Jimmy, an easy space between us as we chatted, filling the dishwasher, straightening chairs.

'Tea?' I said optimistically, filling the kettle, and he shook his head, taking a cloth to wipe the table.

'No, you're all right, thanks,' he replied, then threw the cloth into the sink.

'Go on, Jimmy, don't worry about this. Go and see your friends,' I said after a while, because I knew that was where he wanted to be, to drive to the pub in the next village one last time, like he was, in fact, the one who was emigrating. He hugged me and vanished from the kitchen, which suddenly seemed too quiet. When I went upstairs to try to persuade the children to get into bed, his things were all there at the bottom of the stairs: two nylon duffel bags and a rucksack with his clothes, the cardboard boxes full of kitchen equipment, a duvet stuffed into a bin bag, the one saucepan which had a matching lid, his paintings, all sitting waiting beside his skateboard.

We drove, together, all through the next day, and when traffic slowed to an almost stationary crawl on the M6, I didn't mind. Not at all. So often, throughout his

childhood, I'd wanted to be able to get up and leave, as
Pete did all the time. Now, though, sitting in the car
together, doing exactly that – getting up and leaving,
although taking him with me – I was silently stunned
by the sense of all that time we'd had, spooling away
into the past. I wanted every moment of it back. I had
thought there would be more to it: I had thought there
would be more of those moments as his mother, when
I'd felt myself at the centre, in the middle of it all, with
Jimmy and Dolly and their siblings around me. Taking
Jimmy away to university, and braving myself for the
moment he walked away, I realized I was moving to the
outside. Jimmy was the first of them all to leave, and he
was showing me how complete that movement would
become, over time. Everything had suddenly gone so
fast, and watching Jimmy made me want to do the
impossible and make it all stop, to hold the children's
childhood still, before it was all over.

We left the motorway early, finding a route along
smaller roads crossing bright-green countryside, and
then stopped, close to Manchester, at a supermarket.
Glimpsing Jimmy from a distance down an aisle, as I
returned to the trolley carrying packets of dried noodles
and cans of tomatoes, I experienced that sense of the
wrenching of separation again. I observed him, lingering
in front of packets of coffee, choosing that packet of biscuits then swapping it for another, and felt the painful
tug of the increasing distance between us as something
like the loud tear of masking tape ripping off a roll:
necessary and practical, but also containing within that
sound the sense of something being mended after being
broken, a loss, but also, not a permanent loss.

We played Radiohead as the car edged towards the red-brick student accommodation, sitting bumper to bumper with estate cars stuffed with duvets and cardboard boxes, parents at the wheel but with young faces in the back, as their lives moved forwards. Queuing for the lift to Jimmy's room, smiles passing nervously between students and parents, that electric jolt of time happened again. Two decades containing all of Jimmy's childhood and adolescence were now held in the past; yet, two and a half decades ago, I was standing in another university room, with a tall man who looked somewhat like Jimmy, and would soon become Jimmy's father. As Jimmy found his new home, and I watched him reach across the small room as he unpacked his clothes and books, the time of his sweet childhood dissolved all around me like melting sugar, so that for a moment I struggled to focus on which year, which decade, which room, which dimension I was really inhabiting. The past and present were a Venn diagram, the adult Jimmy forming all the best bits in the intersection between his dad and me. As I turned around to reach for books to unpack or started flicking his pillowcases out to make up the small single bed, the outline of tall Jimmy and his tall father overlapped, and for a split second I feared I might reach out and inappropriately touch Jimmy's face, forgetting, in those dizzying seconds, who is who and when is then and what is now.

I turned to the window for air, trying to push it open, but it wouldn't move more than three inches. I wanted to lean down to the crack of open window and suck on the cold outside, in that way I lean down to suck from the tap when I wake in the middle of the

night and cold water is the only thing to orientate me
through the darkness. Instead, I looked right outwards,
across the city, so magnificently vast, a single sheet of
metal and glass and concrete stretching seamlessly for
miles into the distance. There was nothing green and no
curved edges in sight. It was all completely new for my
son, a new, deep breath, ready to be inhaled.

'Look at the city, Jimmy! Wow, just look at it!' I
gasped, suddenly aware of the high-rise view we had
from his room. 'Look at the cranes, the tower blocks.
Look at all the glass, the space, the new places to go to.
Look at the graffiti!' The possibility of what that city
represented excited me so much, I wished I could grow
wings on the spot and swoop over it. To fly like that
would show me so many more worlds and so many
more homes I knew nothing of. But then I stopped,
because I could hear in my head the same voice – 'Look
at the lorries! Look at the cranes, Jimmy!' – saying
something like this to him when he was two years old, a
baby, crying a bit, strapped into a buggy, trying to distract him from his tears by taking a long cut home past
a building site. Suddenly I was very quiet and went back
to unpacking books. *Understanding Mycelium, Islands of
Abandonment, Slaughterhouse-Five*, those missing teeth
from home taking their place in the jaw of a new bookshelf. Jimmy propped the little blue oil painting of the
American gas station on the shelf above his desk.

'We're not allowed to put nails in the walls, see?' he
explained. 'Pretty cool picture, Mum, just think of
being in there.' He widened his eyes as he nodded
towards the American landscape. Then he laughed,
because he knew what was in my head. 'Almost looks

like home. Might even be home, next time I come home. And that would be all right. Me and Dolly will be all right, wherever you are. We'll come and see you. We'll move in for the holidays! Then you'll be desperate for us to move back here and give you some peace.' He reached across and hugged me. 'Stop worrying, Mum. Nothing's gone wrong.' I hugged him a little tighter, then pushed him quickly away, trying to move around the small space to help. I wanted so much to do the right thing for him. Ask the right questions, but not too many questions; laugh, but not too loudly; stay, just long enough that he should know how much I love him, but not too long either. Do not hang around.

Along the corridor four other students were creating small homes in their rooms: a boy propping skateboard wheels up on his shelving, a girl talking loudly on a mobile phone, the adult sound of someone's mum asking about a duvet. I felt clumsy, unsure if I should just watch him, sitting on the radiator under the window, or crush the cardboard boxes piling up on his floor. I was just about to make myself useful, to take the bags of shopping we had bought in Tesco down to the shared kitchen three rooms along his corridor, when he said, 'I'll put this away later,' and in those words he meant, 'After you have left.'

My car was parked near by, and later I sat there for a bit, mascara running down my face, stunned by the ending I had facilitated. Twenty minutes, perhaps half an hour, passed. Another batch of estate cars slid away at the far end of the street, empty of duvets and boxes, all of them heading in the direction of the motorway, wipers moving slowly against the gentle rain which had started falling. And gradually, with parents gone, small groups of new students started appearing, moving together in the direction of the pub closest to the university accommodation. I sat deep down in my seat, watching from the distant bubble of my car as they trooped past at the end of the road, new friendships forming, some smoking, some with their hoodies pulled up, someone laughing a bit too loudly, excited. Then, unexpectedly, I saw Jimmy, a stranger now, totally separate from me, but his tall lope and curly blond ponytail hanging down his back so familiar, talking with a group of two or three other students. In that moment I was reminded of lingering just outside the door at playgroup, to watch him from a distance when he couldn't see me and thought I'd gone. The terrible and beautiful sense of the child moving beyond your arms, beyond touch, out of sight, creating a new friendship with another little boy in blue dungarees that you'll always be separate from. Now a new, greater distance was growing between us with each step he took down that street, as he moved away from the orbit of our family, of home. I watched him and felt my chest hurting, resisting the urge to jump out of the car so fast I'd leave the door open, to run to him, grasp him by his shoulder so that he'd spin around to face me. 'Come home! You can come home with me! It's all right, it's going to be all right for both of us, neither of us must do this, you can come back with me.'

I drove to a Chinese restaurant a friend I knew through Instagram had recommended. I sat alone at a large, round table, big enough for my whole family, and gulped down a Coke.

'This is very good,' the woman who handed me a menu said, pointing to a photograph of crispy pork with broccoli and garlic. I nodded quickly.

'Yes, please, I'd like that, please,' I replied, smiling at her but barely looking at the photograph or the menu. I would have eaten anything. Outside, tears of rain began to trace down the windows. I hated that the aloneness I'd craved, especially when my ears rang with tinnitus as the children shouted at me in the kitchen, was much less satisfying than I'd dreamed it would be; in reality, it wasn't nice at all. I'd like to have been in the kitchen at home, sitting on a painted wooden chair, with Lester crawling into my lap. Being a mother rarely makes me feel balanced – I crave solitude when the noise the children make is most intense – but the Chinese restaurant felt huge and empty now, embarrassingly silent.

I ate too quickly, dripping soy sauce on to the white paper tablecloth. I wanted to be like Jimmy: capable of leaving, walking away from the past, of simply stretching out to a new city to make a new home in an unknown place. There was a lightness to being so young which could never be replicated two and a half decades later. Jimmy was walking away, but perhaps we were both taking different paths. If Pete continued to press forward, if the visa application was successful, if Dolly got her place at university and stayed in England, and if I stopped resisting, then she and Jimmy would take their own paths, which would be very separate in every way from mine. I'd wanted my five children from two marriages to feel like one family; sharing the same childhood references had been part of that plan. Of course, they'd all eventually move away, scattering like pool balls in

their own special directions, but I'd wanted to create the
same place they could return to, a physical place as well
as a place in their imagination. If we didn't move, their
childhoods would all be framed by the same willow
outside the squat white house, the same village shop
where they'd all pestered me for Irn-Bru and sour Har-
ibos, and of course White Horse Hill, where they'd all
sat with me at many different moments throughout
their young lives, slightly resentfully eating Bourbon
biscuits and hoping it might be time to go home. In
Washington, the younger children's references would
be completely different, their lives stretched apart from
one another.

I shivered, pushing my plate away, wiping my mouth
on the back of my hand. I reached across to the chair
beside me, feeling the absence. Because suddenly it was
Pete that I wanted to be there, not Jimmy. I had become
so used to wearing the separation of lives on different
continents that sometimes I'd forget that we'd set out on
a path together at all. Jimmy had shown me how childhood ends, and that they would all, someday, follow him.
What would be left after that would be the shape of Pete
and me. Pete was my constant, the person I truly wanted
to be with most, the person who truly represented the
place I wanted to be. I felt a sudden overwhelming urge
to speak to him, so I picked my phone up. The connection rang and rang but he didn't answer.

Before I drove home, I found, in the glove compartment, where I searched for a phone charger, a tiny
penknife decorated with a camouflage pattern. Jimmy
had carried it sometimes since he was a very small

child. I turned it over in the palm of my hand. It was a part of Jimmy, and a part of our shared past, that existed whether he was in Manchester, or Oxford, or Washington. It was concrete, a real thing. Location did not change its make-up.

Holding it, clasping my fingers round the little handle, I thought of something I'd read, while trying to understand all those old, old dates, about the Blombos Cave in South Africa, a place considered the cradle of human culture for what it has taught us about cognition in early humans. There, amongst shells used as beads and beneath abstract rock drawings created 73,000 years ago using ochre crayons, archaeologists found more than 8,000 pieces of ochre marked with tiny, intentional, diagonal lines. These, I had read, were the first examples of what cognitive neuroscientist Merlin Donald called 'external symbolic storage'. This term describes the way earliest humans used physical objects such as jewellery, small sculptures and pottery, as well as drawings, to communicate ideas. These ideas symbolized information that had moved beyond the prefrontal cortex, the most evolved region of the human brain, to become part of a shared mythic consciousness. The tiny, marked pieces of clay pigment conveyed meaning, across time and from generation to generation, into the external world: the family, the community. Today the most extreme version of external symbolic storage could be the massive quantity and near-infinite permutations of information stored on a tiny hard drive, but 73,000 years ago people cut marks into pieces of ochre.

After I'd read about the archaeologists who'd discovered these, I liked thinking of them, their headtorches illuminating the dirt beneath their feet in the Blombos Cave, scratching, scratching, sieving, scratching, to discover fragments of the distant past. I'd worried about how easy it might have been for them to have missed these little bits of history! To brush them aside, ignore them, dismiss them as just bits of matter, of mess, on the cave floor. To lose sight or, worse, never to have glimpsed these special objects which marked a change in the way human culture organized itself.

I turned the penknife over, flicking the tiny blade open and shut, wishing Jimmy had it in his hand. But he was gone, so instead I would send it to him. I wanted him to keep it close as a source of memory, his own external symbolic storage reminding him of the things we had done together and the places we had been that had made up the days of his childhood. And I wanted him to have it to tether him to home, whilst he was also walking light and free through that magnificent concrete landscape.

I thought of this as I drove home, staring for hours into headlights, considering the kind of things I'd choose to carry with me as external symbolic storage should we move to America. I had a very heavy brass hare my mother had given to Nell and me, and a string of green and blue glass beads I'd carried with me since I was a teenager, holding them sometimes when I wanted to feel strong and brave, and a very small picture of the White Horse an artist called Ben Edge had done using actual chalk he'd taken from the hill, and a little metal cut-out of a head of Christ I'd bought with Nell in a junk market not long before she'd died. The beads and the head of Christ and the hare glinted in the colours of the speedometer, lit up before me in the dark. And as I got close to home, the headlights moving across the longer grass of the verges reflected in puddles as I turned past the sign for Uffington, I realized that Jimmy had, for several years, carried his own external symbolic storage tattooed on to his body: the wobbly outline of the White Horse, inked there a few years before by one of his friends in the next village. I remembered the evening I'd first caught sight of it, when he was cooking fried eggs on a very hot day in the kitchen, his t-shirt pulled up over his shoulders.

'I thought you'd mind. You don't mind?' Jimmy had said, looking guilty.

'Mind? Why would I *mind*, Jimmy?' I'd asked, reminding him of my own tattoo: the word *TEXAS* inked on to my left bicep, which I'd had done two years before Jimmy was born, on the way to a rodeo in Amarillo when I was twenty-two years old. I'd needed that word to exist on my body, even though Texas had been my home less than two years.

Pulling into our yard, I knew the outline of the horse would remain on his body for ever, even as it faded. I felt relieved. I'd wanted the green hills and the White Horse to be one of the most important compass points in his life, something he could always orientate himself towards. A symbol of something he thought of when he thought of home. Jimmy's tattoo horse reassured me that something of that plan had worked.

In the weeks after Jimmy left for Manchester, I felt air and space inside the house rearranging itself around his absence. The day after I returned, I faced his somewhat empty bedroom, standing in the window as dust settled everywhere in the morning light. I walked around feeling a kind of confusion which came from missing him, wondering where had all that time gone, while also feeling slightly embarrassed because I was acting in character, behaving like a woman in a television drama facing midlife. The departure of my first child to adulthood was both abrasive and quiet, making me certainly feel sad, but also strangely excited. Dolly and the younger children still filled the house, blurring the kitchen as they grabbed plates of pasta or creating havoc simply looking for the pencil sharpener one of them needed immediately, but there was also an absence. That absence was Jimmy, and beside him, fainter, the shape I'd assumed as his mother. I missed the outline he made, standing so tall by the cooker, making a fried breakfast at any time of the day. I missed the kind of music that only he listened to, and the clump of his big leather shoes on the stairs. I missed his energetic presence in the house, even when that presence had irritated me: the frying pan coated in grease left in the sink, the grubby fleece unzipped on the sitting-room floor. Things that were signs Jimmy was at home.

I missed the life and energy Jimmy carried with him: the line of small cars in the yard which meant his friends were over, that sound of them all laughing upstairs, even the smell of weed. The house didn't smell the same. An atmosphere of the illicit had left with Jimmy, and I missed it.

There were also small freedoms that came with this absence. With Jimmy gone, there was less work for me to do: less food to cook, fewer clothes to hang up; he didn't need pencil sharpeners any more. I could move through the room and the day with greater energy, a little less of the sense of burdensomeness motherhood carries with it. I must admit this was a relief. My arms had always been full of a huge load of clothes, cups, coats and odd shoes that I carried around the house, and now I could put some of that load down.

But in putting those things down, I could feel my balance changing. I was so adept at carrying all that stuff, I wasn't completely sure what shape I would take without it. I knew I should feel lighter, but I also missed being the one who knew how to carry everything for him. Most of all, I missed my daily interactions with Jimmy. The shape that had really changed in the house was our relationship as mother and son, the way we had moved around each other within that relationship for twenty-one years. For two decades I had carried with me at almost all times a heightened sense of awareness of where Jimmy was. Of course, when he was a baby and a very little boy, I had known exactly where he was at every moment, since he was almost always within eyeshot. His shape within the house was always there, first taking the perfect little chrysalis of space in a cot, then swelling a little bit as he sat in a highchair to gnaw a piece of toast or lay on the bed kicking his small legs, then crawling across a rug until he was toddling and walking and running, very fast, out of sight. Jimmy was like a little dart as a boy, and wherever we were I carried a feeling around me that was like a little alarm going off – 'Where's Jimmy? Where's Jimmy? Where's Jimmy?' When he was small, it was essential I always knew the answer to that question.

But life had carried him onwards and forwards. This stretching of the spaces between us had of course grown longer and longer throughout his adolescence, when he started spending days and days, and then nights, away from the house. But he always came back. He was always part of home.

Watching Jimmy moving away showed me how a family changes. Being Jimmy's mum now was showing me how it ends: motherhood covers absolutely every surface around the home for about two decades, and then suddenly it's just cleared away, the mess, the noise, the work, all gone, and we are left to squeeze and form our lives into very different new shapes.

Pete, too, was moving forward. He sent me more pictures of houses to look at, and optimistic updates on meetings he had had in preparation for the official interview about his visa. It would take place at the American Embassy in London, and at first the solicitor informed him all the children would have to be present. Pete was in London when he called to tell me this, and we had laughed together about the slightly ridiculous idea of Dash or Lester being interviewed by officials about their intentions to stay in the US. Later, she corrected this information: it was just Pete and me who would need to go to the interview. The questions would only be about his work and he'd receive a training session beforehand. When I tried to call him again, he was on another flight and I couldn't get through.

I hated trying to unpick our life from opposite sides of the world. I'd like to have conveyed to him something of the things I'd been trying to learn about home

THE GIANT ON THE SKYLINE

by looking up on the Ridgeway, as the giant man in black had told me to do, but the separation made it mostly impossible. Because of the time difference between us, and Pete's commitment to his work, finding a time to talk on the phone about home life was often really difficult. I had to work hard to get his attention. 'Listen, I will speak to you of a wonderful dream' are the opening words of an Old English poem called *The Dream of the Rood*, and this was the way I wanted to talk to Pete about our life. I wanted him to understand the urgency of the way I felt about our home and our family's relationship with the Ridgeway and the hill, and also to understand that I was more supple and malleable than I had thought. I wanted him to understand I wasn't straining against him without reason, but we were rarely able to finish a conversation before he was pulled into a meeting, or a child needed to be dried out of a bath or soothed after a fight.

'Listen to me right now,' the writer of that strange poem is saying, my wonderful dream demands your attention, and I am going to talk to you about it because this thing matters more than anything else I have to say. He is not saying, 'Would it be possible we could talk at nine p.m. my time, when the children are in bed and it's three p.m. your time, or possibly one p.m. your time, depending which coast you're on, but before I go to bed and while you are not in a meeting?' as I had to do, to try to get Pete's attention. I needed to address him with the same energy as the poet, although I wasn't sure how to broach things like Sylvia, or the red-brick house, or the school prospectus I'd opened in his absence, while still

maintaining that startling authority the poet had. I
needed to convey to him that something of me would
always remain close to the hill, even if I was forced to
live a very long way away from it. A part of me would
always be here, but I could take my external symbolic
storage with me wherever we went, so I was starting to
believe that the loss was not terminal.

I tried, one night, but Pete was in a car and the signal
kept cutting out as we were talking. He said he hoped
he might be home sooner than he'd thought, but that he
was driving into an underground car park. He cut out,
and when I called back I tried to tell him about the
things I thought we must take with us to America, but
the signal cut out again, and then it was impossible to
get through. After he was gone, I moved through the
house putting my hands on to some of the things I liked
best. The painted chairs in the kitchen that the children
and I had created with some cheap pine chairs from a
charity shop and several tubs of old paint; a purple-and-
black geometric blanket knitted for Evangeline by a
friend who was now dead; a painting I'd bought from
my cousin, of horses standing beside a flooded field;
shelves of poetry books I picked up and put back and
pulled out again almost every day; the brass hare from
Mum and Nell; a collection of little folding wooden
icons picked up in Ossetia when I was travelling regularly for work as a journalist in my early thirties, just
before I fell in love with Pete; a black mackintosh that
had belonged to Nell, its outline perceptibly still hers; a
white-and-pink teapot with a gold lid my dad and stepmother had given me for my last birthday. I couldn't
take the land, but I could I take my connection to the

stones or the White Horse, since that was something I carried inside me. I stayed up late, lying on my bed in the darkness, illuminated in the glow of my phone as I typed short lists of everything that mattered which could be part of home somewhere else: blankets, hares, icons, a mackintosh.

I only realized I had also taken the knife from the kitchen when I stood up very quickly, water rushing from my hands, and it fell from my pocket. I'd been leaning over the bucket, staring at the pewter-coloured, neatly curved shape the water made as it spewed from the thick blue piping in the middle of the field. The sharp silver blade of the knife, tucked into its stubby burgundy casing, had ridden up in my jeans, touching the whiteness of my skin and falling from my pocket. It shocked me, as a bee sting might, although the air was too cold for small insects like bees. I sat back on my heels, looking at the knife where it had fallen into the grass with a small, muffled thud, and I wondered what to do about it. It looked precious, glinting metallic beside the coarse plastic water pipe. Sparrows twittered out from the scrappy hedge beside me, leaving the inside of the black-thorn suddenly still and quietened by their absence. Several months ago, that hedge hadn't been scrappy or black, but was instead dense with the strong white shapes of may blossom which had appeared, so early, in March. The may had scared me, appearing before its rightful time. And it's always made me suspicious any-way, because of the luck it takes with it. A few weeks before her accident, Mum had shown me what the sharp daggers of may thorns could do, hidden within that seductive froth of white blossom. Putting her hand too deep inside a hedge when she'd been opening a gate, a may thorn had left its sharp, black tip in her skin.

'It seemed such a tiny thorn but look, look at all the poison,' she had said, running the tip of her finger around the black dot, making the skin strain red and angry. I remember the thorn tip coming out of her skin, a drop of yellow poison pooling on to her hand.

Mum told me that may was unlucky; that I should never take it into the house, and although she did not use these words, she gave me the sense it was a flower that carried dark secrets.

I was sixteen. Three weeks later she had her accident.

That was three decades ago. Now I stood in the field, transfixed by the pewter water, the sensation of the knife pressing against the whiteness of my skin at that place around my midriff where it is whitest and fattest, marbled with veins and the marks that motherhood has created. I picked it up, flicking the blade open, holding the smooth plastic handle in the palm of my hand. Its burgundy weight was familiar from further back in time. It was the kind of knife my dad always carried. He always wore a ballpoint pen clipped into the pocket of his shirt and he was never without a Swiss Army knife. Mum usually took us on summer holidays alone, driving to Scotland or Cornwall to stay with cousins, but when my father was there we'd always stop for a good picnic on a verge some way from the motorway. Once, he brought a gas stove and cooked fried eggs, but he also always seemed to have on him a pork pie and a small pot of bright-yellow English mustard. The penknife he carried was important, used to cut smooth slices through the fatty mottled pink of the inside of the pie, then dipped into the mustard. He'd given me the knife I'd just dropped, and as I held it, I realized that it could easily have fallen into the longer grass and been lost for a long time, certainly lost to me for ever. I might in fact have died and been lost to people who cared about me before the knife was found, much later, perhaps by a man with a metal detector for whom it would have gained the status of an artefact.

Turning the blade over and over in my hand, I wondered if a part of me wanted to drop it, to lose it in the field. If part of me wanted to stay in the field for ever. Perhaps that part could be the knife. I looked down at it, searching for a green place to leave it under the hedge. The knife lay in the wet grass, as bright and beautiful as a jewel. And I realized then that the artefact I would really like to take to America with me was the Alfred Jewel, the most beautiful work of art I have ever seen, a finely decorated little thing slightly longer than a small matchbox. It's unlike anything you might have seen before, created from gold, with a point on one end shaped like a rounded dragon. Above the point, a small figure, crafted in blue, white and green enamel, is held for ever beneath a slice of rock crystal shaped like a tear. The figure is immobile, eyes wide and hands open, yet the object is not passive. *AELFRED MEC HEHT GEWYRCAN* is spelt out around the edge of the crystal, the tear and the man. *Alfred ordered me to be made*, it reads, because Alfred was the first king who cared about literacy. That same Alfred who stands on a stone in the middle of the square in Black Wantage, where teenagers sit at his feet on their phones, really cared about whether people could read.

As I thought of the Alfred Jewel, it occurred to me
that that small gold thing was part of a long chain of
thoughts, actions and consequences that began with
Alfred, who ordered it to be made, which led to someone holding a book in their hands, which led, further
down the chain, to someone writing text, and later to
teenagers uploading TikTok videos, which are, after all,
a way for people to decipher themselves and find or
bring meaning to their existence.

When I was very small Mum took Nell and me to see
the Alfred Jewel in the museum in Oxford. I have been
to see it many, many times since then, often taking the
children. When I first saw it as a child, the most powerful thing I remember was being told by the museum
assistant that it was found, by accident, by a man working a plough in a field in Somerset in 1693. That fact
seemed to me then, and still seemed to me now, like a
magnificent thing. My adult self can still feel my child
self's wonder at the thought of being this ploughman,
walking slowly through a wet pasture, and it is 1693.
(My child self could only conceive of him as old, since
he existed in 1693, but now I feel bad for him, made old
in this way. Our mother used to tell my sister and me to
imagine our great-aunt and grandmother as young
women, not to see them as old just because that was the
only way we had ever known them. So now I try to
colour him in with a younger life, like the startling
effect when black-and-white photographs of a distant
past are given a colour wash.) My child self feels his
wonder when he looks down into the black earth and
sees this gold and blue and the glint of the jewel. He
reaches his hand down into the earth and picks it up.

And I remember the feeling of a very childish but also ancient delight I registered when the museum attendant told my mum and my sister and me that eight hundred years before the ploughman saw the jewel in the field in Somerset, Alfred had sent it to a bishop there. The jewel was accompanied by a book called *Pastoral Care* by Gregory the Great, which Alfred had translated from Latin into English. The jewel wasn't unique, although it is now, since all its fellows were lost; originally it was one of several sent out by Alfred across his kingdom, to encourage literacy. I experienced a strange kind of relief at the thought of the little jewel being held in so many different hands as it was passed from the craftsman to Alfred, to Somerset, to the ploughman who found it, and then finally into the hands of the museum curator in Oxford, who put it in a glass box in the Ashmolean Museum. The attendant also told us that, for a while, the jewel on view in the museum was a copy, made by a jeweller on the High Street in Oxford, since there had been many attempts to steal it, some of which had almost been successful. That was strange and exciting: the jewel had been held by a robber too. Now the real Alfred Jewel, the true one which Alfred and the ploughman held, sits in a bulletproof glass cabinet in the museum. You can go and look at it any time. I'd do almost anything to put my hands around it.

But 329 years after the ploughman left his plough, kneeling to pick the jewel up from the mud, I was standing in a field in Oxfordshire thinking about him, and the king, and the jewel, while I stared at my penknife, trying to work out if I intended to leave it there or put it back in my pocket. If I left it, someone might find it, maybe 329 years later, although by then the plastic would have disintegrated, because it wasn't as hard as rock crystal. I rubbed the plastic handle. Just a penknife. *VICTORINOX*, it spelled, just a brand. It was passive. Not like the jewel, which had an active life: *Alfred ordered me to be made.*

The jewel had had a place in the world, and it had belonged. The jewel had also moved, crossing counties, and crossing time, leaving something important of itself there. If I was going to be moved, I wanted to leave something of myself too. More than just a penknife, I wanted to feel myself rooted into the landscape I knew as home, even if my physical body was somewhere else. I would like to have left my bones there, if possible, but I wasn't dead yet. I opened the blade again, then loosened my hair from its rough ponytail, grasping it in two places and hacking at a clump to cut a lock a few inches long. I held the hair in my palm, beside the knife, and thought that this was a perfect way to leave some of my physical body there. If I went to Washington, but came back to England for a visit, I could creep into the field and feed it with a bit more of my hair, so that it was always nourished with something of me and in that way I'd never really leave it. I kneeled down, tucking my knife into the grass, leaving it comfortable there, close to the place I'd left my hair, then walked away, back towards the far side of the field, where the dogs were frantically digging for mice in the long, wet grass.

On the other side of the narrow road there was a small wood where people walked their dogs and the local

Brownie group went for excursions with torches and high-vis jackets. I walked on around the edge of the field, whistling to the dogs as Pablo darted into the road, and saw the figure of a man walking silently along the tarmac, his feet making almost no noise at all. In the verge beside him the spiky, oval-shaped heads of teasels pushed closer to the hedge, and a blackbird alighted in a sudden flurry before sensing the man's movement and vanishing. I had seen him there many times before, early in the morning when I took Dolly to Faringdon, to catch the bus to Oxford. I'd often raised my hand to him, a greeting of familiarity to someone I knew by sight but had never spoken to. He had a small, neatly defined face, flushed cheekbones with tiny marks on them as if the tiniest brambles had scratched him. His sandy hair fell to the side of his forehead in a parting, and he motioned his dog – a thin whippet as sandy and slight as he was – on to the verge, looking towards me with some sense of recognition. Pablo ran over the road to his dog and the man lifted his little hands as the two dogs greeted each other but were also gentle together.

'I expect you want rabbits,' he said, staring down at the two animals who sniffed the air around one another, almost courteously, as if with respect. Then, without raising his head, he lifted his eyes up to mine, so that it was as if he was keeping contact with the dogs while at the same time connecting with me. A blackbird chattered overhead, and in that moment, as he looked at me, his tawny hair and slightly ruddy, pointed face took on the look of a small fox. His eyes were bright and black, little clever slits. He had small black boots on and black gloves like skin, so that his hands and feet might have been mistaken for pads. He gestured, too, with the quick, small, clever movements a fox might make with its paws, standing on its back legs.

I swallowed, shifting from one foot to another, and in that moment the fox man looked up at me more directly and I saw he wasn't a fox at all; how ridiculous that idea had been, I thought, as he pulled one glove from his hand and reached down to pat his dog's head.

'A lot of rabbits in the copse there,' he said, motioning with a quick movement of his pointed chin to the thickets where the nettles grew amongst the trees on the far side of the road. 'You should take care of him,' he went on, this time tipping his chin at Pablo, who stood, four-square, looking up at him, his dog head on one side, unblinking. 'A nice dog, a good dog, a good dog, that one. You don't want to lose him.' He reached down to stroke Pablo, barely having to lean forward, since his hand fell to Pablo's height. I started telling him that Pablo was seven years old, and that although he used to run off, he'd stopped that now because he knew where home was. As I was speaking, the man cut in, not interrupting, but simply as if he hadn't heard me.

'Have you ever seen a dog caught in a wire fence after chasing a rabbit, the skin on its back legs skinned right off as if its small fur trousers had been undone, like pyjamas unstripped from small legs?'

His question didn't surprise me, for I had seen exactly that when I was about six years old. The man looked up at me intensely, his hands behind his back, while I told him about my aunt's sandy-brown collie cross, who ran into a wire fence chasing a rabbit. My aunt, who was my mum's sister, found the dog in a field above her house, making a screaming sound so bad she at first thought, as she sprinted up towards him, that her dog must be moments from dying. She carried the dog home wrapped in her coat, holding his skin on to him as he howled and twisted in her arms. I had been very afraid of the wild screaming noise the dog made, but I watched her, later, at the kitchen table where she had wrapped the dog tightly in a towel to stop him struggling and snapping at her, unaware she was working to save his life. The dog's skin under the fur, where it had been peeled back, was black, but she put it back on to his body like a jigsaw made of flesh, sewing the dog back together with a needle taken from a sewing box. The dog recovered completely, the only sign of his accident a scar that ran around his middle.

'And you were right, the way the skin had peeled off and was put back on again was exactly like pyjamas. That's exactly how my aunt described it,' I said.

For a moment I wondered if I had alarmed him, my head too full of Alfred Jewels and penknives, because, as I spoke, a skin knot had formed between his eyebrows. Perhaps there had been a lot of sorrow or tension in his life, which worked its way forward as we were speaking, or perhaps he was thinking of a dog he had lost. Watching his face while talking about my aunt's dog made me think of her so vividly, it was like she too was suddenly there, in the cold air around us. My mum had often liked to tell me about the time her sister had been riding her horse over a ford and saw a brown trout moving in the water below. My mum was so delighted that her sister – her very sister! – was a woman who would dismount from her horse, tickle the trout, then take it home to cook for supper.

Like my mother and my sister, my aunt is dead now. But the man cannot have known about all these other thoughts in my head as he continued to stare up at me with his sharp little features after I had finished talking. It was disconcerting, but his piercing presence made me feel I needed to reassure him in some way, so I said I would make sure I looked after Pablo and not let his skin get ripped off like fur pyjamas.

'I know you will. I have seen you caring for him, when you walk him out in the morning, getting those shoes all wet because you left the house in too much of a commotion to wear boots,' he said quickly, his words moving so fast I didn't have the chance to truly recognize them. 'That's an important thing to do. Creating a space for living things. Looking after the animals, caring for them like you belong to them as they do to you. Caring for the creatures that take up a place in your heart. Not as big as the part that's taken by the children but still, a big part. It's something that matters,' he said, looking out to the field, in the direction I had come from, where the horses sometimes turned around to watch us, then went back to their grass.

'I've seen you before on this road. I often pass you when I take my daughter to Faringdon. Do you live near here?' I asked.

'Oh, yes, I've lived here since I was a lad, my whole life. I live not far from here, up across the vale towards the hill,' he said, gesturing, vaguely, in the direction of the Ridgeway, and in a flash I saw that fox again. It was the slightly sly, knowing way he spoke to me, like he was concealing from me something that I didn't yet know but might soon find out, just as a fox looks when disturbed near a chicken coop, having not yet killed but with the intent to return to do just that. 'All my life I've lived here in the vale, long before you were born, I imagine.' His voice trailed off a bit, leaving a space for me to answer, so I told him that I was forty-seven and he chuckled.

'Well, I'm not quite but almost twice that age, a good age. And I imagine you have moved around a fair bit in your young life and are making a home here now, with all those children.' I nodded again and said yes, yes, that was exactly what I was trying to do. And because he had that interesting, enquiring face, I told him about the feelings I had of needing to actively belong to this place. I didn't mention the Alfred Jewel, though. It struck me that the fox in the man might steal my thoughts about the jewel if I gave them to him too freely. Instead, I told him that I liked bringing the children up here, and I added that it must be a good feeling, to have inhabited this landscape for his whole life. The man didn't blink once as I spoke to him. He looked at me very closely, while also keeping one hand out to pat the head of his dog, who stood with him, listening too.

'Well, you can move around as much as you like, but it's always the same thing you come back to. You cannot change. We do not change, not that much. Whatever the season, we do not change, however much the changing air or the feeling of frost underfoot when it's been cold might make us think we can. You always come back to the same thing, inside. We cannot change our insides, the things we carry in our hearts, that our parents and our first home put there, if we are lucky enough that these are things we want to return to.' He made a little laughing sound so that his dog raised his head to him and wagged his tail, as if laughing too, then he added: 'I belong here, I imagine. I don't belong anywhere else. I've been other places, to visit and so on, but nowhere makes me feel like I do here. Anyway, nice to see you caring for the animals, growing lives here, growing things. You should spend as long as you can on the Ridgeway and up on the hill. That hill. It's always the place to go for answers.' Then he raised his hand, putting his head down, moving quickly towards the next village, his little whippet tagging along at his heels.

As I walked back to the gate, I realized I had forgotten to do any of the things I had set out for. But none of that mattered, because as I approached the house I could hear the children shouting, a wild noise of joy and excitement, and there was a car in the drive. Pete was home.

# Chapter 7

Just as the air in the house rearranged itself when Jimmy
left, it shifted again with Pete home. His suitcase sat
abandoned in the hall as the children pulled him into
the kitchen, his jacket was thrown across the back of a
chair as they clambered on to him, clamouring for his
undivided attention with a new ferocity. Small hurdles
crossed and prizes won during the weeks he had been
away – Evangeline's prize in a dance competition, the
spelling test Lester had conquered, the new Pokémon
cards Dash had traded – all were gabbled out to him, the
children's voices criss-crossing one another's like radio
waves all at odds. Sentences hung in the air unfinished,
snatches of meaning lost, sibling rivalries asserted.
Through the tangle of children I could just make out
Pete, although who we were, our relationship, our marriage, had to necessarily sit in a long queue behind the
kids.

The din of chatter and connection lulled slightly
after a few hours. The boys peeled off upstairs to plug
themselves back into *Roblox*. Dolly went to see a friend.
Pete dropped Evangeline at a dance class in Wantage.

Once he was back and we were alone in the kitchen, re-finding our shared language, the connection between us felt tentative. Reuniting after weeks of separation isn't straightforward. Expectation and resentment run neck and neck. Having criss-crossed multiple time zones, rushed to get an earlier flight home, then worked most of that flight, Pete wanted to relax into home life. Our body clocks and the emotional rhythms of how we communicated were completely out of sync with one another. I was impatient. I stomped around the kitchen, clattering cutlery, slamming a chopping board down, desperate for a clean, clear table in an empty room to thrash out all the questions whirling between us about where our future might take us. But we couldn't even have a proper conversation: the boys were hungry; Evangeline needed collecting; someone had to go to the Co-op for more bread. We were always inside sepa-rate dimensions, and there was a distance too, which made me feel a bit self-conscious and nervous as I made coffee and tried to relax, like Pete was a sort of stranger who had suddenly landed in the kitchen, upsetting the routine I'd created.

Once, at a party in London, I found myself talking to my friend Sophie about what it felt like to exist within a marriage where so much time was spent apart. She was a year into a new relationship then, and I'd often scroll through her Instagram, alone at night, feeling envious of images of the physical domesticity she shared with her boyfriend: late-night shots of them together, sitting up in Sophie's kitchen, the focus blurry because they were both laughing too hard, the novelty of doing something as mundane as walking her little black dog

THE GIANT ON THE SKYLINE          215

through a familiar park, or taking a train to visit a grandparent, the ordinary and everyday elevated by the sheer erotic delight of being close to one another, whatever the circumstances. I told her that we'd been like that, but that now Pete and I spent three-quarters of our marriage in separate places.

'And when he comes home, do you just rip each other's clothes off as soon as he walks through the door?' she asked. I remember the black t-shirt she was wearing because it had made everyone laugh when she arrived, with white letters spelling *fuck you you fuckin' fuck* printed on it, and she was holding a glass of white wine, her face all open and expectant and excited. The room was crowded, people had dressed up, and there was music and the glint of bottles everywhere, but when she said that I laughed so hard that the man behind me turned around, suddenly, and I spilled my drink all over Sophie's t-shirt. When you're apart all the time, I told her, you are forced to create a life that's completely independent from one another, to withstand the separation. You cannot be needy or dependent on one another or everyday life would be intolerable. You separate a bit, because you have to. And so when you're back together, you need to re-find one another, every time, amongst the demands of domestic life. That's not very romantic. I've always felt a physical connection to Pete that still makes me want to smell him and lick him or drink him, but the sheer volume of responsibilities that come between us, almost all the time, make finding each other again after long periods of separation hard. And even when we are in the same house, the same bed, the small figure of a child is often wedging us apart.

Still, the impulse is always there. We both want to be together, even if returning to the same domestic space initially means we both have to break down the little shell, the capsule, we create around our individual lives when we are separate, and breaking that shell usually involves some pain before we reach the soft centre inside. That weekend when he was back, we tried to create opportunities to be together, even if this was just to drive on our own the seven minutes to the Co-op for butter, honey and milk, which we sometimes joked was the mini break we needed, allowing us to talk uninterrupted for fourteen minutes with the music we wanted playing, and talk quickly, feeling exhilarated, just for that short time, by the sense of being alone. Through everything, Pete and I loved being alone. We loved being together. We loved talking. We were one another's best friend.

Or we might walk out into the field. I like being in the field with Pete so much. I love observing his delight as the expanse of the field is spread out before him, and I can sense its irrepressible earth power working into him, even when he's wearing good trainers and the field is muddy. I love it when he tells me that being out there is what he misses most about being at home, and that it's the field he thinks of when he's away, more than the house, and that when he's inside a conference centre in Tucson or Ohio it's the open expanse of the field he craves. It makes me so relieved when he says this, as if the grass of this landscape has won over the concrete he walks on. The fact is, the hills and the fields of this part of England, in fact any rural landscape, don't really feel like home to Pete. I'd brought him to Oxfordshire. It

was my fault we lived here, and it was my need to satisfy
the craving for the squelchy green fields of the hill and
the white chalk thread of the Ridgeway that had guided
us to create our home here. Pete would have been happier in London, or any city really, but he'd gone along
with it for me.

Leaving the children in the house, we went out there
together, leaning into one another, as all the words suddenly flowed between us: the distance separating us
vanished as we talked about what a life in Washington
might look like. He helped me see the streets as something other than a grid, and we discussed the schools,
that prospectus full of happy children, and the red-brick
house, which looked like a home, which he had looked
around again.

We talked about all of this, and I felt my body readjusting with cellular relief at being close to him as we
skirted around deep puddles of water in the slopes of
the ridge and furrow where the perfect outlines of
green grass grew underwater. The willow in the pond
looked bony; it had shed many of its leaves, which
floated sadly on the surface of the water below. Rain
and moisture from the previous few weeks was making
the landscape glisten, the hedgerow in the distance mottled in patches, darker greens smudging into blushes of
dark-purple leaves as the hawthorn changed colour.
The oak trees on the far border were still bright green,
but the changing light cast on to the horizon of the
Ridgeway created an impression of a huge green
expanse of slightly altering shades between fields,
hedgerows, woodland and trees. Pete liked seeing the
horses moving across the field to meet us as I pulled

from my pocket stubs of carrots I'd taken from the
kitchen, and the outline the horses made as a single
shape after we walked on and they moved back out into
the field, moving in a small herd. We talked about the
home we'd created together here as we stood for a while
beneath the stillness of the oak trees in the far hedge
line, and how hard it would be to leave that. And as I
watched him, turning around within that vast green
space, observing the sweep of the weeping willow into
the pond, or registering something like awe as he caught
sight of the ancient horizon of Uffington Castle and the
scratch of white which made up the chalk horse, I felt a
powerful sense of love for him. For what he'd given up
for me. For the way he'd encouraged me to rediscover
the childhood that had been mine, not his, for our own
children. Rural life in a village didn't make sense to him,
as it did to me, but he'd done it because of the way he
loved me.

I wanted more time with him, but we were pulled
back inside, of course, by Dash shouting something to
us from across the railway line. For a few moments,
with Pete in the field, I was in the place I wanted to
be most, with the person who made me feel most at
home.

It felt good being close to him that night. Knowing
he was there to talk to, knowing that I could reach out
and touch the back of his neck, knowing that, for that
night at least, I'd sleep with the solid reassurance of him
beside me, despite the small child bodies separating us,
changed the way I felt about the day. Even when we
argued or fought, and the day of his return to the family
home after a long separation always had the potential

THE GIANT ON THE SKYLINE

for fiery anger from both of us, he was the person I wanted to be closest to most of all.

But the shock of what he was really asking me to do returned the next afternoon. I'd been out, walking the dogs, moving horses around, filling buckets of water, and it was mid-afternoon. The kitchen was quiet, the children all plugged into separate screens in separate rooms, but Pete was upstairs, talking with great focus to a woman with an American accent, her voice on speakerphone filling our bedroom. I moved around the room, checked my phone, lay down on the bed for a moment, got up again, listening to the confident, forthright way the woman spoke. I could tell, quickly, from her language, that she was the lawyer he had told me about, and her voice sounded bouncy when she talked about Pete's visa application, which was clearly moving forward. They were discussing the documents we'd need to pull together for the interview – birth certificates for ourselves and all the children, our marriage certificate – and talked about the kind of questions Pete might be asked about his work. As she spoke, I stripped off my jeans, spattered with specks of mud, pulled off my t-shirt and lay down on the bed, staring at the ceiling.

'Peter, I'm confident that you'll get the visa, and we anticipate that the interview will be scheduled for one or two months' time, in the early new year. This gives us a little more time to pull the documents together, but you will find out on the day of the interview if your application has been successful. They will tell you, there and then, at the embassy. Although you should know, too, that there is no appeal process for at least a year.

You get one shot at this. But if you are successful, your
dependents will all be entitled to the same terms of the
visa too,' she said, then added: 'Your partner and children will be entitled to live and work in the US for the
length of the visa, which is five years, and you can
reapply to have it renewed while you live there. Essentially, if you're successful, you and your family can
expect a long stay in the US, if that's what you choose.'

After they finished their call, Pete looked at me. I sat
on the edge of the bed, in my pants. He wasn't just
holding the prism of our lives in an imagined place but
had already stepped right inside it. Suddenly all the
uncertainty of leaving home, which had sat inside me
for the previous few weeks, spilled out like bile around
us. I pulled my t-shirt back on, locking the bedroom
door, but I didn't care if the children could hear me as
my voice cracked and I shouted at Pete about how
uncertain leaving absolutely everything we loved made
me feel, and about how angry I felt at the prospect of
selling our house and starting again in America. It was
my fault, he returned, since I made it so impossible for
us to be together, since it was my choice, not his, that
we lived in the countryside, and all because I was so
obsessed with being in England.

That had made me angrier, and I turned on him.
'You're the one that chooses never to be here. You're
the one that constantly leaves. No part of me wants to
leave here or sell our home. You are the one making us
dismantle it all. You're the one forcing us to leave a
place that has become very important, which is our
home, our base, where our roots are.'

'Roots,' he said. 'Oh, roots. You can create those anywhere.'

'Maybe you should have married a different kind of person, not me, because you don't understand,' I shouted, louder. 'We see this in a different way. I do not know how to just transplant us all to the suburbs and make this again.' I was standing at the window but turned, gesturing to the green walls of the room around us, then outside, to the yard and the hill in the distance.

'But we can create something new in America. Not the same, yes, that's true, but do it together, properly together, not separated as we are the entire time,' Pete said, and I felt a stab of guilt at the way I'd given so much to my relationship with this place, at the cost of my relationship with him.

I sat on the edge of the bed, twisting and pulling at our green bedspread, and told him, much more quietly, about the way the landscape of home made me feel safe because it allowed me to touch the past. 'Being here connects me to Nell and Mum too. They are part of this land now, and if we leave, I leave them behind too. And if we're living in America, and the older children are in England, are we even a family? We'd be dividing our family for the sake of what? A better life? What would that mean? What would make it so much better?' My questions went on until I slumped on to the bed and Pete reached over, running his hand through my hair, and there was his voice, as he talked about his need, not for the land, but to be with me and the children, for us to be together, and that change might be good. It might be exciting. And of course it would be complicated, with such a big family, and maybe Jimmy and Dolly would stay in England, because they were young adults now, but we'd find solutions. He reminded me of the ways we had always moved forward, of the big challenges we had withstood in the previous decade of our life together, and how proud he was of what we had achieved, growing our family, building our life, unafraid of the losses thrown at us. He leant down and kissed the back of my neck.

'You're the only home I want, Clover, right here, with you,' he'd said. I wanted to lie there quietly, with his hand stroking my hair, his voice around me, reassuring me, but a child was rattling on the door.

'Mum Mum Mum Mum Mum Dash has put some chewing gum in Lester's hair and Mum Mum Mum Mum Mum there's a man here who says the dogs are out on the green and you have to come outside right now.'

Before Pete had to leave again, we spent some time together, alone. He had to drive to Exeter, for a meeting with a scientist he sometimes worked with, and I went with him. Iona would collect the children from school, and the thought of almost an entire day alone with Pete was beautiful. We were much kinder to one another than we had been for ages. Pete's meeting wasn't long, and I sat in a cafe, writing. Afterwards, we drove home, flashing past Stonehenge and taking a detour, away from the A303, to snake back via Avebury. The last time we'd been there together, and alone, had been during the spring of 2010. My mum was still alive then, and I had taken Pete to meet her in a nursing home near Swindon where she lived for the last years of her life.

He had been sweet and gentle with her, holding her hand, talking to her as she stared at him from deep within her broken brain, gently moving her hands in front of herself and making indecipherable sounds.

Afterwards, I took him to the high grass ramparts, up on the hill at Barbury Castle, and then on to Avebury. I could not explain it then, but I understood it now, how important it had been to me at that time to take him to stand on the hill at the castle, and to be close to these old stones. That was a couple of months after we met, and all I really wanted was to become a physical part of him and for my blood and body and fluids to join with his so that we could walk around, always, as part of one another. But I also wanted those geographical places which were so important to me to imprint themselves into him too. I wanted the Ridgeway and Avebury to claim him, maybe, in the same way his physical body and his soul was claiming me.

What I remember most clearly of that day was how luxurious time felt during that period of our life. It had a ceaseless quality. We were together all the time and Pete was never away. Then, we were creating home in the same location and the same house, for both of us. Now, a decade and a half later, as we approached Avebury, I realized I was searching for a way to relocate that feeling of being together, which was the opposite of where we had got to, with a day of fighting behind us and lives so separate that sometimes all we had together was a day or two, a night, a few moments.

The road from Devizes snaked onwards, its smooth and endless horizons, with the downs tracing us on either side, like water, the long, clean lines of the hills where they met the skyline unbroken. And suddenly those curves of the hill, the soaring bright-green spaces they took up where they met the blue sky, as intense as lapis lazuli, had entirely worked their way under my skin, into the corners of my eyes, into my tear ducts. The hills made me cry, and I admitted to myself that I was scared. The road twisted and turned, until quite suddenly the ancient stones were all around us, like small giants.

'Let's stop,' I said to Pete, and we pulled into the car park at the Red Lion.

At the tables outside the pub, we could see a couple wearing colourful knitted hats and knitted coats sharing a pint of amber-coloured beer. A bus with *DEVIZES* lit up on its face sailed past as we crossed the road, then walked through a narrow wooden gate into the bigger field, where some of the largest stones waited. I went to Avebury a bit as a child, and sometimes went to raves close to the Ridgeway there in my adolescence, but I've taken our children there many times, because I was certain making them touch the stones would give them a more literal connection to the landscape of home and help them understand how much place mattered.

I liked strange, bleak Avebury in winter, when the stones were quite solitary, but we'd usually go for the summer solstice too, when we'd arrive before dusk along with hundreds of other people, to be there as the sun set over the stones on the longest day of the year. Lying in the sunshine in their school uniforms, eating sausage rolls and packets of crisps bought hastily in a garage after school pick-up, the children always enjoyed watching the people who gathered there: middle-aged couples in sensible boots and warm jackets, well prepared for sundown when it could get suddenly sharp and cold, gingerly picking their way through groups of teenagers, girls wearing tiny cropped tops and tie-dye shorts, boys juggling with clubs beside small speakers blaring trance music that was lost in the bigness of the skies around us.

'Jimmy,' Dash had once said, after he and Lester returned from walking amongst a boisterous group of teenagers passing joints between them. 'Me and Lester can smell Jimmy everywhere here.' The predictable thump of drums would fill the air, as the flat field and deep ditches around the stones filled with people. Often, by the biggest stones, a group of druids and their cohort would gather. One year we watched as a group of men and women wearing burgundy tunics appeared with props – a papier-mâché lion's head, a staff tied with blue and gold streamers, a small sheet painted like an ocean, and musical instruments too, violins and recorders and more drums – to enact the rising of a new world. It had been quite moving, until one of the men started running around swirling a long length of bright-blue satin to create the impression of a great wave. His movements had seemed out of control, his big sandals flapping on his huge feet, and the children lost interest and dragged me off to try to find the source of the drumming they could hear. Sometimes we'd witness a wedding by the stones, a couple both dressed in long white robes with flowers twisted into their hair.

These were beautiful moments that made me feel a deep, soul-quenching love for my children, for the luck awarded to me by fate that I was their mother. But they were also a reminder that often the best moments I spent with my children were accidental. I tried, but I could not really engineer my children's relationship with the landscape; all too often, if I strained to conjure up the profound, normal life would barge in: they'd have a huge row about whose turn it was to sit in the front on the way back, whose turn it wasn't to carry the picnic bag, who had pushed who or whether it had been an accident, whose legs were most exhausted, who should be given the phone to hold, whose turn it was to sleep in my bed tonight and who should keep the pound coin that had been found on the floor of the car. But being at Avebury with them, as they bickered and fought, reminded me that the strange and powerful osmosis of place doesn't happen in perfect moments when the light is just so, the sunshine is bright, and no one's fighting; actually, it happens precisely when you *are* all fighting, swearing, *living* within a landscape. Perhaps this is why the Ridgeway is such a powerful and magnetic place, because it holds all that shadow and memory of the emotions of the people who have fought and sworn and laughed there for thousands and thousands of years.

As Pete and I closed the gate on to the road behind us, I felt that sense I always had when I approached the stones, which was that they were waiting for something. This sense of silent expectation encircles Avebury, and as we walked between the huge stones, pressing our palms against them, feeling their cool, constant stillness, time itself seemed to be suspended, just as it had been when we were first there. The pressing, urgent, everyday concerns of our busy lives were beautifully absent, and it was much easier to talk there, about how our life would look in America, than it had been at home. I felt less angry, more able to breathe, and closer to Pete than I had for a while. It was easier to see it all, talking together, rather than standing alone at home, stressing over city plans of Washington, or trying to get inside a school prospectus, or imagining how secure the space inside a red-brick house would feel. Pete had all this information in his head anyway. We returned to the conversation with the lawyer, laughing, at last, about how unexpected life was. I told Pete that I'd seen lots of things on the horizon for us, but moving to an American city hadn't been one of them, and as I said it, the image of the red-brick house appeared to me for the first time not as a looming threat but as a bright possibility. The eternal certainty of Avebury soothed me. I could slip my hand around the back of his neck as we walked, and we could slow down; I could step back from the cliff edge where I'd seen our lives teetering. Nothing was dramatically ending. With Pete, and with the old giants around me, I felt the pressure inside my head subsiding.

We walked to the beech trees beyond the biggest stones, along the massive ditches which encircled the site before falling away to rolls of farmland beyond them, like a smooth, distant ocean. I wanted that moment to go on and on, but after a while Pete had a call. He went back to the car to talk, but I walked to the highest point of the deep grass ramparts, because I wanted to think of the children and women and men who'd first stood amongst the stones when Avebury was created.

Possibly the oldest stone circle in the world, its outer edges are difficult to hold in your head, since it's bigger and stranger and more unknowable than anything our minds can comprehend. It was created over the course of about six hundred years, from 2850 BC. No historian or scientist or druid, or any human alive today, really understands it, and everything we think about it – why it was made, what it was made for, how it was made – is speculation. I've read many different accounts of what Avebury might have been when it was created, but as I sat on the grass rampart, waiting for Pete, I tried to arrange these thoughts in my head so that I might see and listen out for the past, conjure up a sense of the rites or ceremonies it might have been built for, as a manifestation of humans' relationship to place, space and nature.

I squinted, covering the edge of my view with my hands to block out the shapes of the dots of houses, the grey snake of road, the pub, the gift shop and post box which jostle for space alongside the stones since the village grew up amongst them. Behind me a couple with a black spaniel marched past, determinedly planting their walking sticks in front of them as snatches of their conversation about a missed bus reached me. Trying to think yourself into the deep past is like performing a magic trick: it's asking your mind to remain conscious of the present, but also persuading it to seek out a place so distant it's beyond the reaches of human comprehension. I squinted again, remembering reading something, in one of the many piles of books beside my bed, that had told me '13,000 years ago ancient people were dealing with an Ice Age'. Trying to visualize the people who had created Avebury, I was straining for a much more recent past, a mere four and a half thousand years ago, but as I tried to quieten myself to hear the very, very distant sound of men pulling huge stones about and a thousand little hammers made from flint knocking them into place, I felt distracted by the comedy of an ancient woman 'dealing with' something like irritation or frustration or boredom. I tried to picture her dealing with the same emotions I was while waiting for Pete. Shut my eyes and I could see her rough, blackened face, her big hands pulling at her matted hair because her children were thin and shivering, everything about her was turning to ice, her toddler would not stop scream-ing and the man the child had come from had gone to move stones about.

Often, reading about ancient history, I'd been con-fused by the number of ices ages that came and went but I really wanted to understand what it felt like to be a human around the time of the Last Ice Age onwards. But since time and space before then is so unimaginable, I might as well have tried to make myself comprehend the emotional life of an alien. I'd liked reading how it was possible to interpret the last glaciers of the Last Ice Age as a physical barrier in time between the people of the inconceivably distant past and the people of now, a now which included both the men and women who had dragged the stones of Avebury into place, and me, sitting on the hill waiting for Pete, trying to understand them.

And I'd been interested to read that, about 12,500 years ago, a human in Robin Hood's Cave, in Derby-shire, took a section of the rib bone of an animal, and after polishing it to turn it into a small canvas, scratched on to it a perfect and almost heartbreaking image of a pony, its foreleg just visible in movement, its mouth slightly open, eyes narrowed, as if moving. Afterwards, that human made scratch marks across the drawing into the bone, as if displeased or disturbed or frustrated by the image. It was confusing and even frightening to try to imagine how the same people who could create a piece of art like that must have felt, living at the outer edges of the Last Ice Age, as the glaciers retreated, a time which also created the green ripples of hillside making up the Giant's Staircase beneath Uffington White Horse.

In the gathering dusk, teatime traffic snaked along the road, people returning from jobs in Devizes and Chippenham, or buzzing past on the school run, seemingly oblivious to the fantastical ancient mysteries the stones they drove between represented. As well as the books I'd thumbed through on the secrets of Avebury, I'd also listened to a podcast which had tried to simulate the sounds of life in Neolithic Britain and watched a YouTube series which had had a stab at simulating the demands of life several thousand years ago. I'd even read an article about a man who'd moved with his wife and two young children to the Highlands to try to live for a year in the conditions experienced by a Neolithic family, but my overriding memory of that was that the wife got scurvy and eventually left, taking her children with her.

How these people's lives really felt remains a mystery, and probably always will. I thought of this as I skirted around the far edge of the ramparts, and tried to push against the shadowy barriers of time, wondering how it might have felt to be a human eleven thousand, nine thousand, five thousand years ago, one of a band of men and women, perhaps with a memory of a bone-white, ice-cold landscape in their genes, and the sounds of mammoths and sabre-toothed tigers in their souls, moving across this landscape. Perhaps they carried a memory of the flood too, which came in a single day eight thousand years ago, in 6100 BC, when movements in the seabed off Norway caused a massive wave, thirty metres high, which submerged Doggerland, and the landmass of Britain became an island. I tried to picture them moving together across the tangled wildwood on the downs, all eyes searching for the same shifting shapes in the landscape around them, of rosy-brown deer, of wild cows, elk and boar, as they picked their way through birch and aspen, clambering among the spreading, tangled, endless branches of lime, elm, hazel, oak and pine trees.

I circled around Avebury, following the hollows, which were so steep in places, trying to imagine what had driven people to create these huge, artificial hills. The job to move that quantity of earth was vast, their tools no more than bones and antlers. From the top of the slopes, I could just make out the car park of the Red Lion, and the outline of Pete, head down as he paced backwards and forwards on the tarmac, engrossed in his call. Tiny spits of rain had started falling, like the lightest pinpricks against my cheeks, but I wanted to stay out amongst the stones, to listen for the ancestors.

I leant down, to pick up a flint that lay on the little path that tracked around the top of the ramparts. I held its cool shape in my hand, looking closely at the dark outline of hardest rock where it was smashed in half. The flint felt solid, but unwieldy too, and I imagined using it as a tool which defined my survival: to kill a deer, butcher the carcass, rip flesh from the hide and from that hide create a cloth to protect against the bitter cold. Because for thousands of years, before humans realized that mixing molten tin with molten copper created bronze, the substance of flint had been everything. It was used to cut down trees and undergrowth, build houses, kill animals, butcher meat, fashion clothes from skin. Straining to prolong the magic trick of time travel, I shivered, trying to ignore the gathering spots of rain which tugged me back into the present.

When I had taken the children to Avebury, or Uffington Castle, or on to White Horse Hill, I'd attempted to distract them from fighting over who should get to hold the pleasingly straight stick one of them had found by asking them to imagine themselves into the space their ancient human ancestors walked through. Mostly they ignored me or rolled their eyes. It was easy for them to think of Neolithic humans as crude, violent, stupid, blunt instruments, capable only of dragging great rocks around, and forget how precisely they knew the landscape, how closely they understood the plants, which to pick and which to avoid, how to feed the people around them and treat illness or salve wounds, how to create real shelter, how to *live*. They were rich, I realized, and very clever too. Alone, now, I tried again to visualize a man, half closing my lids, imagining a hunter and the shape his breath made in the cold air, the imprint of his foot on wet dew, the way he grasped his spear, the accuracy

with which he threw it, the relief he felt when the deer
fell. I tried to inhabit the feelings inside him as he ripped
open the deer's flesh, stripping meat from bones, rubbing the animal's skin clean, the carcass smelling sharp.
That smell of flesh and blood must have been around
him all the time, in his hair, his teeth, in the skins he
wrapped around himself. And the meat must have tasted
so good – beyond mere taste, representing existence
and survival itself – blood and meat and fat sizzling and
bubbling over the flames he fed with a crackle of sticks.

In my mind this man was never alone, but always
part of a bigger body of people who looked and walked
and smelt and moved like him, and it was exciting to
think of the words they might have used to communicate together, and the stories and memories they shared:
recollections of which green plants they could eat,
which red berries might poison them, which mushrooms would keep them strong and which might send
them wilder still, which plants like comfrey and mead-
owsweet might be used to salve wounds, and how to
create fire and keep it burning through the wildest, wet-
test weather. I thought of them sharing new words to
communicate their understanding of which sticks and
flints and bones made the best tools, and how to fashion
antlers into spears or arrows strong and sharp enough to
kill. I liked to think of them sharing that knowledge,
too, to create a necklace or bracelet from animal teeth
or pleasingly coloured stones, to decorate themselves.
And I often imagined the man, squatting by his fire,
reaching for the tools around him to create rituals which
put stories around his life and the lives of the people
around him.

I shivered. Above, in the beech trees, there was a gathering blackness as the dark clumps of rooks grew thicker, cawing to one another. Dusk had started to draw in and most of the other walkers had returned to their cars, or the pub, or had hurried to the Henge gift shop for crystals and essential oils before it shut. I glanced around me, alone among the stones, apart from a few rabbits hopping and sniffing and nibbling the grass around late, dying clumps of ragwort. I pulled my collar up and turned towards the car, although I didn't want to leave behind the man who I'd been struggling to find and who had appeared to me. Thinking of him there, I imagined him holding the head of a still-warm red deer in his lap, running his hands over the antlers and imagining a mask for himself. I'd seen a skull mask just like that at an exhibition about Stonehenge I'd been to in London some time before. Now I imagined the man cutting the top half of the skull open, then carving eye holes in it, creating something he could wear to become part deer, part human. I imagined the cold smell of the earth and the grass and the downs, green all around him, and I saw the man's face, blackened with soot and grease but lit by the glimmer of the fire, as he placed the antlers on his head, his breathing long and low, like the shape of the hill, while the fire crackled yellow and sharp and white. I thought of the way that becoming whole with the deer might have made something move deep, deep inside him, making him truly feel the energy of life and loss happening all the time around him, an energetic presence he could manifest when he stood in the flicker of firelight with those deer antlers on his head. These rituals of life and death, acted out with that deer skull, might have felt indistinguishable from the life and death that defined his every day.

I hunched up my shoulders as the rain started to fall harder and laughed to myself. Everything was speculation, but still, it was fun to speculate. It made me feel the landscape more than simply observing it. Home had not been a fixed place for the men and women and children walking across the downs, along the Ridgeway, five or six thousand years ago, since they moved with the seasons, the weather. Archaeologists have found scatterings of flints, a Hansel and Gretel trail of pieces of stone which marks the movement of Neolithic people, although those movements across the land slowed right down, starting to settle around 3000 BC. I knew, too, from the reading I'd done, that this nomadic life of the hunters and gatherers had changed when they learned that the deer and boar and massive wild cattle they followed could be trapped, not killed, but fed and cared for, then bred from. I'd enjoyed reading about the Beaker people – they sounded so lyrical – who arrived from across the Channel around four and a half thousand years ago, bringing their knowledge of which grasses and plants to grow, and how to master the environment, separating their crops from the wildwood, the tame from the untamed. All this happened over vast periods of time, thousands of years passing, so that gradually the hunters slowed, no longer moving across the land to return seasonally to familiar places. When this slowing of movement happened, people, families, communities started binding themselves to a place, then imposing themselves on that space too, changing the physical shapes of the green around them, pressing their hands downward, scraping at the ground to find fertile soil, then tending, watering, growing, farming.

The man who had crept through my imagination as a hunter-gatherer became a farmer when he learned to clear the wildwood so he could grow crops closer to the enclave where he now slept, night after night, his family around him. He had created a place, a world within a world, where family, food, crops, sat close beside one another, and this place – this home – where he slept, with the people around him who must have mattered to him, came to be associated with the life of a person. I remembered the words in one of the books I'd read, which had veered, delightfully, outside dry geology and the bare scraped facts of prehistory, to describe the landscape of the downs that these people walked through as one of the mind, as much as the hills. Their relationship with the land must have been psychic as much as it was literal. I thought of this as I paused beside a huge stone, smoothing my hands over the crevices, pushing my fingers into the holes of its face before pulling my hand away, ashamed of the intimacy of what I was doing. Perhaps the stones were a representation of how the sacred and mundane were part of the same thing to these hunters turned farmers. Perhaps there was no division between normal life and another, non-visible life: their ancestors were all around, living with them and part of them, all the time. Living deep within the landscape and depending on it for everything, the spirit of the place they lived with must have seemed real. Once, I'd walked up to West Kennet long barrow with the children, just outside Avebury, and built before it, in 3650 BC. There, a massive mound of chalk rubble holds five tombs, with monuments of sarsen stones standing at the entrance. The bodies and bones of forty people were buried inside, over a period of a quarter of a century; the old and the young, men and women, were entombed separately from one another, but over time the bones were mixed together: a skull separated from its skeleton, vertebrae of many different people alongside one another. But the land around the tomb had been farmed too, so perhaps West Kennet long barrow represented the impulse of a group of people to say, 'This is our home, this is our land, this is where we belong.' I had read about the idea of this 'ritual landscape', those two beautiful words, which harmonized when placed beside each other. A ritual landscape described the trenches, mounds and hills people created on earth thousands of years ago, when they dug the ramparts of Avebury and dragged the stones into place, scratched the shape of a white horse on to the hill, fashioned the massive earthworks of the hill forts at Barbury, Liddington, Uffington, constructed the long barrow at Wayland's Smithy and the many, many other, mostly forgotten, barrows and henges and enclosures across this special area of the south of England.

As I walked closer to the car, and to Pete, I could also make out Silbury Hill, the massive, unnatural mound of land that rises, like a giant green upturned pudding bowl, almost vertical to the sky, just outside Avebury. All these hills and ramparts and earthworks were certainly a feat of creation but also a feat of the imagination, the mounds like Silbury Hill lifting the people who dug them up, up, up, closer to the heavens, and the divine. And near it is Windmill Hill, the huge artificial earthworks of another causewayed enclosure, where archaeologists have found so many pig bones, fire pits, shells and jewellery that they can say, to the point where speculation is almost fact, that this was a place for ancient communities to come together, for feasting, trading, breeding, being.

Beyond doubt, this ritual landscape is a very real, very vivid and still-living physical reminder of how much we matter to one another: these places cannot have been created for solitary contemplation, but instead are, as Danny had said, like stadiums, places where the bonds of humanity were formed, where cooking together, trading with each other, talking and touching one another could happen. The ritual landscape, more than anything, was a place that bonded lives together.

It was dark as the edges of the stone circle retreated behind me, and the man with matted black hair, wearing his skull antlers, holding flints and skins, retreated, and then vanished. I left him, stepping forward towards the present, but I was grateful for what he had shown me. Because as I looked towards the car, I could make out Pete, his call finished but his head still bowed over his phone, and I could see that what really mattered was a place that brought people together, connecting them through growing, creating, making and being together. Avebury, Wayland's Smithy, Uffington and the Ridgeway were all places that drew me towards them again and again because of the way they represented not a distant, lonely wilderness but a real, almost tangible sense of the human past, and the human present too. That was what mattered. That was what I loved.

It was almost dark when I reached the car. Pete looked up and smiled at me.

'Each time we come back here, I'm surprised again how strange and extraordinary the stones are,' he said, putting his phone into his pocket, reaching out and pulling me closer to him. 'I understand what this means to you to be here. I know it. And I know that leaving it is hard. Taking the kids away from this place that's their home is hard too. So let's not think of this as for ever. If I get the visa, we could go for a few years, make it feel less final. Not for ever, but for a while. And anyway, the stones have been here for thousands and thousands of years. They're not going anywhere. They can wait for you for another couple of years.' Inside, I felt myself letting go of something I'd been holding very tight. Leaving for ever had seemed so impossible and painful. But as we drove home, the idea we might go for a few years, keeping hold of England in some way while experiencing America, took hold. I thought of what Aaron, the farrier, had said to me weeks before. Maybe there's another way.

At the weekend, just before Pete returned to America for another long stretch, we took the children out together. I'd read about a field close to Avebury where hundreds, maybe thousands, of sarsen stones dotted a valley, running from a place called Piggledene, just outside Marlborough, to Overton Down. The stones were called grey wethers, because the local word for a castrated male sheep was a 'wether', and the stones must indeed have taken on the outline of the flocks which once grazed everywhere on the unfenced downs. These grey wethers were peculiar enough to arouse the attention of Daniel Defoe, and Samuel Pepys, who passed them while travelling to Bath on 15 June 1668: 'it was prodigious to see how full the downes are of great stones', he wrote, 'and all along the valleys stones of considerable bigness most of them growing certainly out of the ground so . . . thick as to cover the ground'. I wanted to see these stones, but most of all, before Pete and I were separated again, I wanted to do something, together with the children, that we'd all remember, and that was beautiful and meaningful.

'This is the most unbelievable boring waste of a Saturday I have ever known,' said Dash, kicking a sarsen stone with his glittery red trainers which Evangeline had just grown out of. Lester sat beside him on another stone, his back to Dash, one hand bunched beneath his chin, looking pale, scowling into the middle distance. Evangeline trailed behind, wincing at her brothers and complaining how very much her feet hurt.

'Oh, come on, guys, this is great fun,' I said, glancing at Pete, who made a funny face at me.

It had taken so much effort to get here. We'd driven up and down the road between Marlborough and Avebury for about an hour, stopping, eventually, to pull into a turning at Overton Hill. Parked up at this point, which is where the designated Ridgeway National Trail officially starts, were a white Transit van and a burgundy-coloured horse box with a chimney on top. There were a few other cars scattered about too, and a tent and a small campfire. These vehicles are the echoes of the New Age traveller convoy, a hard core of people holding on to a life on the road. Sometimes the vehicles change, and occasionally Jimmy has driven from home to a rave here, just as I did at his age. At the last solstice, the site was so heavily policed that all vehicles were banished from this spot, although they do no harm at all. Now, a man with long grey hair pulled into a ponytail was sitting out the back of his van. Inside, I could see a wooden interior converted for living, the back windows covered in stickers relating to XR and low-impact living. I chatted to him for a bit, and he told me he always returned to this spot, even when he got moved on. The police were all right, he said, except around the solstice.

'But we keep the vibes positive and the vibrations high, and they don't really bother us so much,' he said, pulling on a rollie. He smiled gently, his eyes a bit droopy, and beside me I could see Dash's nose twitching as he smelt Jimmy somewhere near by. The man said he knew Piggledene.

'Not the easiest to get to. You could walk, three or four miles along the Ridgeway, then take a right by the tree. It's just a tree. Few miles down there. Can't miss it. Or drive back towards the garage on the main road and park in the village. Take care crossing that road, mind. Lethal.'

He'd been right about the road; it was fast, despite the peaceful scenes beside it, where a brook glittered in a field below the bank, the shining water tangled with mint and the fuzz of beds of watercress, so bright-green and so very clean. Beyond the water were acres of fields, where sleek black ponies grazed, heads down, in neatly fenced paddocks, but the road was vicious, with bikers who appeared suddenly in my rear-view mirror then zoomed ahead, tailgating cars, hustling to pass. Pete said it was nuts to even attempt to cross it, and after we'd

parked in a village off the road, then walked down an
ever-vanishing verge, I'd had to pause, squeezing Dash
and Evangeline's hands very tightly, questioning why
my need to understand the landscape of our home was
so great I'd actually risk crossing such a dangerous road
holding two of the most precious beings in my life. We
did it anyway, skittering across during a break in the
traffic, throwing the children on to the far verge, oblivious to nettles as we fell through a gateway, gulping in
relief, laughing, to skid down a steep bank. It was like
magic too, because beyond the roar of the road, a curving river of stones revealed itself in the valley, flowing,
unending, beyond the furthest point any of us could see.

As we passed into the field, I felt like these strange
stones were taking us through a portal in time. Sarsen
stones hold time within them, although in this part of
England they're also familiar. I've seen them many
times, dotted through the villages around the downs.
They're named after the Wiltshire dialect for the medieval word 'Saracen', which referred to anyone who was
not a Christian, and they are post-glacial remains of
silicified sandstone which evolved sixty-five million
years ago when the chalk sea bed rose and then emerged,
much later, when the glacier which shaped the downs
retreated. You stumble upon them all the time, sometimes sitting, strange and lonely like a lost walker, high
on the Ridgeway, or unceremoniously plonked in a
gateway by a farmer to block an entrance to a field.
Sometimes they're embedded in a cottage wall or form
part of the building blocks of a house or a block of
kerbstone on the steps into a church. Alfred's blowing
stone at Kingston Lisle is a sarsen stone, and they make

up the heel stone at Stonehenge. They stand to attention, their flat faces forwards, at the entrance to Wayland's Smithy and West Kennet long barrow, but I've seen them used as gateposts too; wherever they are, they belong within the landscape, like Danny, or the man on the bridge. They are beings of this place, and, moving among the stones, I pressed my hands to them, as if they might provide a route into a different time, but Dash's voice interrupted me, repeating himself.

'Why do we have to come and see all these old stones when it's literally the most boring thing we have ever done? And if we *have* to talk about history, even though it's sooooo boring, what I actually want to know is, is it more violent to live on the planet today than it was in Roman times? How did people actually kill each other? That's all I want to know.'

We walked on through the stones, as Dash ran through as many ferocious ways to die as he could think of. I wasn't sure where the stones were taking us, or what the point of them was, but it was so delightful to be together while the children whined and mewed around us, rather than alone in the same situation, and the sun was high, the sky unusually blue, the air warm after days of wet and dark. I'd read about three stones making a dolmen burial chamber called the Devil's Den, near to Piggledene. I'd seen it first in a painting by the same artist who created the little chalk outline of the White Horse which might make up part of my external symbolic storage. In his painting, there was a representation of the Devil, horned and red, standing before the stones. And the words 'burial chamber', if not the promise of more big old stones, was at least enough to entice the children to keep walking.

We left the footpath, following a map I'd pulled up on my phone. It didn't really resemble the landscape we were walking through, but the hunt was interesting. We walked for an hour or maybe two, up a steep track edging beside a ploughed field, passing a lone cyclist who lifted a hand in silent greeting, and then onwards, through a field littered with great pieces of farm machinery. A huge red plough, a yellow combine harvester and the green out-line of a chain harrow sat apparently abandoned in the landscape, and for a moment they made me think of the carcasses of decaying giants. The children had to be squeezed and coerced onwards as we dropped down, though, away from the machinery, through a rough field of set-aside boundaried by hawthorn hedges just begin-ning to reveal swathes of dark-red berries, onwards, until far ahead, in a fenced-off area of long rough grass, the last of the afternoon light hitting it, we saw the stones. As massive as some of the stones at Avebury, they were propped up like a Neolithic church.

The children scrambled between them as Pete and I sat together, quietly triumphant to have found this site. All the resentment and expectation around his return a few days before had dissolved and we were, for that afternoon at least, parents together. It was a rare and beautiful feeling. He left again at four a.m. the next day, a taxi arriving in the yard as Pablo, disturbed so early, started barking. Even in half-sleep, I felt something inside me plummet at the thought of his departure. 'Don't go, Pete, please don't go,' I murmured as he leant across and kissed me in the darkness. 'I only want to be with you.' Then he left, the front door closing, a car door slamming. Pete gone, again.

# Chapter 8

Sitting in the kitchen, in that perilously short time in the early afternoon between finishing a sandwich and three p.m. suddenly arriving, when I'd have to be back at school, I scrolled through emails. The interview at the American Embassy sat on the horizon like a looming exam, and my inbox had been filling with exchanges between Pete and the lawyer, which I was now copied into. Reading the correspondence, I felt like a child who has been asked to step into the dining room and join the adults' table. Until now, I'd been in the playroom with the kids, drinking squash and eating Wotsits off paper party plates, but now I was at the mahogany table and there were linen napkins and cut-glass tumblers. She might ignore every question I asked about the process, but at least I could observe as she and Pete set up dates for a practice interview. In her emails she ran him through the process. He might be asked the ages of our children, but it was clear that, while I was expected to be at the interview, my presence was symbolic, and I almost certainly would not be asked anything.

One of the ginger cats gently batted at my fingers as
they scuttled across my keyboard, tipping her head on
one side, her little whiskers moving as inquisitively as if
my fingers were mice. Watching Pete walking forward
within our emails, towards the questions that the lawyer
asked him, I felt something like freefalling, although, for
the first time, it was as if Pete was holding out his arms
to catch us. For the first time, I felt something liberating
in the idea of letting go. Every corner of our kitchen was
layered with memory, so that simply glancing up into
the room – towards the painting of cherry blossom
Evangeline had done propped up above the sink, to the
photo of Jimmy and Dolly as they left to visit their
father one Christmas Eve, to the speckled teapot with
the pointed spout I'd bought with Evangeline after I
stopped drinking so that we could make mint tea
together, to the brass knight my friend had given me to
remind me how to be brave, to the little jewelled bag
Nell had once left hanging over a picture, which had
never been moved – was like looking into a kaleidoscope
of love and people, which altered subtly every time I
moved my eyes. And as my gaze darted from one corner
to the next, I realized I had been holding on, so tight, to
all those memories bound up with our home, but that it
wasn't just OK to let go, it could also be a relief. Like the
team at the school tug-of-war who had suddenly given
up, I could stop straining with all my will and drop the
rope. I didn't need to go on pulling so hard in the opposite direction to Pete, as I had been doing for so long. I
could at least allow the fully formed idea of a life in
America to settle in my mind and see how it felt.

Sometimes, in the previous weeks, walking through

the wet autumn grass in the field, where tiny brown-grey mushrooms were ringed in small patches on the higher ground, strewn between the precise glitter of strings and strings of spangled spiders' webs, I'd turn back to our house, a distant white oblong on the far side of the railway, and practise the feeling of it moving away from me, the walls no longer mine, the garden out of reach, another family's car parked outside, them making it their home. A few months earlier that sensation had felt like a form of physical pain and would send me hurrying back to the house, as if by stepping back through the front door, moving around it to make food or rearrange some furniture, I could reassert my hold over it. But now I let that feeling sit there. It didn't make me wince. Rather than letting go of home, I experienced a stronger feeling of moving towards Pete, and that felt, truly, like a place of comfort and relief which struck through at least some of the pain of leaving.

I shut the emails. The ginger cat had left my mice fingers and was stretched out on the cooker top. Beside the cooker was a wobbly handwritten note from Evangeline.

*Can we buy some pumkins and halowean things today after school pleese Mum?*

Later that evening, half-eaten plates of pasta pushed away in front of them, the children and I talked about the kind of rituals we might create, or enact, or find, in Washington DC. I'd read, a bit, about the cherry blossom in the Tidal Basin, about the trails for riding in Rock Creek Park, about the hothouses and magnolias

in the National Arboretum, about the marshes on
Theodore Roosevelt Island, and about the bald eagle
you might be very lucky to spot above the Potomac
River. There was a novelty to hearing certain American
placenames we might go in the children's voices: we
could drive to the Catskill Mountains, or out into West
Virginia, Tennessee, Mississippi. Texas, the place I'd
had tattooed on my arm, I'd loved it so much, would be
within striking distance. I wasn't sure how I'd relate to
any of these places as a mother. I wasn't sure where or
how I would create our connection to place there, but I
was more curious about how it would feel. What rituals, or connections, we might find that would provide a
thread of continuance between these years and those
that would follow.

Inscending, and turning my eyes inwards, to the
landscape I loved, to the people I loved, to the memories of home I loved, reminded me that of course the
space of home would change. That was inevitable,
whatever happened, but ritual, underlined by memory,
would have planted something of this place inside the
children which would grow as their memories of it
strengthened. I didn't want their sense of home to
become a haunting, as Minety had become for me; I
didn't want it to be a bomb in their brains, but instead
be a place of strong, colourful memories which had
formed them, and which they'd carry onwards wherever they were. It often seemed to me that creating this
sense of continuance was the entire point of the parenting I was trying to do. The world is insecure, terrifying
and beautiful, but if home is something vivid, deep
inside them, it could become a place to return to, in

memory, if not literally. In Washington, Pete and I would sew new experiences into their lives, which would turn into memories we had created together. That felt like a beautiful thing.

Driving home from school, the fields on either side turning rust-coloured in the late autumn, the children and I were reminded that nature is a sorcerer. Swooping low over the blackthorn hedge on the last lane before home, the barn owl who belongs to this landscape appeared. In that moment, the tangled, excited spikes of the children's voices which filled the car suddenly ceased as the wide white wings appeared, truly as if by magic. 'Stop,' said Evangeline, 'stop, please stop,' and we pulled into a muddy gateway on a rise in the road, by a barn with a collapsed roof, like a half-sunken sailing ship, which we passed every day. We squelched out of the car, the children's tatty school shoes submerged in deep puddles as the barn owl flew in a huge circle, turning his head like he was watching us. His wings were striped with thin lines of yellow and brown, dotted with spatterings of black, drawn there in exquisite brushstrokes. Evangeline held my hand, squeezing it tighter and tighter as the owl swooped around us, sometimes turning his strange, round face right to us and looking at us with something approaching absolute familiarity.

'Remember this, kids. Put this memory inside you and keep it there to take out later,' I said to them.

As the yellow of autumn smudged into the darker colours of winter, I found myself returning with the children, again and again, to familiar places where ritual and action could join to create even stronger memories. Finding ritual meant taking them to the same stretch of beech trees on the Ridgeway, copper-gold against the grey autumn sky, so they could pile sticks into dens in the same place and look for squashy damp mushrooms, where we could sit on the same logs and argue with one another about much the same things we had for years. Ritual was chasing them to the top of Dragon Hill, the steep green mound below the White Horse, where George was said to have slain the dragon, the bare patch of grass signifying where the beast's blood was spilled. Ritual was a Sunday-afternoon picnic of cheese sandwiches and orange squash at Wayland's Smithy or visiting the brook at Letcombe Bassett, where they could dare each other to walk barefoot through the bright, clean water where cress once grew so thick and green, it was sent to London daily. The children liked unpeeling their school socks and paddling in the water while ignoring everything I told them about the famous 'Letcombe cress' and a book called *Jude the Obscure* with a village in it called Cresswell, which was where they stood, their voices echoing off the water as they hopped about, their ankles turning white and numb. History lessons always fell on deaf ears, but it didn't matter. I wanted the green of the hills to drench them, as it had me. Creating ritual around the places within this landscape we returned to, again and again, felt like a process of threading the coloured beads of memory and action together, to create a talisman bracelet of green beads they might understand the true value of as they got older.

And ritual was also visiting the fish and chip van in Uffington on Tuesday evenings, for chips drenched in vinegar and cans of Fanta after Lester finished Beavers in the village hall, and stopping for reduced chocolate bars at the garage on the way back from Wantage after dance class on a Friday night, and it was saving up for a comic at the village shop. When Halloween arrived, we created more home-made rituals, trawling the charity shops in Wantage, hunting for china cats, orange and brown mugs and red candles we could dress our table with, alongside the pumpkins, and conkers collected from the horse chestnut trees in the churchyard. We pulled a clump of the strange grey gossamer threads of old man's beard from a hedgerow down on the village green and piled it up in the middle of the table, spreading tendrils of it over a length of heavy, silvery cloth Nell had given me years before, when we had created our first death table. It had been her idea, to collect animal skulls and feathers from the fields around her house to dot between piles of sweets. We did this together for a few years, the last years before she died, and the children and I have continued the ritual, to honour her, to tether her to us.

Evangeline lit one of the bright-red candles we'd bought in the charity shop, and it filled the kitchen with a sickly sweet smell of synthetic cinnamon, which reminded me of Texas, where I went to live after university, talking my way into a job on a ranch. Nell had visited me there, and her arrival in that alien landscape of jagged red rock and sharp yellow bluffs in the Palo Duro Canyon had broken the spell cast on me when I'd first arrived. Until then, I'd been living in an illusion that I was creating a brand-new life for myself, where the past could not cast shadows, where I really thought

I could be a new person. In Texas, I could not taste or feel or smell home anywhere. The landscape wasn't green but red and dry and dusty, ragged with mesquite bushes growing under an endless sky, which was almost always a sunny blue. There was hardly any rain in Texas; it was never damp. There were no hedges, no cow parsley, no blackthorn or bluebells or blackberries. Every few weeks I went to Walmart, with the wives of the cowboys I worked alongside, and the aisles smelt like that red candle, of synthetic cinnamon and chewing gum, the same smell I'd noticed in the chemist in Washington when I'd been visiting Pete.

In Texas, I slept in a bunkhouse, under a blanket decorated with blue-and-white embroidery of the American flag. Everything I ate and smelt and tasted was new: Mexican shrimp grilled on a barbecue with hot sauce and lime and big cups of iced tea, or beef jerky stuffed inside my pocket for a long workday, even the sugary cheer of Dr Pepper. Nothing was familiar. There was no ritual, no reference points, no history, personal or national, that I understood or could touch as my own. Every time I slammed the door on the pick-up truck I was driving, I sensed a new version of myself stepping out. I was convinced I could become a new person, one who had not ever experienced a mother's brain damage, who did not have the language of intensive care, long-term prospects, chronic illness, in their vocabulary. I truly believed that if I moved away from the pain, the pain could not follow me. I had a lot to learn, and until Nell arrived to visit me, I had felt completely free.

But when I saw her, walking across the yard, her blonde hair blowing off her face in the hot air, her

strong stance, the way she moved her hand to her face
and dipped her head when she was uncertain of something, everything about the landscape, which I had
thought was reinventing me, vanished into nothing.
With Nell there, suddenly the cactus, the bunkhouse,
the veranda that wrapped around the little wooden
cookhouse, the pick-ups and horses and corrals, all
seemed insubstantial and almost unreal.

In that single moment, I felt a crumbling sense of dis-
appointment and relief. I knew I could not escape the
past, and also that I could not leave Nell either. One
afternoon, during that week she was with me, we
walked away from the ranch to an abandoned schoolhouse, way out on a flat plain, as if flung there,
surrounded by the hum of crickets with the crackle of
yellow, dried grass underfoot, and we talked about the
fields we'd grown up in together. I still remember that
afternoon so clearly, like a brilliant dream that has
stayed with me while almost all other dreams vanish.
We lay on the grass, remembering how it had felt to be
children growing up in Minety, the reassuring feeling
of the thick black hedges and the squelch of wet clay,
and the almost soporific effect of the sweet smell of the
bluebell woods that to us were simply the place we
played, and the way we had felt scared by an abandoned
tractor under the pylons near that farmhouse where the
siblings and their pigs had lived, and the pain of picking
a path through a nettle patch with rusty barbed wire
hidden in it. Imagining a life for myself in Texas had
been foolish. As we talked, returning to these places in
our imagination together, I understood very clearly
that the red rock and mesquite and tumbleweed, the

dustbowl of Texas, these were all in my heart like a
lover who had fully owned me, but they must be left
behind in the same way. They would never be in my
soul, as the green of England was.

I'd thought I could not live without Nell either. But
the years since her death have proved that that was wrong.
I can live without her, although really living takes a new
kind of intent. Grief is a volcano whose lava destroys the
old landscape around your soul. But when its heat has
passed, when it has cooled a bit so that it's not perpetual
agony, something new and beautiful can emerge. The
rituals, I thought, as I smoothed my hand across the shiny
threads woven like darts of silver through the length of
heavy fabric I'd thrown across the death table, helped me
hold on to a feeling of what Nell and I had shared
together, even as life rolled onwards. And this was why,
as the idea of moving to America started solidifying, the
death table, the Ridgeway walks, and my love for the wet
green fields, the nettles and brambles and clay, felt more
violently precious to me than ever before.

'Why do you put pumpkins on a death table? It's not as
if you could take a pumpkin with you when you die.'
Dash was sitting on the table, at the end of autumn half
term, rolling the pumpkin head precariously close to
the edge so that I had to keep leaning forward to stop it
from smashing in a mess of orange flesh. He said that
death was stupid, because you could not take with you
the things you liked best from life. 'What like, Dash?' I
asked. 'What would you take with you, a long time
from here, when you're an old man?'

'Well, Pablo, of course, I'd take Pablo more than

anything. Also Lester. And my Lego. Pokémon cards.'
He paused. Then he started crying, realizing that he
couldn't take any of those things with him when he
died. He was also worried he'd become a spirit who
wanted to go back into its body. 'Because we know
about spirits who want to leave their bodies and go on
to the spirit world, like Nell did, but what about a spirit
who doesn't want to leave their body? Or who leaves
their body and then wants to go home? Imagine being a
spirit and leaving your body and then realizing you
want to go back to your body?' He cried harder when
he thought of this, a tiny torrent of tears flooding from
his eyes, and I caught the pumpkin head halfway from
the table as it fell.

'Maybe, Dash, you carry things inside you, inside
your soul, bigger things than stuff like Lego or Pokémon
cards, that mean your home is always there with you?
Maybe even a soul feels that, which is why it doesn't
need to go back into its body? Maybe the body was just
the vessel, holding all that energy which is the soul?'
Dash thought for a bit as we started scraping seeds from
inside the pumpkin, and then he seemed cheered up by
the thought of this. Even more so when we looked in
the cupboard and found chocolate fingers, marshmal-
lows, Jaffa Cakes and some orange tortilla chips, and
laid the table so that death and life could come together
around it.

Later, much later, after I'd found their uniforms for
school the next day, rubbed a flannel across their faces,
crouched by their beds remembering the moments of
this half term together to lock into their hearts like little
jewels, and then gone back to the kitchen to clear the

mess of pumpkins and conkers away, I returned to the thought that had been tapping on my eyelids with increasing urgency: these rituals to connect them to home were all very well, all very vivid, all very beautiful, but they were missing one crucially important thing – their father. Pete had missed out on so much of the children, and they had missed him. What, now, was the point of home if he wasn't there?

Sometimes, driving home at half past eight after first ballet then musical theatre had finished on a Wednesday night, Evangeline persuaded me to stop off at another nearby village, to nip into the Co-op for chocolate and instant noodles. Once, having persuaded me to make the detour, she spent the extra driving time explaining to me how her dance school was *home*, a place where she felt most happy because she was with her dance *family*. Her little voice chattered to me through the darkness of the car, an intimacy between us, her pale, almost luminous face lit up by approaching headlights. We spent so long in the car each week, driving the same roads, but at that moment I felt grateful for the enforced hours of time together it had given us. When Jimmy was an adolescent, that time in the car was a moment to connect with him. Parenting a teenage son had been a white-knuckle ride of expulsions and a policeman suddenly arriving in the driveway, of slamming doors and a lot of shouting, but the time we spent together in the car had been a way of talking, even when he was fifteen and I, his mother, was the last person he wanted to speak to. Evangeline's words cheered me: if the warm and loving feeling she got from being in her dance family made her feel as supported as she did within our real family, then she was showing me how home, too, could be an intent rather than a place. We splashed through the darkness, Evangeline gasping when we passed a row of houses with Christmas lights strung along a garden fence, a halo of yellow glitter cast from a window where a tree was already up.

'I just love the days we get to go to the Co-op with you, Mum,' she breathed, and we laughed together. I felt it too. When the village shop in Uffington is shut, I have always felt extraordinarily grateful to this place that seems to always be miraculously open, even at 9.40 p.m. on a Sunday evening, and where the woman with tight grey curls always says, 'Hello, Dash, had a good day, have we?' when he charges in shouting for sweets. Now Evangeline only needed Pot Noodles and a can of squirty cream to make a shopping trip truly delightful.

Sweets at the local shop, *Modern Family*, the dark drives to Wantage: they were all rituals, in some way, of my life in the countryside with the children which I was now viewing, from a place of some distance, as our date at the American Embassy drew nearer. Months ago, America had appeared in my mind like an artificial, distant shimmering platter of piled-up toys, but now it was all so real. Pete and I had spoken about it the night before when he'd called me from a hotel room in Houston, both of us ragged and exhausted by months of separation, and nervous too about the outcome, longing for certainty either way. There was no guarantee of getting the visa, he'd reminded me, and now I felt a prickle of discomfort at the idea that it might not happen.

'If we get refused, I don't know what we'll do. We'll

have to rethink everything.' He was homesick, he said, missing the children, missing me. The food was terrible and the air conditioning depressingly sterile. I turned over in bed as we spoke, the shape of a sleeping child nestling against me, and was reminded how much Pete needed the comfort of family life around him. 'I want us to be together. I want you and the kids here with me. Sometimes I feel that without you and the kids with me, I can't really breathe, that I am not really living, just existing.'

One morning just after that, before the children broke up for Christmas, I went to the woods. I would not like to live in the nest of a wood, with the darkness of branches obscuring the way out, but sometimes the wide-open curves of the downs and the hill are too exposing. Often, walking on the hill surrounded by so much sky made me feel like my head was scooped open and laid bare. Mostly, I went to the hill consciously to feel this openness – to scoop my head and heart open. Up on the bigness of the downs I could scream, even when I was making no noise. But there are times when I want to be held by landscape. Different landscapes offer different gifts. That morning, I wanted to be quietened, to find solitude and green silence. I didn't want to join up with all the ancient people on the Ridgeway. I wanted to separate myself from them and their pull over me, make myself vanish in the safety of leaves, to concentrate on what was really happening now as the reality of America loomed before me.

So I drove to a small wood on a hill outside Faringdon called Badbury Clump. In spring the place is electric blue. Too blue, I have found, as the bluebells growing there have become very famous. Where once, just a couple of years ago, you could park in a little clearing off the road, now there is a car park, tarmacked, with a visitors' board with a map marked out on it, and a lot of notices about the work going on there. In the spring, the road beside the clump becomes backed up with cars, and people stand in front of the blue to take just the right photos for social media. The bright, bright blue of the bluebells is almost artificial, like very good-quality plastic flowers, so they look outstanding in a photograph. I understand why people want to record themselves there, but because so many people have this urge, it's not an especially lovely place to visit at that time of year, at the weekend, for anything other than a photograph.

But this was not spring, and it wasn't a weekend either, so the car park was empty. Mid-December, but the real cold of winter wouldn't arrive until new year. The air was mild, and I was almost relieved by the coolness among the beech trees, their spreading branches cocooning me, casting a gentle, calming shade I was looking for after the thin, high air and outrageous bright light of the downs. A robin flashed red up ahead, seeming to pause and observe me before it pecked at a tiny spider or bug amongst the leaf mould, then flitted off.

The ground felt springy, only slightly damp, and I chatted to my dad on my phone as I walked, following a path under the canopy of leaves which were thinning as autumn moved towards winter. Rosehips on a tangle of bushes edging the path now changed from orange to a darker brown, and beyond the trees the hillside fell away, revealing the outline of Faringdon, and High-worth beyond.

I talked to my dad about America. A few weeks before, on the phone to my stepmother, I had cried, overcome with worry about how I could tell my dad that, yes, we really might be moving to Washington. I was very afraid of how the idea of that might hurt him. I was with him when Nell died and had heard the cry he had made as death took her from the room. I would have done anything to protect him from great pain again, and I was worried he might think he was losing me, his only other child, if we moved permanently to the other side of the Atlantic.

'Clover, you must take the path that is yours. You should never stop yourself from doing something that feels right for you, simply to protect your parents. I feel that very strongly,' my stepmother had said.

That had helped a lot. I talked to my dad on the phone most days, and over that autumn I started to tell him about Pete's conversations with the lawyer, about the red-brick house, about what the school prospectus had looked like, although I'd always ended our conver-sations about it with a dismissal. 'It probably won't happen,' I'd say. 'Lots of people fail in their visa appli-cations, we may well not get it and we won't be able to appeal for ages if we don't.'

'I think it's a very exciting future, for you and Pete and the children,' my dad said now, as I perched on the edge of a log, tugging at the furled edge of bracken beneath my feet. 'We'd miss you of course, but we'd visit, you would visit, and there's FaceTime and social media. We can still feel connected.'

After we finished talking, I sat for a bit longer, staring at the graffiti carved into one of the beeches before me. On the far side of the clearing, a man and a woman were walking with two springer spaniels, throwing sticks backwards and forwards for them. For a while, I sat and watched. I was feeling lonely, and it was reassuring to watch this couple, who seemed so pleased with their dogs. They looked happy, and I envied the sense of them in the bubble of their world. They leant into each other as they talked, one putting a hand on the other's arm and pointing out the sunlight falling between the trees. It looked rare and precious, that chance to talk and walk on a Tuesday morning. The smaller of the two dogs had gathered a stick close to the log where I sat, and he ran over to me, dropping it between my feet, wagging and wiggling his body, trying to enthuse me. I picked the stick up and threw it between the trees, the dog bounded after it again and the man raised his hand in a friendly greeting.

It was almost snug, and certainly reassuring, to walk amongst the trees with a sense of the present all around me. I followed the track where I had once seen boys on BMXs biking, and as the path curved I caught sight of a man in a green zip-up fleece, his face slightly flushed with the exertion of pulling brambles and branches into the back of a pick-up parked near by. The ends of the branches were very pale, and there were piles of saw-dust all around, as if a chainsaw must have been put away very recently. An older man stood with him, leaning up against the edge of the truck. The way he was leaning made it clear he wouldn't be breaking into a sweat, but neither of them looked up at me as they were completely absorbed in their conversation.

'And up in the clearing I've seen a buck, clear as light, with a pair of tights around his head,' the older man said, pausing as he leant back a bit further, to make himself more comfortable against the van.

'Oh, right,' said the man with the flushed face, who had unzipped his fleece. 'And what does that mean?'

'What does it mean? *What does it mean?* The buck has a pair of tights right over his head,' the older man went on. 'Stuck there. I need to catch him and take them off. But that means, that *means*, someone has been getting their knickers off in the wood, right?' They both burst into laughter. 'As good a place as any for it, isn't it?'

I walked on, the sounds of their voices discussing how to catch a buck, and their laughter, receding as I clambered over the trunk of a fallen oak, glancing upwards to the mottled, shifting blanket of dark, dark green leaves obscuring the sky. I breathed deeply as I walked, enjoying the thought of tiny particles of leaves and trees and undergrowth, the nettles, brambles, oak, beech and hazel trees, moving into my lungs and becoming part of my insides. Then I started suddenly, catching sight, between the trees a little way off, of the outline of a girl, pacing a little and humming a soft sound. She saw me, stopped, turned, then sat down quickly, her movements small, darting, as she settled on a fallen tree trunk. I lifted my hand in apology for disturbing her, but she smiled a bit and shook her head quickly, so that, as her hoodie fell, her long, glossy red hair tumbled around her face.

'Nah, it's OK, you're all right,' she said, and pulled a wad of leaves from a low-hanging branch near by, ripping them into strips, little flakes of green confetti that caught on the sleeves of her top and her black leggings. She shivered, despite the relative warmth of the afternoon, and something in the slight, sharp way she moved made me think she might just vanish. Her hair was magnificent, a bright copper sheet of flame shot through with golden strands which tumbled over her shoulders and halfway down her back as she leant forward, throwing the leaves to the ground and then rubbing her face with both hands, shivering again and pulling her sleeves down over her hands.

'I used to think these woods were haunted, when I came here when I was a kid, with my brother, but now I wouldn't mind a few ghosts to keep all the people away,' she said, staring towards where I had crouched down, skimming my hand over the damp ground. I stood up, because it was me who had walked into her space, but she gestured for me to sit.

'Nah, nah, I'm kidding. You're all right. Seriously,' she said, pulling her hair back over her shoulders and leaning forward, as if settling in for a chat. 'It's barely getting colder, is it? It's been so warm for so long, and people are saying it was too warm, but I'm just grateful, where I live.' She stood up, fishing around in the pocket of her hoodie for tobacco. 'Don't mind if I smoke, do you?'

I shook my head. 'Do you live near here?'

'Yeah and no. Did, properly, until a couple of weeks ago. Do still, in a way. Live here. At least for now. I live here today,' she replied, and snorted. 'I live here for now. Is that good enough?'

She drew heavily on her rollie, the silence between us companiable, easy. 'So where do you live, then?' I pressed, after a minute.

She told me she was born in Faringdon but moved away when her parents split when she was seven. 'I left then to live with my mum, and we moved all about, Wantage, Swindon for a bit, Cricklade, Highworth too,' she said, stretching her hands out wide as if showing me a mighty landscape, when the spread she was describing covered no more than twelve miles. Her words fell over one another as she spoke, because she seemed to like chatting, her eyes widening as she told me about her mum, who had found work as a cleaner at first, then, when she was good at it, became a housekeeper. 'So we always lived in other people's houses, in an annex to a bigger house, or in a cottage or in a granny flat, that kind of thing. We never owned anything, but I know my mum always really, really wanted it. She really wanted her own place. Mum says she's getting too old for it now, she wants to stay in one place. Stop all the moving around. She wants to feel grounded – not like me, I don't care where I am.' Her dad was a butcher, or at least he was when she last saw him. 'Great butcher. Crap dad. Haven't seen him for a good five years. Since I was fourteen. But it's just one of those things, isn't it? Not going to let who my dad is, or wasn't, kill me now, am I?'

I nodded. 'And what are you doing now?'

'I'm staying in a van. My van, if you can call it that, which you can't. Although tonight, I guess it's my van. But not for much longer.' She'd been living in the van with her boyfriend until recently. 'Then he fucked off one night, out of the blue, just like that, no idea why. But he has been kind of distracted and a bit angry for a while, always on Snapchat, always on his phone, and so

now . . .' Her voice trailed off. 'His dad wants the van
back. It's parked behind his place, on a drive behind his
house, near the new estate on the Coxwell Road,
y'know? And he wants it back. Which is kind of a
fucker for me, but he has a point. I'd want it back if I
could. And it's his van. Something my boyfriend never
told me. Mind you, there was plenty he never told me.
So I've got to get out. And I can't stay at my mum's any
more, she's got a boyfriend, her own life. She makes me
welcome enough, but she doesn't need me hanging
around.' She ground the end of her cigarette into the
edge of a log, then dug a little hole for it in the soil,
beneath the leaf mould, where the ground was damp,
covered it over and swiped her hands together. 'Why all
the questions anyway?' she asked me, sitting back on
her heels, smiling slightly.

I laughed, then said, 'Because I'm trying to understand what it means to live here. That's all. I don't mean
to pry.' And now it was her turn to tip her chin towards
Faringdon.

'You from here, are you?' Her green eyes narrowed
slightly as she tilted her head on one side, waiting for
my answer, testing me perhaps.

'Not right here, about half an hour away, near Cricklade. But I've lived here for a while. My kids all went to
school here. It feels like my home, I suppose. And the
Ridgeway, I love the Ridgeway and the hill, that's really
why I first moved here.' She grinned at me quickly,
nodding something of recognition.

'Yeah, I get you. Before he fucked off, my boyfriend
and me, we were parked up near the Ridgeway. We had
to move a bit now and again, but it was beautiful. I

loved it there. Waking up beside all that space. It was like waking up by the sea or in a desert, someplace where no one else is. But it wasn't very practical living there. I couldn't get far from there. I couldn't get a bus from there. You can't live a normal life like that. It's fine when you want to be on the edges of things, but not if you have to get stuff done.' She snorted. 'Use bus time-tables, go to college, have a steady job, things like that. I was at Swindon college for a bit, doing catering, but I ended up leaving, couldn't get there so easily.' She looked down, scraping at the earth again, and I could smell the rich, dark aroma of leaf mould, like the smell of the earth exhaling. 'Now I'm not sure what I'm doing, to be fair. Now that I don't have the van much longer, I don't know what I'll do. Leave here, I imagine. Leave here, stay here. Move to Swindon maybe. Bristol. Anywhere, really. Not a lot keeping me here now, without the van, and what's that anyway? An old vehicle. I'm probably better shot of that. And my boy-friend.' She stretched, extending her arms and yawning extravagantly. Then she hunched her shoulders up quickly, shook her hair back and leaned forward, con-centrating. 'My boyfriend's dad says I'm lucky. Free as a bird, he says. Which is true, in some ways I am. Anyway.' She shook her head again, letting her red curls tumble around her shoulders. 'I like it here best. If it was up to me, I'd sleep here. That's why I come here. I've been coming here since I was a kid, probably know these woods better than any houses.' She laughed again. 'I love the trees, the bracken, the wetness that's held here. That's why I used to come here. To feel all green.'

   She looked around, at the oak trees stretching

overhead, holding us so carefully, so safely, beneath their branches, the flecks of bark and leaves, the springy wall of bracken on the outer edge of the clearing, as if this was a space created just for us. Underfoot, the ground felt soft, the leaf mould almost like a humid carpet.

We sat together in the silence, and I thought of what the girl had said. If it was up to me, I too would like to lie down on the ground, which smelt all cosy, and stare up at the pattern of leaves which flattened and criss-crossed one another, a jigsaw of different greens marked with sharp little diamonds of white where the light pierced through.

Somewhere behind us, I heard the two men I'd seen earlier laughing, and then the metallic cackle of a chain-saw firing up.

The girl stood up, stamping and brushing herself down, coiling her hair into a knot at the back of her neck and stuffing her hands into her hoodie.

'My name's Jade, by the way. No chance of a lift back to Faringdon, is there?'

I was thinking of Jade later, as I slowed on the bridge just before home, and a man crossed the wide verge in front of the field. His straight, silver-grey hair fell below his ears, and he wore a neat backpack and heavy shoes. He lifted one hand, gesturing to me to stop, and I slowed right down, pulling in opposite the wicket gate into the field.

'Is this your home?' he asked, tipping his head towards the railway track and then the space of the field beyond it. I nodded. He'd walked from the far side of

Wantage, close to Didcot, he told me, and was looking
for a place to sleep. Did I have space? Yes, there was
space, plenty of space, I said, I would show him. Even
though the ground squelched as we walked into the
field, water sitting in some of the lower areas where the
ridge and furrow fell, there was certainly more space
than we could ever need.

Walking beside him as we crossed into the wide-open
plain of the field, I could sense him exhaling as he
smiled. 'Magnificent,' he said brightly. Beyond us, the
Ridgeway and the hill revealed themselves as a patchwork of bright green stitched through with the darker
greens of hedge lines which edged up to clumps of trees
mottled all over the incline. 'This is perfect,' he said. He
told me he was researching theories of extinction by
walking ancient routes and tracks across Oxfordshire,
Berkshire and Wiltshire, to trace the vibrations of
energy in those paths, and that this 'research, understanding and work', as he called it, had brought him to
the Ridgeway. 'In the meantime, I need a place to sleep,
and someone suggested you might be open to people
passing through. That's what they said in the village. I
spoke to a woman driving a truck and she said you
might be a place to try. So here I am. Just a space for a
fire, space to pitch a tent, not more than a few feet
squared. There I will continue my research, understanding and work while I sleep, since this is the first
place here beneath the hill. Would you mind?'

I shook my head, told him of course not, I would
love him to stay here; and as I spoke, I wondered if his
research, understanding and work might overlap in
some way with Danny's preoccupation with vibrations

and extinction. For a second, I considered messaging him, so that these two men could compare the things that mattered to them, but first I needed to show the man, this camper with his serious project, the tap in the field, and direct him to the higher ground where there might be a patch that wasn't sodden and damp. 'Oh, yes, this is perfect,' he repeated, tapping the air with the flat of his hand at waist height, as if patting a table. 'Just here is smashing.' He pulled his rucksack from his back and looked again towards the horizon. The mid-afternoon winter light was thin and pale, and I could hear the twitter and chatter of crows gathering as they cawed amongst big clumps of mistletoe balled in the high branches of the copse on the far side of the field, right up in the top of the trees where the light got in.

'This landscape. This is a magnificent place. A sacred place. You're very lucky to call this home, you know that?' he said, without taking his eyes off the horizon, and I nodded, murmuring, 'Yes, yes, I really do.'

It wasn't yet dark when, later that evening, Evangeline put a book out on the kitchen table and asked if she could use my computer. Her project, she told me, was to research the meaning of a certain colour.

'Green. I want to look up different shades of green, and find out what they mean,' she said, and as she did so, Jade stepped back into my mind. I remembered the quick smile she'd given me as she leant down, resting on the car window, while I punched my number into her phone. I wasn't sure what I could really do, but if nothing else we could keep in touch.

'Thanks ever so much for the lift,' she'd said. 'And for

listening. Not being funny, but I wasn't sure about you when you first sat down. But it was nice, chatting. I hadn't really thought about it all so much, where I'm going next and all, until you asked.' She'd pulled her hood up and grinned at me, her pale features glowing translucent, her big green eyes framed by her red curls. 'I reckon I'll go to Bristol probably. My brother's there. He'd put me up for a bit. He's a chef in a pub. I could stay on his couch. You never know, he might have work in the pub. I've got other mates, down in Southampton too. Could head there. Or Devon, my mum's sister is there, I could go that way.' She shrugged and grinned. 'Anyway, there I go, living the dream.' She'd turned, smiled quickly, then vanished through a wooden door in a fence beside the back of a house.

'Green is the symbol of vitality and fertility, also of healing, rest and security.' Evangeline's voice interrupted my thoughts as she read from a website about colours. I picked up one of the green pencils she'd lined up on the table and coloured a corner of one of the pieces of printer paper lying beside them. We scrolled around. 'Viridescent' means slightly green, from the Latin *viridis*, a weaker colour than green that was vivid and verdant. 'Celadon' was the name of a character in a French novel by Honoré d'Urfé, but also a Chinese word to describe a translucent pale-green glaze used in porcelain-making. 'Emerald' was first used by Shakespeare, Evangeline read on, stumbling over a Latin word, *viriditas*, so I pulled the computer towards me and ran my eyes over a paragraph describing the philosophy of Benedictine abbess, mystic, philosopher, writer and visionary Saint Hildegard, who lived in Germany in the twelfth century. Her philosophy of *viriditas* related to the idea of engaging with the living force of creation, and the idea that greenness, freshness, vitality was essential as a creative force in a life lived well. I pushed the computer back to Evangeline, took a thick green felt tip and wrote *VIRIDITAS* in broad strokes all over the back of my piece of paper.

We chose more pencils, and felt tips too, both of us colouring in patches. 'Chartreuse' came from the greenish-yellow hue of the liqueur invented by Carthusian French monks. 'Paris green' came from a toxic powder used to kill rats in Paris, but 'Brunswick green' was from the pigments formed in copper compounds, and named after the city in Germany where it was first made. Then there was 'Hooker's green', named after the botanical illustrator William Hooker, who created it by mixing bright Prussian blue and a deep yellow called gamboge. But the green I liked best was 'harlequin', a shade falling close to 'chartreuse' on the colour wheel, but which also referred to the Old French meaning, of a malevolent spirit.

As Evangeline read, I coloured, blending different shades of green into one another, listening to her sweet and bright voice, stumbling sometimes over some of the words, but reading slowly and clearly through the colours. When the paper was almost covered, I remembered the sound of Jade's voice as she recounted her own movements through this little patch of landscape we had both called home. I sat back in my chair, admiring the paper so pleasingly coloured with so much green. I felt sleepy, remembering that urge I'd had to lie down on the damp earth, under the bower of the last of the green leaves of the beech trees of Badbury Clump, and remembered, too, the copper sheen of Jade's curls, the way she shrugged and shivered when she spoke, so completely untethered, free as a bird, as she had said, and so full of *viriditas*.

'Jade,' I said to Evangeline, leaning forward, pulling my daughter back into focus. 'What does jade green symbolize?'

'Jade,' Evangeline read, 'symbolizes serenity, harmony and balance. It's a colour that those who are indecisive or directionless should keep close to them.'

The camper was there, later, beside his small fire, when I picked my way back through the thick, ink darkness, holding up my phone as a glow-in-the-dark guide through the wet grass. He'd pulled one of Jimmy's pallets from the far side of the field and was sitting beside the darting firelight, his hood pulled up. A pan of water was balanced on two stones beside the fire, and by the light of the flames I could see him carefully stirring a packet of instant noodles in a plastic cup.

'Do you mind if I eat now?' he said, and I shook my head.

'Of course not,' I replied, regretting not having thought to bring him one of the pork chops I'd cooked for the children's supper. Instead, I'd brought him two cans of cider I'd found in the larder, but he quickly put his hands up when I offered them to him and said very kind, but he wouldn't as he hadn't drunk a drop for thirteen years and his body preferred it that way.

'You've a nice set-up here,' I said, crouching down beside the fire, holding my palms out to the heat and nodding at the warm yellow light glowing from the torch hanging in his tent.

He glanced up from his noodles and said indeed, indeed. 'Not too cold, is it, either, for this time of year. Not cold at all, as long as it's not raining.'

He told me that he often walked straight out of his home into the landscape of the south of England, so that he could inhabit it more fully and with an intent that wasn't possible when he was in his house. He said he'd like to live here very much indeed, but he lived in Reading, working as an engineer in a water supply facility, a job he'd had since he was a much younger man. He didn't have a car, he told me, and I agreed that it wasn't a very practical place to live without a car, since there were very few buses and the nearest train almost three-quarters of an hour's drive away.

'But I like to be able to come out here, to camp, to stay the night. Sleep on the land. Just to be close to it. But it's very hard to find places for that. People don't want you on their land. Always assume the worst. Which is a shame because, for us humans, being close to the land opens something fundamental within which might otherwise remain closed. Although, of course, a few bad apples spoil it for everyone. I won't leave litter or gates undone. I'm not a vagabond or thief. I'm not a landowner or a farmer either. Just to be here, it means the world.' The fire crackled, and across the other side of the field a train rushed past my house, the violent speed cutting through the silence, taking something of the feeling of the distance and darkness of the night with it. 'It's very pleasant to be here,' he went on, 'even in winter like this, and even with a train so close. I shall certainly take this with me when I go back to Reading. The feeling of the hill and the night, the field and the stillness of it. It's very pleasant.'

I sat with him for a little longer. Somewhere far away a fox barked, that short, choking, dry sound of movement in the dark. I liked the smell of the fire, the reassuring deep glow of the lit orange stumps of sticks as they burned down a little. As the night thickened, I pulled the hood of my long puffer jacket up around me. On the far side of the field, where the hedge line ran closest to the wood, the distant sound of an owl suddenly filled a small pocket of the night sky, and we both turned, looking behind us towards the sound.

'Sitting under a dark sky like this, it always gets me thinking of something,' he said as he put the cup he'd been eating his noodles from upside down on the grass, wiping the fork neatly beside it. He brushed his hands together and then gestured upwards, as if putting his palms out to test for falling rain. 'These fields and this land. It's the same place where our ancestors walked, but it would be almost unrecognizable to them now. If they saw it they might not know it, because the tanglewood has all gone, replaced by houses, so many houses, and the fields with the barriers made by hedge lines and strong metal gateways. I often wonder what they might make of that change. But look up,' he said, gesturing upwards with his palms, to the sky, which was pierced with the yellow-white dots of stars stretched like a canvas above us. 'Look up, and the night sky is unchanged. If you're lucky enough to live in a place as dark as this, the stars and the night you see now are the same as they have ever been. That's a truly marvellous thought, isn't it? The stars are unchanged, and so the ancient lives on with us in the present. When we are long, long gone, the same sky will sit above this beautiful field, just as it does now. Time rolls on and on and things remain unchanged.' He fell quiet, but I nodded at him silently in the dark. Then, after a bit, the night was getting colder, so I said goodnight and left him to his little lit-up tent, and the warmth of his campfire.

Early the next morning, when I walked through the field to take him some milk and teabags, the man and his tent were gone, leaving a small, black circle of earth where his fire had been. It vanished within days, covered by a mottled patch of thin winter grass.

Sometime in late January, I caught an early train to London to meet Pete and we stood in a queue for an hour outside the American Embassy. There were vigorous security checks but eventually we filed into a huge hall with perhaps a hundred other people, our hushed voices swallowed by the high, shiny walls of white marble surrounding us. The space was like a modern cathedral, every line of the walls and staircases sharp and perpendicular, light flooding through tall windows, as if we were standing inside a transparent glass box. An electronic counter called people forward when it was their turn. We tried to chat as we waited, but both of us were distracted. I had to keep swallowing as I watched other people around me: a couple with three children looking exhausted, a single woman carrying a well-organized handbag and a cup of coffee, a man wearing a puffy black leather bomber jacket who stood stock-still, staring ahead until his number was called. So many stories and lives contained within this huge space.

When we were called, we both stood in front of a Perspex screen separating us from a man with very neat, short dark hair and a strong American accent. His consular uniform was sharply pressed, not a crease out of place. He fired questions at Pete, about his work, his intentions in America, his plans for the next five years, and after each answer the man ran his eyes intently over the computer screen beside him, clicking between multiple documents as he also checked paper birth certificates, our marriage certificate, signed photographs, more forms. I felt my hands sweating, the sharp, insistent click click click of his mouse inside my head, as if that was the loudest sound in the room. He paused, searching through more documents, frowning as if something was wrong, then nodded slightly as he pushed some papers back at us under the screen.

'You need to take these documents to the far end at the right, to be stamped,' he said. Then he made eye contact with Pete, and then me, for the first time. 'Your visa has been approved. Congratulations, and welcome to America.'

# Chapter 9

It was as cold as bone for the rest of January and long into February after that. The sky turned white, and the dark, blackish green of the winter grass frosted like crystal which glistened and shimmered, each tiny glass stem shattering underfoot as I barrowed hay out to the horses. They pawed at the frozen ground, impatient as I scattered the feed in separate piles, their warm breath melting spots of ice as they nuzzled their soft noses into the hay. Beneath their winter coats, my dun mare Mavis and the Blagdon grey Sexy Legs were thickening out, their bellies growing rounder. In the cold, I'd pull my glove off to run my hand around their outline, imagining the babies growing silently deep, deep inside them.

One day I walked into the middle of the little pond. It had been ravaged by drought in summer but was now frozen solid enough for me to edge slowly on to it. From inside the ice I heard a sound like a deep, ancient groan, a creaking as I shuffled tentatively across, the dogs watching me, Pablo with his head on one side, but the ice didn't give. Even if it had, I knew the water was no more than knee-deep. The willow, whose roots had appeared like a tangled ball of bones in the summer, was now submerged, as if up to the neck, in rock-hard ice which gripped the curving trunk of the tree. Some truncated branches, which had fallen into the water over the winter, now emerged from the ice like the tentacles of a wild being lashing to get out but held stock-still. Ice sat on the horses' buckets too, as solid as thick blocks of concrete that no amount of stamping in leather boots would break. Sometimes I carried a kettle out to the field with me, and I left a tiny trickle of water running from the blue pipe, to try to stop it freezing solid. It worked for a few days, until the temperature plummeted overnight to minus nine, then minus eleven. One morning, Sally stopped in her white truck as I barrowed plastic canisters of water out to the field. It wasn't yet seven a.m., and the children were still sleeping. I was grateful to stop on the bridge to chat with her, enjoying the smell of her cigarette, the jingle of her radio, her always-bright smile. Her shiny blonde hair was pulled on top of her head, the bright pink of her sweatshirt peeking out from a bomber jacket zipped up tight against the cold.

'Hard work right now,' she said, nodding at the water canisters. 'Everyone on Instagram keeps saying how beautiful it is, with all their pretty pictures, but when you've got horses to water, this weather is no joke.' I batted away her offer to help me lug the water out to the field. She had half a dozen mares of her own to water in the next village anyway, and then she asked if there was any news on that American move? I bit my lip and looked down, kicking the edge of her tyre because I felt uncomfortable telling her I was going. I felt guilty to be leaving and Sally was the person I'd miss the most.

'Yes,' I said, 'it's come through. Bit of a shock, to be honest, I was still getting my head around it. Moving to America is the last thing I expected to be doing right now. And I'm going to miss everyone so much.'

'I think it's exciting,' she replied. 'I'd do anything to be going out there – not for the cities, mind, but to see those massive American landscapes. Just think of that. But it's a big, big move, it's not surprising you feel weird about it. We'll all miss you. And the kids. We'll miss you a lot. I'm not sure I could do it myself, but good luck to you.' She smiled, her eyes crinkling at the sides, her cheeks flushed with the hours she spent outside, every day, tending her horses. She drew heavily on her cigarette as I glanced up and stamped a bit. 'You'll be back, though, won't you? Don't tell me you're leaving us for ever, are you?'

No, I could tell her, we were not leaving for ever. As it turned out, Aaron was right, and there was another way. Because over the course of that winter, while holding the image of home in our hands for so long, turning it over and over, looking at it in half light and darkness and bright daylight, leaning down to squint at it close up, pulling away to see it from a distance, spread it right out to get a big picture while also looking at the smaller details, it became quietly clear that selling up and leaving permanently was too final for Pete, too. For so long, we'd been looking at the future as if through a telescope that was always slightly out of focus. When

we walked out of the American Embassy, both completely silent with shock, the lens suddenly came into
focus, startling us both with its clarity, encircling an
image of us standing, for the first time in many years,
very close together. The sense of straining against one
another ended as we walked down the steps, and part of
me felt, You've won, Pete. You've won, and I'll go with
you, wherever you take me.

During the last weeks of the winter, when Pete was
at home for a few days, we found moments to go out to
the field together, walking out alone after the children
were at school, to talk about how we might make the
logistics of a new life in America work. Sometimes I felt
like we were engineers, trying to build a machine with
many complicated moving parts, trying this plan, then
that one, talking and talking and talking to try to fit
the pieces of our life and our children's lives together.
We still argued a lot, of course. We often shouted at
each other, and we swore, or one of us would storm off
to the far side of the field saying the other was being
ridiculous and unreasonable. But then we always walked
back towards one another to fix the temporary crumple
we'd made in our relationship. This part of our marriage was teaching us both how to put together the
pieces of our life without forcing them so much that
they fractured or broke.

And we both recognized that a permanent move to
America might shatter something sacred at the heart of
our family life. Neither of us wanted to let go, and renting rather than selling our house meant we could return.
I also like to think that the field worked its green mag-
netism on Pete; it was, after all, the space he said he

missed most when he was away, more than the house itself. Fate intervened, too. That red-brick house, whose face had sent me up on to the hill at dawn last summer as it blinked inside my head, came back into view. Sometimes the pieces of life fall into place in the most unexpected ways: Sylvia called Pete and told him the owner of the house had decided he, too, did not want to sell the place that had been a family home to his children when they were younger. Instead, he wanted to rent it to another family, to enjoy as much as he had.

In March, two months after our visa was approved, Pete moved into the red-brick house. And four weeks after that, I stood in the kitchen at home, running my eyes over the essential layers of life contained in that room, making decisions about what I could pack up back home to send in a cargo ship across the Atlantic.

'I want it to feel as much like home as we can make it, when you and the kids arrive in August,' Pete said, one evening when we were talking on the phone, late, as usual, when he was in Washington. Behind him, the muted outline of another hotel room had been replaced by a background that was becoming familiar now. As he moved around the house, I could make out the kitchen cupboards which would soon be full of our plates, the bright-green curtains in the bedroom where Lester would sleep, the yellow-and-blue embroidered chair that the owner had left in the sitting room, as his kids had liked it and he thought ours might too. Pete was starting to know the city well; he'd found school places for the children, so could chat with the boys about the big, friendly elementary school where they would start in the autumn, and help Evangeline prepare for a bigger move, to junior high. He'd found a dance school within walking distance for her and Lester, and a basketball club for Dash. He'd been right: it was an adventure, an exciting, funny, strange adventure. And then he said, 'I don't think it will ever actually be home, here in Washington, for us as a family. I respect those people whose home it really is, who belong here, who really know it, and I love being here. I love being in Washington, but the Ridgeway, the field, I see why that will always be home to us together.'

I'd been sitting up on the bed as we spoke, pulling at the fraying edge of my blue pyjamas, but when he said this I flopped backwards on to the duvet, all the air taken from my chest. Until that moment, I'd felt a tremendous pressure to create a sense of emotional permanence for our family in America. But I was also certain it wasn't something I'd ever truly feel. And hearing this said aloud by Pete liberated me. It freed me to look forward to the idea of enjoying it as an adventure, rather than a trap that would shut me in and take me away from where real home was.

I thought of this as I looked around the kitchen, reaching for things to take with us that would sprinkle a sense of home over our new house in America. We hoped what we shipped would arrive just before the children and I flew out on 1st August, after school had broken up. Moving big pieces of furniture was expensive, and anyway, sofas were simply sofas. Beds could be bought easily. But layered on top were parts of home we could peel away and take to the house in Washington, whose pale-grey walls and cool, empty interior was

just waiting for the colour of our shared life to be plastered upon it.

I walked through the house, unhooking fifty-five
pictures from the walls. The hall filled up with frames:
a painting of moonlight a friend had done for Lester;
another I'd bought with Nell, of a horse in front of may
blossom; some oil paintings of landscapes and kitchen
scenes I'd found in a local auction house; wobbly drawings the children had done that I'd glorified in frames;
embroideries bought from charity shops; photographs
of people I loved. I lifted rugs from bedrooms, shaking
dog hairs out of the windows, squashing them into neat
squares and stacking them alongside a vivid pink throw
pulled straight from the kitchen sofa, a favourite picnic
blanket, bedspreads from the children's rooms, and a
beloved embroidery usually on our bed, bought from a
seamstress I met on Instagram, with a dazzling image of
the White Horse cut out in lace and overlaid on green
velvet. I trailed backwards and forwards through the
house, plucking favourite anthologies of poetry and
unread novels from shelves. I wrapped newspaper
around a pile of plates decorated with a rose pattern,
bought with my stepmother one holiday in France,
nestling them inside a big cardboard removals box
alongside Evangeline's doll's house, packed beside a box
of Lego and one tiny tin of Pokémon cards that Lester
couldn't live without. I packed a collection of ceramic
Madonnas I'd bought in Seville and Lourdes, and a gold
lustre jug I'd found at a gypsy horse fair in Gloucester-
shire. For the first time, I felt I truly understood why
pioneer women packed their precious dinner sets in the

back of wagons when they headed out west with their children.

Finally, the only piece of furniture we chose was my mother's kitchen table. It was Pete's idea, and he insisted we take it. With a thick grain and sturdy legs, she'd bought it as a young bride in Cambridgeshire when she married her first husband. The table is marked with some compass points of graffiti my eldest brother and sister left on it as children, and I'd sat around that table with some of the people I love the best, during all the most important moments of my life. After my mother's accident, our house at Minety was sold, and for a while Nell had the table in her home, until she passed it to me. It made me and Dash laugh, to think of it bobbing across the Atlantic. 'When you say that, I think of it floating upside down like a boat across the sea with its legs in the air,' he said.

That evening, I sent Pete photographs of these pieces being loaded into the removal van in the yard. And after I'd moved the garden table into the kitchen, refilling the blank spaces on the walls with a mismatched selection of other pictures taken from upstairs, I felt a strangely exhilarating sense of relief, as if I'd just stepped out of very cold water.

Visualizing leaving, and then making that happen, was much easier once we knew for certain that we would return. I'd found it simply impossible to imagine leaving Jimmy and Dolly behind, but while there were practicalities to organize if we left for a couple of years, there was an emotional impermanence to the plans that I could cope with. And as I started packing up our life,

I saw that their lives were changing too. Jimmy was flourishing, away in Manchester, and when Dolly was offered a place at university, in a much smaller city, more pieces of the jigsaw fell into place. That trip I'd taken back to Minety had shown me that my fate was not that of my mother. I was not snatching home away from Jimmy and Dolly in a permanent way, simply readjusting it slightly, for a few years. Jimmy had all those friends he could stay with in England during the holidays, if he wanted to, but Dolly was excited at the prospect of long visits to America.

We couldn't take all the animals. Pablo, who was a faithful friend to Dash especially, and slept in his bed every night, would come with us, but it was impossible to take three dogs to a house in the city. Instead, we arranged for the other two, Cracker and Stow, to go to foster homes, with my uncle and with a friend, for a couple of years, with the promise of returning when we did. The ginger cats would go to another friend, but could also return later. I found it much harder to imagine where the horses would find homes. Sexy Legs and Mavis were due to have their foals in the early summer and even trying to envisage selling them was painful. Solstice was growing into a beautiful dun-and-white cob. I didn't know how to do it and so, for a while, I just closed my eyes to it.

Around this time, in the late spring, I was invited to contribute to a podcast. I was asked to talk about what was sacred to me, in relation to the values I tried to live by. I liked this question, and the day before the recording, as I tramped around the edge of the field, enjoying the watery squelch of wading through big puddles where the water was deepest, I turned it over in my head. After the cold, white winter, the hedgerows around the field were turning a sharper green, hawthorn leaves starting to unfurl, with the white tips of buds tentatively appearing. In the shorter grass below, clusters of bright-yellow celandine created a vivid dash of colour amongst the deep, green grass. Evangeline had said they were so bright, they reminded her of tiny, tiny fluorescent jackets. This made me smile, thinking of that which was sacred, looking up to the lip of Uffington Castle and the Ridgeway. As I walked around the field, I could just make out the narrow road which snaked up the hill, between Dragon Hill and the White Horse. It wasn't always so, but when the sun hit it in a certain direction it resembled the pale grey of a distant stream rushing straight down the hill. Sometimes, at night, I'd see lights on the Ridgeway, strange and dazzling as they moved around on the felt-tip-black crest, where there was no road. But there were no lights now, just the reassuringly familiar long, bumpy outline of the hill, so upright in relief against the flat land of the vale below. I paused to look at it again, putting my head slightly to one side, enjoying the way I could find, in the outline, the shape a huge human being might make, shoulders protruding, lying on one side. I'd first recognized this when I'd walked into the field two years ago, and once I'd seen it, it was always there: the hill was like a giant figure lying down, and if that figure stood up it would break the hill open and fill the entire skyline. Even on a warm day, as spring slowly unfurled, the idea of that made me shiver inside.

Because the podcast was loosely based around ideas

of faith and belief, I was uncertain whether I should talk about God, and what I did or did not believe in, since that was different from things that I considered sacred. Because when I thought about what was sacred in my life, I thought about God a lot less than I thought about my relationships with my dead mother and my dead sister, and how those sacred bonds were represented by wet green fields, by the pale clay lying so sticky under my boots, by the blackthorn which would soon arrive, by the nettles growing so thick near the gate, by my relationship with the scruffy, hairy horses who followed me across the field, knots in their mane, pushing at my elbow with their soft muzzles. Could I talk about these things on a podcast about things that were sacred? Could I talk about the fallen branches of a willow in a murky pond with dead nettles growing at its throat, or the loops of baggy barbed wire red with rust in a wet field edged by black hedges thick with may blossom and a ditch throbbing with the huge yolk-yellow heads of kingcups? Could I tell the host about the smell of leaf mould and ivy in a woodland where the beech branches were so thick overhead they cut out any chance of light? Would I be allowed to talk about the quiet way a horse moves as it walks through strings of finest cobwebs in wet spring grass, and the exact way the movement of that horse's head and ears really made me feel? Was there space to talk about the words of different poems which contained my life, or the special place where I carried the people who were gone, like a precious talisman inside me? And could I describe my love for these things as the yearning for home I'd held inside since I was very small, like fluid that filled me up from the tips of my toes to the top of my head, so that my body was just a vessel to contain it?

I lingered as I walked back across the field. It was dusk, and in the taller oak trees on the hedge line, a cluster of rooks were flapping about with twigs in their beaks, tending to a nest. In the shorter grass, on the tops of the ridge and furrow, a patchwork of different col- oured moss had settled, like soft, vibrant blankets. And everywhere was the chatter and busyness of blackbirds, flustering around with their mates. Behind me, Sexy Legs and Mavis had tailed off towards the pond, drop- ping their heads and working their way silently through the longer grass as the darkness thickened. My connec- tion to these beloved beings and things was what was sacred to me, and this landscape where we had slowly created a home was the place that held them all. But I realized, too, that this yearning, which represented everything that mattered most to me, was a feeling as much as a place, and I'd probably always carry it with me wherever I was. That knowledge was liberating, but it didn't fix my problem about what to do with the mares.

I slammed the wicket gate behind me, then walked back across the bridge. On the bend, just before the house, a truck slowed down. It was Luke and Kat, with all their boys bouncing around in the back seat. 'Hello, Clover, hello, Clover, is Dash anywhere near by?' said their eldest, Ryan, poking his head out of the window, his dark mouse eyes shining.

'All right?' Luke grinned at me. I leant up against the truck, my elbow on the window as we chatted for a bit. They'd come from a neighbouring village, where they'd been looking at a paddock to rent for the three ponies they kept for their kids. They were always running out of grazing, but the paddock opened on to the main road. 'The traffic's deadly, that part of the Stanford Road. We'll keep looking. It was too expensive anyway. Silly money they were asking for it.'

I told them about packing up bits of the house to ship to America. Luke whistled.

'That's a big move. A big thing to move your whole family, 'specially from somewhere like this,' he said. 'I've got some respect for Pete, making that happen for you all. Think you might end up staying there? For ever, like?'

I shook my head. I told them I was certain we would come home. I told them about having found foster homes for the cats and dogs. 'It's the horses I'm struggling with. I can't sell Mavis and Sexy Legs, or Solstice. I just can't do it,' I said. Then Kat leant forward in the cab.

'We could help you. We could keep an eye on them for you. We drive past here every day anyway.' She smiled brightly. In the verges all around, the cow parsley was gradually starting to appear, later this year than it had been for a while, because of the cold days. It would be another couple of weeks, into May, before the verges along every road would turn to the white froth of cow parsley heads growing everywhere. Behind me, I heard the whoosh of a train approaching, other lives rushing on to new places. I looked down and quickly back up at her. It all made sense.

'Would you do that? Really?'

'Of course,' she replied. 'What are friends for, if we can't help each other out?'

And as we chatted, another piece of the puzzle

arranged itself, revealing a very pleasing picture. Luke and Kat would move their ponies into the field. It would mean they could halt their endless hunt for grazing, and I could keep another thing that was sacred to me.

One afternoon in late April, I was waiting for Dolly in Faringdon. I was early, looking for somewhere to waste an hour, but everything was closed, even the bookie's, even the charity shop. On the far corner of the square, a solitary light shone in a fugged-up window. I'd noticed the window before, and thought it was an exercise studio, with rooms for yoga and maybe massage, but I was curious, as I could make out a figure moving behind the misty glass in the appealing glow of yellow light.

I ran across the grey town square, past a couple of teenagers sitting on a doorstep staring at their phones, and pushed open the shop door. Suddenly there was colour everywhere, like an old and intricate fan being dropped open. I blinked in the dazzle of purple, orange, yellow, green and indigo light. It was like stepping inside a jewelled box – a shop where every inch was crammed with cushions, fabrics, bags, clothes, picture frames and shelves holding miniature mirrored boxes, patterned copper water bottles, painted candlesticks, tiny ornaments and glass boxes, shimmering gold earrings, necklaces and delicate, chained bracelets. The shop smelt unfamiliar, nothing like the dark smell of the earth and cold spring grass that was always with me in the field. This was rich, almost hypnotic; smoky and scented. Coloured plates with glass domes covered a wooden counter, protecting small cakes with white frosting studded with scattered pistachio nuts and dried rose petals.

'Come in, please, you are welcome,' a voice said, and the figure I'd seen outlined from across the square transformed into a man who now left the coloured blankets he was folding at the back of the shop, wedging them deftly on to a shelf above a rack of dresses and shirts covered with floral and paisley patterns. 'Come in, come in,' he said again, and gestured gently to a cushioned bench in the window. I asked him if it might be possible to get some tea, and as his accent moved up and down an unfamiliar scale, but with its very own lilting melody, he replied, 'Of course, of course. Darjeeling? And pistachio cake?' I nodded enthusiastically, noticing his t-shirt, which had a print pattern overlaid with the words *JUST GO WITH THE FLOW*.

I sat for a bit in the window seat, tapping away at my laptop, which looked grey and unnecessarily plastic against the hot colours of the shop.

'Here, would you like more hot tea? Another cup maybe?'

The man appeared next to me, smiling broadly, nodding to my cup. He had very bright eyes, thick black hair, and simply being in his presence made me feel at ease.

'I'm sorry, I didn't mean to let my tea grow cold,' I said. 'But it's so nice, sitting here in the window, and I was distracted.'

'I can see that. You look very busy. What are you writing?' he asked, gesturing to my laptop. I glanced down at the Word document I had open.

'Well, it's something I'm working on, about home. I'm writing about this area, the Ridgeway, and about what it might feel like to leave it, and to miss it.' I glanced back down at the screen, and then at the man's wide-open smile.

'Oh, home,' he said. 'Yes, home. That's a big question, isn't it? I can tell you about that certainly, because you can probably tell, I wasn't born here, or anywhere remotely near here, in fact.' He told me his name was Hari, as he pulled up a little stool beside the bench. 'My home – that is, my first home – is in southern India on the Tungabhadra River. It's a sacred place, called Hampi, and famous too, because there are many temples there, and stones. Big stones. Massive stones,' he said, gesturing wide with his arms. 'It's somewhat like Avebury, near here, do you know Avebury?' He paused, and I nodded quickly, so he went on. 'Well, Hampi is full of strange and beautiful stones, and like Avebury it's a place you just want to be close to, and many people want to be close to. It's very relaxing and it's so beautiful.' He talked quickly, his voice lilting upwards, not like the rounded accent of the downs, the echo of hills that softened Danny's voice, but more melodious, so that when he told me about the heat of the sun on the big stones of Hampi, and the sparkle of the river where he swam as a child, it was as if I could feel it too, for a few moments.

'Here, let me show you,' he said, reaching for my computer, tapping words into the search bar then pulling up pictures of temples, rocks, a green, verdant, vivid landscape. 'See?' he said. 'Great rocks everywhere, very, very ancient stones covering the landscape, which is green too, but the stones show everyone, beyond a moment of doubt, how very, very special Hampi is. That is my home.'

Together we scrolled through images on my computer, as Hari zoomed in on a temple he loved, showing me pictures of the village where he grew up. He told me that his grandmother first took him to Hampi when he was eleven, and he laughed, remembering how, on that first visit, more than the temples and the rocks, he was fascinated by the children he saw, of his age, selling postcards to tourists. 'I had never had any money, but I had never needed it either, living in a village. But after that time, I knew I wanted to learn English and I wanted to go and see some of those places on the postcards. From that time onwards, I knew I wanted to travel out from home, to leave home.' After that he worked very hard to perfect his English, even when his friends laughed at him, then worked as a guide around the temples at Hampi. He found that he liked meeting the tourists, and especially the backpackers.

'They were usually in their early twenties, and they were all looking for something. Searching and wanting something else. That was why they were in India. That was why they had left home, that yearning, that longing. I understood so well why they felt this way. They wanted to find something to change them on a spiritual level. They had a yearning, all of them, although sometimes they were not able to say what it was for. That's why they were all there, travelling half the way across the world, rather than staying in their own little town, in England or Australia. All of those travellers wanted to find what they were yearning for, as we all do,' said Hari, looking more serious, gesturing towards the window, and the almost-deserted town square.

Outside, it had started to drizzle and a light in the
Old Crown Inn opposite flickered. The bus from Swindon swept in: one lady pulling a shopping bag on wheels
alighted, and two teenagers climbed on before it
whooshed out of the square again, towards Oxford.

'It is my yearning that brought me here,' Hari said,
laughing softly. While he was working as a guide, he
met Carrie, who was running a small travel company
out of Faringdon, leading guided tours in India. 'You
could say that her longing took her to India.' Carrie had
two young daughters, and for two years they tried to
have a long-distance relationship. 'But we wanted to be
together. We needed to be together, not for short periods
of time but to live together, to have our lives together.'

He paused, crossing his arms and looking down at
the floor as he remembered this time. 'It was very difficult, at first. I arrived in the winter, several years ago. In
winter! You know how England is at that time, especially in the countryside. When we arrived in Faringdon
from Heathrow, I thought, my God, where are all the
people? Where are the leaves? Where is the life? It
seemed there were no people, no animals, no colours in
Faringdon, at all. It was very shocking, and I was confused. But a few days later, there was snow. That made
me so happy. I was so excited and happy because of this
snow. And suddenly it was all fascinating to be here,
although I was confused because I was not used to
people living so separately. And Carrie told me, she said
people live in a box here. And I wasn't sure I could ever
make my home here.'

Hari shook his head a little, remembering, and then
something passed across his features, a relief, and he

smiled. 'But when the spring came, I could see life changing all around me. When the blossom came out, I felt happier, and then everything was green and bright. It was more relaxing. But, you know, it was meeting people that changed the way I really felt about England.' He explained that the shop was just an exercise studio at first, but slowly he and Carrie expanded it. 'And then people would come in and we would talk, at first about the weather, because now, I see it, you can have four weathers in a single day. But even when we just talked about the rain or the sunshine, the energy changed, and things started to flow.'

He leaned back against the cushion propped on the window seat, smiling again as he remembered this time. And what did he miss, about India, I asked, pressing him onwards, since I was certain he was showing me something that mattered. He frowned, pushing the teaspoon from one side of the saucer to another, turning the cup around.

'I missed the temple, the people there and the flowers and incense. So, one day, I went to the church in the town, here in Faringdon. It was a few weeks after I had arrived, the weather had gone from snow to blossom, and I had been through such big changes, mentally and physically, leaving my home and making a new one here. I wanted to share that feeling with God and with a community. But when I got to the church, I was sad. There was no one there. Or just a few people. But what made me saddest was the idea that this ancient building was being lost. I could not help thinking of all the people who had got married there, or been buried there, or prayed, cried, lived around there. And that was so sad, that it was empty, because a church, and any building, needs energy and it needs people. A building, and stones, mean nothing on their own. It is the people that bring a place alive. All any of us are looking for is connection, isn't it? To be seen, to be understood. That is where our truest sense of belonging comes from.'

He told me how he created a temple in the flat he shared with Carrie, over the shop, and how the couple returned to Hampi at least once a year to buy the colourful fabrics, cushions, clothes and jewellery they sold in the shop.

'Now I have all the flowers and incense I need in my little temple in our home. But something happened for me when more people started coming to the shop. I made my own sense of home, right here, in this shop. Returning to Hampi is important for me, to go home, but Faringdon is my home too.'

I thanked him, telling him he had helped me more than he could know, and told him, quickly, about moving to America. How leaving our home had been a decision I'd found very hard to make. He listened, nodding in recognition, then stood up and went to a glass cabinet on the far wall, which was filled with delicate gold jewellery. Hari took something out and handed it to me.

'Here, take this,' he said. It was a small green pendant engraved with the coiled outline of a dragon. 'A gift. For you. It's jade. It will help you to feel more certain in your journey, so that you know the direction you are taking is the right one for this point in your life. It will help remind you there is nothing to be afraid of.'

I turned it over in my hand, thanking him, clasping

my hands around it and feeling the cool, green softness
of the stone which held the dragon in its form.

'There is something special about seeing your home
from a distance too. It makes you love it even more, you
understand,' he said brightly. 'I am not yearning for
anything now. Hampi will always be there for me. I
love it. But I love it here too. And it was the people,
here in Faringdon, who brought me home.'

It was a week later, and I had stopped at the Co-op so
that Evangeline could post some sweets and a card she
had made for her cousin, who had had a recent birthday. Ahead of me in the queue at the post-office counter, beside the till, was a woman wearing tight riding
jeans spattered with specks of mud. She was posting
several items to Australia. Each package had a long post-
code, which she read aloud like a numerical incantation
that would move it from there, inside the shop, all the
way across the world. I imagined the parcels leaving the
woman's hand to make a long journey to a completely
new land, like the Alfred Jewel moving across time, or
our kitchen table bobbing, legs up, across the Atlantic.
And as I listened to the numbers being read aloud, then
checked again and re-read, I realized I was staring quite
hard at the man behind the Perspex screen. He had dark
hair flicked across his face and spoke downwards, as if
dropping his words on to the ground. I could see his big
hands, reaching under the screen, and the quick way he
made eye contact with the woman, thanking her
politely as he took each package. His broad shoulders
completely obscured the tall shelves on the wall behind
the counter. He wore a black fleece zipped up to his

collar, which looked as if it had been washed many times, since it was faded from black to something lighter, more like the colour of dusk. As I watched him speaking with the woman, I shifted from one foot to the other, and a thought settled in my head; that I had seen him, or an impression of him, in another place.

After the Australian packages had been magicked away, and the woman peeled off, thanking the man profusely as they exchanged smiles, I moved forward, my eyes on his face as I tried to place him. I passed the parcel for the cousin under the Perspex barrier and he smoothed it out, then looked up at me quickly, his hair falling across his eye. He flicked his head sideways to make better eye contact.

'Sorry about this, but you need to add your own address to the back of the parcel,' he said, big dark eyes looking down at me as he pushed a pen under the screen. I scribbled my address on the package and he took it back, running his finger under the words I'd written as he typed them into his computer to print out a postage label. And when he saw the name of my village, he smiled broadly.

'I know it. Know it well. Beside the railway?' he asked, and I nodded.

'Yes, that's it,' I said. 'The railway runs right past our house.'

'I know that house. On the bend, beside the old schoolhouse? Great place for finding things there, trains and so on. Lovely spot.' Something shifted again inside me, as if everything inside me had been righted, and I almost gasped. 'Beautiful place, with the hill ahead of you. Uffington Castle, the White Horse, and the Ridgeway. I've spent a lot of time there, a lot of time. It's a place I often find myself.' I could feel my heart thudding as I smiled back at him, because I wanted to stay, and thank him, thank him so much for everything he had shown me, but there were people waiting, and he was suddenly brisk as he scanned the label.

'Now, is that cash or card? And a receipt. Would you like a receipt?'

I was walking back from checking the horses one evening when Danny's familiar white van approached on the bridge. He pulled on to the verge beside the gate, where buttercups rose as a spatter above the tall grass. A grey squirrel darted along an elder branch near the gate, where a flash of young green ivy was growing, and two magpies swooped down to the edge of the road on the other side of the bridge, pecking at the remains of a rabbit carcass left there the night before.

'Clover, you're just the person I wanted to talk to,' he said, killing the engine, then reaching for something small in his glove compartment. He got out and we chatted for a bit, both of us leaning against the railway bridge, as a train hurtled beneath us, deep within the cutting.

'Here, I wanted you to have this, to take to America. For luck. A talisman, maybe.' He held out his hand and in his palm was a small ingot of silver, about an inch long. 'Go on. Take it. It's for you,' he said.

I picked it up, turning the little silver lozenge, which felt cool and heavy between my fingers.

'It seemed a shame when you first said you were going,' he went on, 'but you've made the decision now and it's a brave one. Go out there and honour your relationship to Pete. It's a great thing. Good on you both. Make sure you come back, though. Look after that too.' He nodded to the piece of silver in my hand. 'It's no bad thing, putting your money in bullion. Shouldn't just rely on a piece of plastic in your wallet. That's what they want, you know. A cashless system. Don't let them. Keep hold of your sovereignty. Got to keep fighting back against it.' He dusted his hands together, and smiled. 'Honour the things that matter to you.'

I thought about that idea – honour the things that matter to you – as I lay in bed that night, with the cool green walls of our bedroom surrounding me. We would not be leaving for America until August, but I wanted to find a way to honour the landscape that had given me so much. I'd walk out into the field and on the Ridgeway many, many more times before we left, but I felt an urge to do something more significant. I remembered the crowds who gathered at Avebury for the solstice. It would be very easy to lazily mock the sects of druids who gathered there, looking vague while wearing papier-mâché crowns and carrying staffs, but I liked the way they established their connection to place through action. Through their dialogue with the elements, the stones and the landscape, they seemed to hold on to something – or at least attempt to hold on to something – that mattered. I needed to find a druid to talk to, and for a while I thought about going back to Avebury and hanging about at the Henge gift shop.

'Don't you know that all the druids live in West Sussex now?' my friend Kate said, while we were chatting on the phone one evening. I was leaning on the fence by the barn, watching a pair of pudgy wood pigeons flapping heavily in the taller branches of the willow tree beside the gate. 'I mean, I do know one, but he's a bit smug. He told me he'd had the Covid vaccine but didn't want his wife to know.' Overhead, the snap of wings was like the sound of someone suddenly clapping. Kate said she'd move to America immediately if she had the chance, but, reflecting on the vaccinated druid, we concluded that it was impossible to ever really know another person, even one you were married to. Life was essentially lonely, wherever you lived.

A few days later, staring into the glassy glow of my phone while sitting in Wantage waiting for Lester and Evangeline to finish their dance class, I found myself deep within the social-media feed of a druid who I soon realized lived three villages away. He was advertising a pilgrimage that weekend across the landscape of the White Horse. The cost was £47, which seemed expensive but would, I read, take in sacred places and secret springs, and involve song, prayer and ritual. Driving home, with Evangeline in the seat beside me chattering about jazz shoes, I felt that £47 was a reasonable price to pay for something that might help me finally untether, with meaning, from the landscape I was learning to say goodbye to.

That Sunday, I was holding Evangeline's hand as we stood on White Horse Hill with two dozen other pilgrims, each carrying a look of anticipation. Some were dressed in well-worn walking boots and anoraks, one woman wore a bright-purple puffer coat which was like a duvet zipped around her, head to foot, but another woman was dressed in a light-burgundy dress with a poncho over the top and wind chimes attached to the straps of her backpack. A woman in a long red skirt and a very tight black jacket wandered around the group, greeting familiar faces, while sipping from a Costa cup. The way the druid looked pleased me a great deal: he had very thick, curly, shoulder-length silver hair and he was wearing various shades of muddy-green, and open-toed walking sandals, despite the spring chill. He held firmly on to a staff made from twisted wood as he welcomed us into the group, and smiled all the time, as if constantly deep in an enlightening conversation. Beside him was another woman carrying a leather bag and wearing a thin crown of ivy on her long blonde hair, which sometimes blew across her fine features. She was an apothecary and told us that she was carrying oils we would be welcome to try when we got to the springs. The druid encouraged everyone to stand in a circle, holding hands, then told us all that the pilgrimage was an act of *intent*, and by committing to it we had all entered into the voyage together not just with intent, but with a *magical intent*. We should, if we were able, use this day to embrace that intersection, existing inside us all, between the mundane domesticity of the day-to-day, and our desire, as sentient beings, to find meaning in our lives.

'A pilgrimage is, in some ways, a place where being and nonbeing meet,' he said, his voice scattering in the wind that sliced across the hillside as his white curls whipped around his face. 'But today you have all the chance in the world to deeply feel and see and know everything you encounter. We all have cauldrons inside us that are out of kilter, and a pilgrimage is a way to turn these cauldrons the right way up. The hill, up here, is a good place to do that, as there is sovereignty in high places.'

When he said that, I thought of Danny's obsession with sovereignty, but as I did so a gust of wind cut through my jacket and I shivered, my whole body shaking, making the cauldrons inside me turn over again like fairground rides all out of control. The druid told us that our day-long pilgrimage would take us across White Horse Hill to Uffington Castle, then to Wayland's Smithy and home again, but that our voyage would be informed by visiting the springs which lay in the spot where, he said, the White Horse's hooves first fell when it jumped from the hill a long, long time ago. He smiled even more broadly as he said this. 'We will be touching time itself at the springs, since how you touch that water now, today, will affect the flow of it in the future. Put your hands, your feet, into these ancient springs, and you will be touching both the past, and now, and the future.'

I had walked on the White Horse many times, and I had slid down the Manger, but I had never even heard of the springs which lay further down in the valley, below the ripples of hillside left by the glacier, and further, still, than the flat land beneath the Manger where sheep grazed. At the crest of the hill, with the White Horse just above us, we dropped down, some people sliding along on their bums since the hill was so steep. I edged down, sometimes walking sideways so as not to fall, marvelling at the way Evangeline ran down the

slope, her hair loose around her shoulders, laughing
with the druid's daughter, a little girl with hair as curly
as her father's but coloured a rich auburn. As they ran,
they both threw their heads back with the confidence
that comes from a child-like certainty that the hill
would cushion them even if they fell.

The wind dropped as we reached the pancake-flat
land in the bottom of the Manger, which sits like a
green lake below the hill. The pilgrims gathered around
the druid, who encouraged us all to turn and look back
at the escarpment. When the melting water of the glacier retreated after the Last Ice Age, the druid said, that
same hill I could see from the field where I walked every
morning would have been bright white, the chalk freshly
exposed, before it turned to browner soil, and the wildwood, grass and heather gradually covered it. The
bright-green ripples were a permanent reminder of the
now-melted glacier: gone for thousands of years and
yet its presence was still there, in the mighty imprint it
left in the rumpled shape of the hillside.

Evangeline was beside me again, and holding her
hand I turned back to look at the high line of Uffington
Castle. Up above, a red kite wheeled around, the sharp
points of its tail piercing the sky, which was softening
from sharpest white to very pale blue. The wind had
fallen now, and thin rays of spring sunlight were forcing
their way across us, casting shadows amongst the pilgrims as we turned as a group to descend further, into
the tree line where the druid had pointed to the place
where the horse's hooves had fallen. The springs lay on
the far side of the narrow, fast road that snakes beneath
White Horse Hill, and after the pilgrims scattered in

groups of two or three across the road, we waded through waist-high grass, plunging down again into the damp, warm enclosure of the trees, clambering over a tangle of trunks and branches covered in the frizz of bright-green moss. Here, beneath the mottled canopy of leaves, I could make out the sparkle of the springs which ran so clear over a shallow chalk gravel bed, stems of mint fluttering in the water.

'Chalk streams contain an ancient magic which has always brought communities together,' the druid said. He explained that almost three-quarters of the chalk streams of the world are in southern England, producing this special, silky smooth and exceptionally clear water. The pilgrims were silent, crouching on the edge of the bank above the springs, or perched on logs, listening to the quietly reassuring sound of the ever-moving water. 'Chalk streams are the white blood cells of the body of England,' the druid added. 'These springs would have been part of the reason why people ever came here to make their homes underneath White Horse Hill. These springs were essential for life itself and represent some of the earliest impulses of human civilizations to come together.' He paused, crouching down and submerging his hands in the cold water. 'And you could say that these very springs are representative of the earth reaching out to enable people to feel a stronger sense of their shared humanity.' He looked up at us and laughed softly. 'That's all we are doing today, isn't it?'

The druid encouraged us to submerge our hands, our feet, any parts of ourselves that we could, in the cold, cold water. I stripped off my socks, rolled up my jeans and stepped into the grasp of the water, which hurt my ankles but felt so good too. Someone sang a song in Gaelic to Saint Brigid, who represented the start of spring, and the druid encouraged us to ritualize the moment with our own prayers or songs, as we saw fit. The pilgrims spread out around the edge of the water, some crouching right down beside it to splash their faces, holding their wrists under it, or submerging little crosses they had made from woven sticks and grass. The woman with long blonde hair who wore the crown of twisted ivy pulled some tiny vials of oil from her bag and went around the pilgrims offering drops to everyone who wanted them.

'Rub it on your face, your wrists,' she said gently, picking her way between people who held out their cupped hands or the gentle inside of their wrists to her. 'Or swallow it if you prefer. The oil contains gold, and we are all born with minute amounts of gold in our hearts,' she said. When she left a drop in my palm, I held it up to the light, examining the small golden globe of oil which sat there, before I licked my hand, swallowing it quickly. 'Consider this oil like the inner hammering of your heart, creating certainty and strength inside you,' she said. When she'd been around all the pilgrims, she took a small brass cup from her leather bag, lit the stub of a candle in it, then crumbled some herbs into it, crouching down beside the water so that a wispy trail of smoke snaked over the top of the cold, clear spring.

I had come prepared with my own sacred offering. Calling Evangeline to my side, I pulled a small red velvet pouch from my pocket, and from that we took the tiny, bright lock of my sister's hair, given to me three years before by the undertaker who had cared for her on her last night before she became part of the earth. The woman offered me the brass cup, where the flame burned bright, and I held the strands of my sister's hair to the heat, letting the gentle flame whisper through the fine blonde strands. The ashes from Nell's hair scattered into the clear, clear chalk water, as I let go of her, sending the last, precious physical part of her that I could touch back into this landscape which had formed us.

Afterwards we sat by the springs for a bit, surrounded by the quiet sounds of pilgrims' voices as they pulled socks back on and dried their hands, finding fallen tree trunks and ledges to perch on. People pulled sandwiches from their pockets, and water bottles and apples from backpacks. I shared a cheese sandwich and a packet of salt and vinegar crips with Evangeline, and when we finished we sat together for a bit. I squeezed her hand quickly three times, a silent signal she returned. *I love you.*

Slowly, the pilgrims started gathering cups and silver foil together, taking a last swig of water, finishing a final biscuit, as we prepared to ascend the hill, back up to the White Horse. The apothecary who'd administered the golden oil told us all that chalk was a substance she loved to work with.

'You probably know that chalk is calcium carbonate, but it's long been prized as an important and powerful substance which helps calm the fire in your nervous system,' she said, then explained she sometimes made tinctures from it, once she had pounded it to a fine powder, since its properties were deeply soothing to the human psyche. 'Chalk makes you feel safe. It makes you soften and feel calm. But be careful too,' she added, glancing up, motioning with her chin through the trees, in the direction of the hill. 'If you find yourself power-fully drawn to this landscape, or yearning for it when you are away from it, it's because the chalk is working on you. Chalk can be addictive.'

A pilgrimage, the druid had said, was to set out on a journey with magical intent. Perhaps, I thought, as we left the spring, wading back through the long grass, that was all that this journey had been about, although I hadn't seen it clearly, to start with, that early morning when I furiously ran up the hill, searching for some-thing. Running back across the fast road, then catching our breath in the broad expanse of the flat land beneath the steep rise of the hill, I remembered the sense of painful uprooting that the red-brick house had first cre-ated in my mind as the email containing its picture landed in my phone. It had made me frantic to find a clear definition of what my home really was.

We climbed the steep sides of Dragon Hill, pausing there as the blanket of the vale spread before us, the hedges and fields and woods knitted together with clumps of houses, the rising spire of Uffington church, the white prongs of the windfarm near Shrivenham and the hill at Faringdon, with its folly, and the tumbling blocks of Swindon edged by black flashes of solar panels, and the spread, further further further into the distance, of hills and plains and landscape and homes that were sacred to other people.

And as we ascended again, up the almost-vertical, verdant sides of White Horse Hill, then beyond that, towards the ramparts of Uffington Castle, the word pilgrimage chimed in my head, a little bell that rang there insistently. The search for home had taken me on a pilgrimage to the places that mattered most to me. I had not followed the track called the Ridgeway, or walked around the stones at Avebury, or sought out the lost village at Snap, or tried to understand Black Wantage, or circled Barbury Castle, or stomped through the stones at Piggledene and the Devil's Den, simply to enjoy the view. I had gone to these places to find meaning, and I had found it, although that meaning hadn't always been clear. Sometimes I'd gone to the Ridgeway, the stones, the White Horse, the long barrows or the little market town looking for a connection and seeking out a certain feeling, and had simply found some very old stones, or a cold, distant, muddy track, or a Greggs wrapper plastered to a wet pavement. But this did not mean my pilgrimage had failed. If anything, those moments when the landscape seemed emptiest and quietest or least fulfilling had been the most valuable. Because on those occasions, I'd been most aware that what was important to me was not in the grass and the stones, but inside me, in the memories that came to me when I was there.

Sharp spring sunlight was seeping across the green as we neared the top of the hill. In the distance the first dazzle of yellow of the returning oilseed rape had started to flood over the fields, and they would soon be turned into oceans of bright gold, as if the sun itself was trapped in the ground. Before we reached the wide expanse of the castle, and with the outline of the White Horse flat on the hill behind us, I left the well-worn path and

peeled away towards the longer grass, amongst the rabbit burrows. I turned around, my eyes focusing suddenly on the huge plain below me, stretching from
Wales to the edge of the Chilterns. I felt myself doing
what I often told the children to do when we walked
through the fields near home, or they ran between the
stones, which was drinking it all in, letting this landscape flood into my soul and simply settle there. Below
me, beyond the cluster of houses and the imposing
church that made up the village of Uffington, further
past the copse, I could make out the corner of our field,
and beyond that, the low, flat, white outline of our
home. It had been there all along.

Meaning, I realized, had only become clear because
of the way people had shown it to me: Aaron, hammering red-hot iron, and Danny holding so tight on to his
sovereignty; Cathy, with her strong, green oils, and the
man with his research, understanding and work, who'd
camped in the field; Jade, with her tumbling red hair
and lightly worn freedom, the man with the fox face
who seemed to understand it all, and the giant who had
returned to me again and again on the bridge. They'd
shown me what it meant to feel at home. And Hari had
been right: there was nothing to be afraid of, because
home would be a place I could recreate and share with
others. Home felt good in a certain place, but what
really gave it its warmth, as Hari had stated, was the
bonds between people.

Suddenly, high, high above me, a skylark tore into
the afternoon sky. It hovered overhead, moving into
the gentle breeze, its wings beating so fast it hung above
me, a flag of bright, sharp sound rippling over the

landscape. Below, the outline of the White Horse reminded me of the giant roll of time, the Mesolithic giving way to the Neolithic, the hunter-gatherers becoming farmers, the bright brilliance of the Bronze Age smelting into the hard black metals of the Iron Age, and society changing, evolving, breaking into smaller groups, into communities, into families, into home. Home had been created and recreated across thousands of years, evolving and reforming itself, just like the chalk, which had once been millions and billions of sea animals but could now be pounded into a fine white powder and used in a tincture. And perhaps the White Horse itself, so open to interpretation – a dragon, a horse, perhaps something else altogether – was the feeling of a horse, more than a horse itself.

'Mum! Come on, Mum!' Evangeline's shrill little voice pierced my thoughts. 'Come on, Mum. It's time to go home.' I turned towards her, waved to show her I was on my way, then stopped to pick up a small lump of chalk, the size of a hazelnut, squeezing its soft, round form in my palm. As I walked towards Evangeline, I felt sunlight on my face, and thought of what the apothecary had said, about chalk being an addictive substance. The skylark fluttered and sang above, and I squeezed the little chalk pebble in my hand, holding it tight, as Evangeline ran to meet me, her face lit up in the sun, her hair like long streamers in the evening light.

# Epilogue

I wasn't sure if I would ever see the giant again. After we had made the decision to leave, I thought he might not return to me or appear on the bridge again. I wasn't sure, but each time I'd seen him there I had always felt as if he was waiting for me. I went into the Co-op many times in the weeks before we left too, but I didn't see the tall man from the post office there either. It was very hot that summer, and sometimes, walking across the bridge as we went out into the field to check the foals, I'd tell the children about the very tall man in black who seemed like a giant, and ask them to look out for him for me. They would laugh at me like I was really silly, and run ahead, throwing handfuls of grass over the railway bridge, climbing over the wicket gate even while I told them to open it, not climb over it, as that way the hinges would break again. But after a while I realized that he'd never be there if the children were there, so I stopped telling them about him.

Slowly, the house was emptied. Books into boxes, pictures stripped from the walls, the layers of memory and ritual and home removed, packed away, but carefully, to be unpacked, Pete promised me, in a few years' time. On a damp, warm night in July, lots of our friends filled the kitchen, arriving in the house with drops of rain in their hair, jostling over paper bowls of chilli and laughing, embracing, celebrating friendship and love and time and the continuity of all these things. When it got dark, Jimmy and his boys, and Danny and his friend James, lit a bonfire in the field and turned up the speakers of a sound system, and the field and the night echoed with the proper loud techno vibrations of a rave.

Three days later, I went out alone to the field. I wanted to walk amongst the horses before spending another day surrounded by books and blankets and toys and pictures lying in messy piles, by charity-shop runs and to-do lists which were never finished, by packing boxes, black marker pens and gaffer tape. It was very warm as I walked out of the gate, along the last strip of concrete making up the track on the village green, and crossed over the railway bridge. Little white butterflies, with the faintest outline of green veins in their fragile wings, flitted and fell ahead of me, and I followed them, my eyes down as they dotted through the grass. When I looked up, by the edge of the bridge and just before I turned into the field, he was there.

'Didn't really think I'd leave without saying goodbye, did you?' he said softly, barely looking up, and I knew he didn't expect an answer. He wasn't standing, as I'd usually seen him, but sitting on the ground, leaning with his back against the bridge. His overshirt was a much lighter grey now, and the soles of his flat canvas shoes, laces untied, were worn very pale and thin. He brushed his hands in the light gravel and dust beside the edge of the verge, using his big forefinger to trace a curved figure-of-eight pattern.

And so I knelt down, and I told him that I had done what he'd said. I had gone to the ridge, and I had looked, as he had told me to, although for what I wasn't quite sure, but I had done as he had said I should and looked amongst the stones and the hills and the castles.

'I know you did it,' he said, his dark hair falling over his face again. 'I know you did it because I was there with you all along.' He paused. The tall grasses in the verge beside him shimmered in the morning light, and a very faint breeze sent tiny seeds of thistledown moving between us. It was quiet, no white vans passing, no dragon trains roaring past, so quiet that I could hear his deep and slow breathing. Then slowly, very slowly, he brushed his huge palms on the thin, pale, dark fabric of his trousers, pressed one hand to the ground and got to his feet. I looked right up at him towering above me, he was so tall, and then I stood up too. Behind him would be the ancient horizon of the Ridgeway, a tiny scrawl of white which was the chalk horse, and the sweet, precarious lip of Uffington Castle, but his shoulders were so broad he filled all the space around me. I looked up at him and watched his face as he asked me, 'And did you find what you went out to look for all the time?'

I nodded, realizing that what I had wanted when I first saw him was to feel connected to the earth, but what I understood I needed, now, more than ever, was to feel connected to love, to Pete. But I didn't need to say these things aloud, because he understood it anyway. Then he turned and walked towards the hillside, and for a moment, as the sunlight dazzled across the horizon, I was certain the green cracked open so that the giant could return to the Ridgeway, from where he came.

# Acknowledgements

For some time before I started writing this book, a thread of conversation ran between Pete and me about the question of where we should live for the next bit of our life. It was an idea which bounced between us but didn't take significant shape, since other bigger bits of life continually interrupted that conversation. My sister had been diagnosed with cancer a couple of years before we really started discussing it, and it was impossible for me to conceive of moving abroad, away from her. Her death in 2019 was very sudden and very, very shocking and made thinking about anything but her almost impossible; the pandemic a few months later threw everything – for everyone, everywhere, of course. But when the confusion started to clear, I realized that the shape America might take in our life together had persisted; it wasn't going away.

It was this that inspired me to write this book, and while the question of whether we would uproot our lives and move to the States is at its heart, the theme of home is something which has preoccupied me, or obsessed me, since I was very young. Home and the

feeling of home have always been important for me. As
a child, it was a place I never really wanted to be away
from and homesickness is one of my earliest memories:
I am upstairs in a house in Oxford and my mum is,
uncharacteristically, away for a night or even two, and
although my friend's house is welcoming, her mother
kind, and there is the smell of something comforting
cooking downstairs, like the sweet, familiar scent of
onions as they make their way towards a bolognese, I
feel a desperate, overwhelming need to be back at home.
Being close to my mum was the thing that assuaged
my feeling of homesickness. At the very start of my
A-levels, I left my home in Oxfordshire and started at
day school in London. The sense of missing home was
visceral; it made me sick, and I only lasted at that school
for half a term before I took myself back home and
went to a local sixth-form college. Mum had a massive
riding accident just two weeks after that, and the shape
and colour of home changed completely. Home didn't
really exist after Mum's accident, and so the feeling of
missing, wanting, searching for home started, and didn't
calm itself, beating like a second heart inside me, until I
met Pete in my thirties.

The Giant on the Skyline is my fourth memoir. Memoir
can be many things, but I am interested in using it to
explore the complex, terrifying, beautiful feelings any
of us may experience in the course of a stone-cold
normal day. And as I write these acknowledgements,
the person I am most grateful to is Pete, who trusts me
while I write about the most precious stuff of our life
together. I want to thank him for that. And I love the
sense of home we're continually creating, which is

showing me that location and geography ultimately matter less than the presence of one another.

As much as landscape and memory, this is also a book about community, and I am grateful for the mesh of friendships that forms the community in my home village and the villages of Uffington, Shellingford and Fernham – especially the people who provide moral support and jokes whenever we stop on the road for a chat, to say nothing of all the invaluable plumbers, mechanics, electricians, roofers, vets, fencers and therapists, there for me at times of need. Thanks to Louise Church and Darren O'Sullivan, Nicola Cale, Sarah Cale, Pam Cale, Rose and everyone at Uffington village shop, Bill and Sally Lea, Jane Darling, Linda Jones, Charlie Buxton, Isabelle Barber, Denice Fage, David and Sue Owen Smith, Chris Foster, Joy Reid, Hilary Deakin, Tessa Hingston, Viv Maton, Antonia Jones, George Reade, Dave and Sheila Shirley, Ricky and Vicky, the Matthews family, Andy Payne, Emma Packford Garret, Emily Hedderley and Chris Tomlinson, Olena Civan, Jillian Clipsham and Tracey Stutt and all of Evangeline's American Dance family, but especially Cheryl Prior. Huge thanks to Suzanne Pullin for being the best friend, and for keeping me sane through that giant move.

The echoes of many voices have contributed to my writing, and I am also grateful to Jade, Andy, Katy, Danny, Sam, AJ, Emma, Tom, JJ, Annie, James, Jason, Sarah Jane, Sean, Rich, Amy, Teyte, Jacob, Katie, both Jonnys, Henry, Max, Ollie, Matty, and of course Josh Legge, for being the local legend he is.

I am forever grateful to Rupert Lycett Green for helping me understand and see this landscape of the

Ridgeway, and for the very real friendship and much fun he has given to Pete and me and all of our children, especially his godson, Lester.

For mystical wisdom I thank Chris Park and Charlotte Pulver, and of course Hari Lambani and Carrie Rossiter. You are all absolutely golden.

I am grateful to Anna Dillon for the outstanding cover illustration. Anna understands the emotional power of the Ridgeway so well and her creative involvement in *The Giant on the Skyline* means a great deal to me. In 2013, when I was still living in Oxford, I saw a rich, green illustration by Anna of this landscape published in a local magazine. I couldn't forget the beauty of that image, and I thought, *I want to live there*. Ten years later, it has been a complete joy to have worked with Anna, whose creative interpretation of my writing is entirely her own.

Thank you to all those people who have offered me precious spaces to write, including Jane and Mark Cracknell, Aude Echalier, Kate Rothschild, Claire Kramer Mackinnon and Katie Le White. Thank you to Iona Quigley, for being there for the kids and for the many hours we spent wrangling Shetlands together, and to Dave Motion, for being a pal and always knowing all the passwords. Thank you to Annabel Brousse for so much encouragement while I was writing, and huge thanks to my very real Instagram community for their support and belief in me. Their messages mean a great deal.

Thank you to my agent, Robert Caskie, for motivating me when I was struggling with an early draft and for helping me to think of myself as a minstrel.

And I am grateful to my editor at Doubleday, Susanna Wadeson. Susanna is an outstanding editor and we worked very closely together, especially during the last six months of writing this book. I love the way Susanna believes in me and pushes me to take my writing further; I also love the fact that she didn't baulk when I told her that a giant and many Neolithic people had walked into my psychic landscape and would soon be walking on to my page. She is part of a tremendous team, including Alison Barrow, who takes publicity to a new art form. I would like to thank everyone who has worked on the book, but especially Katherine Cowdrey, Kate Samano, Lorraine McCann, Marianne Issa El-Khoury, Sara Roberts and Cat Hillerton, as well as Tom Chicken's amazing team. Many thanks to Gillian Stern, who understands my writing so well, and Faiza Khan for her sharp editorial eye.

And thanks, and love, to my dad and stepmother, Rick Stroud and Alexandra Pringle. And to my children, Jimmy, Dolly, Evangeline, Dash and Lester. Because it's you, kids, who make our house a home.

**Clover Stroud** is a writer and journalist, writing regularly for the *Sunday Times*, the *Guardian* and the *Saturday* and *Sunday Telegraph*, among others. She also hosts a popular podcast called *Tiny Acts of Bravery*. Her first book, *The Wild Other*, was shortlisted for the Wainwright Prize. Her critically acclaimed second book, *My Wild and Sleepless Nights: A Mother's Story*, and third book, *The Red of My Blood: A Death and Life Story*, were instant *Sunday Times* bestsellers and rated 'best books of the year'. She is currently living in Washington DC with her husband and the youngest three of her five children.